hunt   091176

14.95
13.95
12.95
11.95
10.94
9.95
8.95
7.95
6.95
5.95
4.95

D0312396

THE JACKALS WILL BE THERE

Sandy with his gun bearer (left) alongside the man-eater

THE JACKALS WILL BE THERE

by

Michael G Harrison

Ashford Press Publishing
Southampton
1987

Published by   Ashford Press Publishing 1987
                1 Church Road
                Shedfield
                Hampshire
                SO3 2HW

British Library Cataloguing in Publication Data

Harrison, Mike
    The jackals will be there.
    1. Big game hunting — India — History —
    20th century
    I. Title
    799.2'6'0924   SK235

ISBN 1-85253-028-6

Designed and typeset by Jordan and Jordan, Fareham, Hampshire

Printed and bound in Great Britain by
Robert Hartnoll (1985) Ltd., Bodmin, Cornwall

Contents

List of Illustrations

Preface

I grew up in India, spending my childhood days with jungles, rivers, mountains and marshes almost at the doorstep. I had few friends of my own age, for the families in the neighbourhood with young children were sparse and so I became very close to my parents. Father being very keen on shooting, made it his business to include me on his outings and if necessary, to have me carried by a servant. This early initiation to shooting played a vital role in moulding me to his way of life, a healthy active life which he enjoyed to the very end.

I did not go to a boarding school till I was about twelve years of age, and consequently I neglected studies to revel in a hectic outdoor life in the surroundings of our property in the Simla Hills, Ambala and Roorkee. Of course, I landed in all sorts of trouble, including being bitten by a snake, a mad dog, and scorpions.

A boarding school eventually accepted me and made my life hell for a couple of years, for I was determined to continue with my interests, and later went on to prove that where there's a will there's certainly a way.

Shy of society and keen for adventure, I combined work with pleasure to make the countryside my second home. Youth is a wonderful thing and I'm proud of not having wasted it on a glamorous city life.

Every year the once mystic East advances more deeply into modern methods and rapidly loses its ancient culture, charm and, above all, its jungles. Fortunately, as a precocious child, I developed an interest in what lay beyond and, as the years advanced, I penetrated deeper into the unknown, travelling through the Western Himalayas, the United Provinces, Punjab, North West Frontier, Baluchistan, Sind and Central Provinces.

Being a Police Officer, I had the chance to probe the districts thoroughly and, having an obsession for what some folk call "blood sports", I not only satisfied my desire to shoot, but reaped the knowledge of the wilderness. Knowing most of the local dialects, adapting myself to what the land had to offer – good, bad or indifferent – and taking an unbiased attitude towards the natives I gained their friendship and respect and was hospitably accepted amongst them.

The basic theme of this book is travel and shooting, encounters with man-eaters and wounded big game.

Whilst shooting is sometimes despised, let it not prejudice you against reading this book. Incorporated in these authentic experiences will be found numerous references to tribes, their way of life, customs, feuds, witchcraft, problems with wildlife, legends, superstitions and humour.

I extend my gratitude to those who so hospitably accepted me amongst them, paved the way to places of interest and, above all, to the brave ones who, unarmed, voluntarily jeopardised their lives to participate in highly dangerous sport.

My desire for an outdoor life, admittedly carried too far, caused an unhappy situation for my wife who found she was burdened with a husband she could neither tame nor keep in captivity. She has my deepest admiration for patiently tolerating one whom she frequently refers to as "a man who does not have blood, but gunpowder in his veins!" Those responsible for igniting the explosive, were my elder brothers, Ainsworth and Charles! Last, but not least, I had my beloved mother and father to thank with words yet to be found. Yes, they had their full share of anxious years with a problem child, yet they supported my hazardous hobbies and wholeheartedly gave me everything, including the freedom of the wilderness which, now looking back on the past, I abused.

This book, too, is dedicated to my granddaughter Elizabeth who I hope will enjoy an outdoor life with camera, pencil or paint brush.

Translation of vernacular words recurring in text

Sarpat	Pampas grass.
Charpoy	Bed.
Sarsi	Nomadic tribe.
Jheel	Marsh, quagma, lake.
Nullah	Seasonal stream, generally with steep banks.
Machan	Hide built in a tree.
Bund	Causeway.
Shikari	Hunter.

*Dedicated to those who shared with me
the adventures, and to those who are now at
eternal rest below the Himalayas*

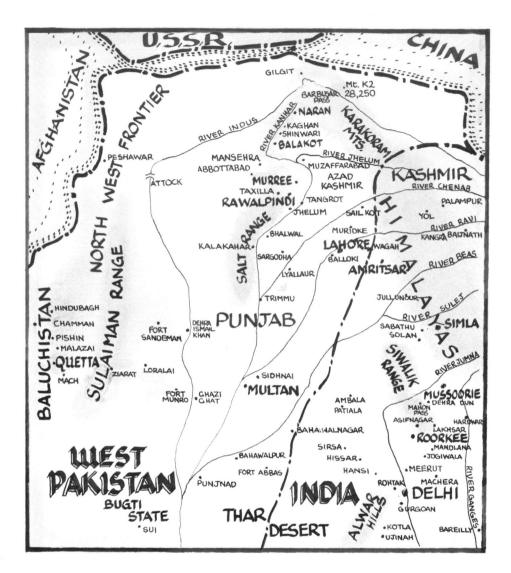

Above is a sketch of the shaded portion shown on the rough miniature map of the sub-continent (left). This is intended solely as a reference aid for the reader to the places described in the book.

Chapter One

Born in 1926, the youngest but one of a large family comprising six brothers and three sisters, we were brought up during the Raj in northern India, shuttling between our property at Solan in the Himalayas and Ambala and Roorkee in the plains.

Encouraged by Father, a very keen Shikari (hunter), some of us followed in his footsteps, especially Ainsworth and Charles, the two eldest of the children, followed later by myself.

Father retired in 1932 from the Punjab Civil Service while I was a six-year-old, which was to my advantage for he now had plenty of time to pursue his interests to which I was now being introduced, carried if necessary by a servant in a "kilta", a long basket used by the hill tribes to carry merchandise. I grew up under his guidance, learning more and more about the countryside, developing my own interests and hobbies, studying the behaviour of birds and animals, their alarm calls, their breeding habits and collecting birds' eggs, butterflies, moths and beetles.

The environment had its hidden dangers. These were constantly being pointed out to me by my parents, but I took little or no notice of their warnings. I went through the common insect bites and stings from bees, wasps, ants and beetles, then came the scorpion stings which were a painful experience, not to mention the terrible swelling.

We spent the summer months in Solan to get away from the heat of the plains. Our small estate with terraced fields, a few fruit trees, a spring, cow shed, servants' quarters, dog kennels, aviary and a bungalow called Marjorie Ville with an annexe, was a place at which I spent many of my childhood days. There was no electrification, but we made do with Petromax lamps which were as bright, if not brighter, than electric lights.

The estate was a mile beyond Solan, going towards Simla. We had a fine view of the motor road and Kalka Simla Railway which ran alongside each other with a level crossing just below the house. Solan itself was a pretty little hill station with a British Garrison stationed in the Cantonment area with limited accommodation for married familes. In a nutshell, it comprised a bazaar, a railway station, a post office, Combined Military Hospital, football field , church, cinema and the garrison school which I attended.

Surrounded by mountains, some in excess of 7,000 feet, the majority of the slopes were almost devoid of trees, yet carpeted with long lush green grass during the monsoon season. This would dry off during the winter to be cut and taken away to villages to provide fodder for cattle. Many of the

My "Kilta" in which I was carried by a servant

Arriving at Solan to get away from the heat of the plains. My sister Dorothy (left), Mother, myself and Father.

valleys, however, were clad with pine forests, lantana, the thorny wild yellow raspberry, figs, apricots, pomegranates, medlars and walnuts.

In these valleys I spent some very enjoyable times shooting with Father or my elder brothers when they were home for their winter holidays from college. Of course, during the summer months in the ensuing years I often slipped away by myself, unknown to my parents, to add to my collection of butterflies or birds' eggs, armed with catapult or air rifle. I had some great experiences, a couple of which remain very vivid.

The behaviour of birds when they utter their alarm calls one day took me to a spot where I guessed I would encounter a reptile or carnivorous animal. Armed with a BSA 177 air rifle I cautiously approached the spot where bulbuls, mynas, shrikes and drongos were behaving in a very agitated manner. I didn't bother to look in the undergrowth because all the activity was taking place high in a walnut tree.

Manoeuvring about under the tree I saw a snake coiled around a branch, its head in a drongo's nest, obviously eating the newly hatched chicks or sucking the eggs. I recognised it as a cobra when it lifted its head, hood outstretched, to fend off the attacks of the parent birds.

I knew how fast a cobra could move but as it was coiled around a branch I thought I had the advantage, especially armed with an accurate air rifle which I could use efficiently. I waited for the right opportunity. The cobra lifted its head and I placed a pellet into the base of its neck. The snake's head dropped, while the rest of its body formed a tight knot around the branch. Like a boxer, I sensed the beginning of the end. I put more pellets into this knot, but losing patience, I climbed the tree, broke a thin branch, and the cobra slithered to the ground from about 30 feet.

Overwhelmed with excitement and what I thought a great accomplishment I took it home to show Father. He was indeed pleased to see that I had come to no harm by using an air rifle on a cobra, but he played hell with me for taking such a chance.

That year the monsoon had come in with vengeance, day after day, week after week with continuous rain, keeping everything under cover except frogs, snails, beetles, leeches, snakes, millipedes, centipedes and myself! There was always the rare day when the sun did shine, and it was on one such evening when I roamed off to sit on the crest of a hill. On the edges of the terraced fields appeared black partridge, Kaleej pheasants and peafowl. Later, as the sun dipped over the hills, I saw a jackal leading a litter of cubs along the bank of a stream. A jackal cub. What a nice pet that would make, I thought! Dashing out from a concealed position I ambushed the family. They split up and I cornered a cub, having chased it into an alcove where child faced cub. I thought I had the advantage, but the cub was no push over. It growled, snarled and snapped at my hands as I drew nearer.

To add to the problem the cub yelped which brought its mother to its aid. She was a terror, coming at me with wide open jaws and at times I thought she would sever my hands or legs in one bite. I fought back as best I could, kicking out, right, left and centre, picking up and throwing stones at her until I finally beat her off to a safe distance, then grabbed the cub even though its razor-sharp teeth bit into my wrists.

With the cub safely tucked away, I rushed home to present it to Dad telling him I'd captured it single handed and, in my judgement, heroically. I wanted to keep it as a pet, but the request was refused in spite of continuous pleading. The cub had to go back to where it belonged, and I'm glad to say, in fading light the mother was there to greet it!

In the ignorance of childhood, I worried cats, monkeys, squirrels, rats etc. until they, too, left their trade marks on me. So far these had all been minor events ... then I was bitten by a rabid dog! By no means as painful as the scorpion, yet it was more serious and 14 anti-rabies injections into the stomach were terribly painful, real killers! Fortunately I survived; the dog didn't!

Repeated warnings over the years failed to change my ways. What my parents feared most was snake-bite and this soon happened. On 18th October 1934, I was in a Muslim graveyard at Ambala looking for a horned owl which flew into a mango tree. Suddenly I felt a jab like a pin stuck into my right ankle. Instantly I ran my hand down to the affected spot to feel the smooth, cold outline of a snake! I looked down to see it in the act of biting me just above the fold of the sock. I immediately jerked the snake away with my hand, jumping on it as it tried to wriggle away. Having killed the snake which I recognised as a Krait about 18 inches in length and very poisonous indeed, I realised I was in deadly danger. I had been bitten and very shortly I would be dead.

I cried with the agony of pain and the fear of death. Everything happened so suddenly and I just could not believe this would ever happen to me. The more I looked at the dead snake the more I cried. Not having taken any notice of the warnings given by my parents, how could I now go home and tell them I'd been bitten by a snake? I decided to stay put and pass away. I sat down against the mango tree, helplessly watching my ankle swell, the throbbing pain becoming more acute.

After a few minutes a railway employee, the level crossing gatekeeper, appeared before me to enquire why I was crying. He spotted the snake lying beside me, asked no more questions and, presumably knowing where I lived, picked me up and was on his way to the house. An elder brother, Edwyn, met us at the gate, to be told I'd been bitten by a snake. He remained calm (bless his soul, he died in 1965 of a heart attack) and asked me to point out exactly where the snake-bite was. I showed him the spot which he cauterised with a penknife, adding to the pain I was already experiencing.

He then clasped my thigh with both hands to arrest the circulation of blood. Meanwhile Bryan, the youngest brother, had arrived on the scene under the impression I was being thrashed by Edwyn! He was told to bring a rope or string in the shortest possible time. Bryan, fully aware of the thrashings I'd been given by the elder brothers, thought that Edwyn was in the act of hanging me so he returned with a bootlace, thinking he was doing me a favour! However, Edwyn told me to remain standing and keep a tight hold with both hands around my knee until his return, which was very quick indeed. He used a bandage to improvise a tourniquet and rushed me to hospital on the crossbar of his bicycle. I was immediately given an injection, the only one remaining in stock for snake-bite! This injection, like those given for rabies, was administered to the stomach, once again a very painful affair.

After the injection I was made to sit up, with strict instructions to remain awake day and night! This was difficult but nevertheless it was complied with, Mother making sure by sitting at the bedside for over 24 hours until I was discharged, shaken but not yet beaten.

Unknown to any member of the family, including myself, our servants had arranged a function in the servants' quarters to have me treated by a "Sadhu" (witch-doctor). He was an old man, wearing a yellowish brown robe with a metal chain around his waist to which was attached a long pair of tongs. He had long matted hair, a white beard, his face smeared with ashes and broad white and orange lines painted across his forehead. From his neck dangled strings of large brown beads.

I sat in front of him while he extracted juice from a young, tender, succulent banana plant. To the juice he added a thimbleful each of four different types of dried herbs, mixed them thoroughly in a cup, added a little water and gave it to me to drink. Reluctantly I swallowed this bitter, revolting mixture. Then I was made to lie face down on a "charpoy" (bedstead). There was no mattress or sheet on the charpoy, so I was able to see through the rope meshing what was going on below me.

A layer of green leaves was first placed under the charpoy, followed by a further layer of what appeared to be dehydrated weeds. He then put a match to the dried stuff which burned steadily from end to end, emitting a dense yellowish smoke which almost suffocated me. In fact, I was so worried that I attempted to make a run for it but was held down with an assurance that no harm would come to me.

He turned me over on my back, dusted me with smouldering leaves, ran his hands down the length of my body, over both legs and feet, across both arms and hands and then told me to get up. I was free to go, henceforth protected against further snake-bite!!

With these nasty experiences over, things began to change for the better. I witnessed my first shoot in higher circles which took place in October 1935 along the mountains between Solan and Simla. Father was invited by the Maharaja of Patiala State, His Highness Bhupinder Singh, to join his shooting party. This was an elaborate affair; special tracks and butts had been constructed through his preserved forests and his personal surgeon, ADC, and other VIPs were in attendance. I'd never seen so many beaters before, a conservative estimate would be no less than 200.

The area shot over was rough, considering the altitude was about 7,000 feet. The beaters walked shoulder-to-shoulder, controlled by his forest officer and guards and noise was encouraged, the louder the better, so tom-toms, large tins and rattles made up a successful beat. The timid muntjac (barking deer), goral (goat family) and the langoor (black faced monkey) emerged first. They were allowed a free passage, but Kareej pheasants were shot, though the majority rocketed through the guns unharmed.

A large black bear moved swiftly across a grassy hillside, then stopped to look back towards the beaters. The Maharaja had his rifle levelled but for some unknown reason lowered it and let the bear go free. Later we learned he didn't think it was sporting to shoot the bear. However, in the beat which followed, a panther came out in leaps and bounds, at which he fired, wounding it with the first shot. When it took cover in a few isolated bushes, the beaters were informed of its position by means of a loudspeaker. On nearing the spot stones were pelted into the bushes without the panther breaking cover. Only when a large rock was rolled down into the bushes did the panther leap out, not away from the beaters but towards them. The Maharaja was fast and accurate! The panther collapsed amongst the beaters at his second shot.

At the conclusion of this shoot, the Maharaja was not pleased because neither he nor anyone else had seen a ring-necked pheasant nor a red deer, which he had imported and introduced to these forests, hoping they would establish themselves in their new environment. We later heard that the gamekeepers and forest guards were sacked for allowing poaching of these pheasants and the deer, though vermin must have accounted for most of them, the panthers which abounded in these hills finding the alien deer easy prey.

The following winter at the end of January 1936, the Maharaja of Patiala State invited the entire family to the annual gundog field trials about 10 miles outside the town of Patiala. This was a grand occasion with no expense spared and guests included ICS Officers, State dignitories, Senior Police Officers and Senior Army Officers posted at Ambala Cantonments of, I believe the Cheshire Regiment.

Guests arrived at Patiala Railway Station to be met and taken by chauffeur-driven Rolls Royces or Bentleys to the State Guest House, annexed to Bhupindersager Palace, the official residence of the Maharaja of Patiala State.

At the annexe all guests stayed for the duration of the field trials, which lasted a week, living in sheer luxury. Theodore, my immediate elder brother, then aged 13, was seen by Father sitting in the main lounge with a

The Maharaja of Patiala State (centre), Col. Hutton left,
Prime Minister of Bhagat State, Father, Edwyn, Ainsworth
and myself extreme right.

A portion of the road to Mussoorie above Rajpur.
(now derelict having been bypassed by a new less
picturesque road)

bottle of beer, a tin of State Express 999 cigarettes and a bearer in attendance awaiting further orders! Those orders came from Father – "Out!"

Each day eight guns were invited to participate in the shooting of partridge at the field trials. Transport was always available for guests, whether they wished to go to the shooting grounds or sightseeing. We went daily, using an array of elephants to take families in stately fashion sitting in howdahs (enclosed seats attached to the elephant's back) to witness the dogs retrieving the partridges.

On the day that Father, Ainsworth and Charles were amongst the invited shooters, our elephant took up its position behind them, which made up the right flank. The beaters, armed with sticks and wearing red shirts, positioned themselves five yards behind the guns. The column extended about 300 yards. Those shooting were briefed by the Safety Officer to observe shooting etiquette – no cross-firing, no swinging back to shoot and no firing when a dog was being judged in the act of retrieving.

On the sounding of a whistle by the Beat Master, the column moved forward. Within 100 yards the first shots were fired at grey partridges. Birds fell and the column was brought to a halt. The retrievers, labradors and spaniels – the majority being labradors – were selected to do the retrieving within a time limit of ten minutes.

An incident arose when Father shot a black partridge. A spaniel failed to retrieve it in the specified time limit, however the owner insisted that the partridge was a "runner", but Father was quite positive that it was a dead bird. To settle the affair, "Flying Squirrel", a famous champion gundog, was brought in to settle the dispute. He also failed, convincing the judges that the bird must have been a runner. To their embarrassment and Father's irregularity, he walked straight to the spot where the partridge fell and picked it up!

During this stoppage some pintail duck approached from the right flank, flying surprisingly low, but as they crossed in front of Ainsworth and Charles they began to climb. It was too late and between them they shot three with the state-owned 12-bore double barrelled shotguns made by Holland & Holland. In the process of retrieving the third duck, a large solitary wild boar was disturbed. It immediately attacked dogs and beaters alike, causing panic, and then attacked an elephant alongside ours. This elephant ponderously ran forward, completely out of control, much to the discomfort and fear of the family in the howdah as it tore through thorny acacia trees. Fortunately the elephant was eventually pacified and brought back to the column where an inspection of its legs revealed deep lacerations caused by the boar's tusks. No wonder it went beserk; its pride had been hurt!

In 1938 I was finally admitted to boarding school in Mussoorie, Queen of the Hill Stations. I say "finally" because it was difficult to get into a boarding school in spite of there being eleven of them, one Indian, one American and nine British. As a matter of fact, Mussoorie had the most boarding schools in India at the time with long waiting lists for admission.

I was most unhappy in the first boarding school. I was away from home for nine long months without a break, and excessive caning for minor infringements of school regulations made life a misery and, worst of all, I was deprived of the freedom to explore the surrounding hills. Anyway. I survived two long terms in this school, then a vacancy arose in Allen Memorial Boys' High School, also known as Bala Hissar, the name originating from Afghanistan.

When visiting the school in 1983 I noticed many changes, prominent amongst which was that the old Bala Hissar had become a multi-story building, a section of which, the science laboratory, has been dedicated to Major Bahuguna, Kumaun Rifles, a junior pupil of my time who died tragically in an assault on Mount Everest in 1971 by the International Expedition.

I happily completed my education in Allen Memorial, enjoying each term and looking forward to the ten days' holiday each August followed by the 13 weeks' winter recess. I was fortunate to be able to go home for the August recess, for Roorkee was only about 60 miles away, faintly visible on a clear morning, while the lights were distinctly seen on a clear night!

I much preferred the long vacation in the winter when I was able to get about without a care in the world, spending most of the time in the wilds or with Ainsworth and Charles who were both in the Punjab Police but posted miles apart in different districts. However, they always coincided their leave to do a winter shoot together and including me in the trip. Father, though always invited on such trips, usually declined the offer because he felt he would be a handicap to the younger generation, unless he knew the area to be plain sailing.

Generally, Father made his own arrangements by booking a Forest Block in the Siwaliks for the purpose of "shikar" (shooting). Forest Blocks comprise vast areas, with or without, Forest Bungalows. Some such blocks were popular for big game only, though every block would have jungle-fowl and peafowl. Permits were issued for blocks, limiting the number of animals to be shot over a specified period. These shikar programmes were very popular, more to get away from it all, than for indiscriminate slaughter of wildlife. Our practice was to shoot for the pot and enjoy the recreation. There were times, however, when a heavy toll of peafowl substituted turkeys for Christmans Dinner at officers', sergeants' and B.O.R. messes.

The year 1942 brought some changes to the family, some good, some bad. The bad first. My eldest sister Millicent passed away in her late twenties, leaving a young daughter Anna, aged two. Ainsworth got married, followed by Charles. Good or bad news? I'd say debatable! But undoubtedly the good news, was that Mother had inhertied "Charters Ville" which belonged to

9

her parents Major W.C. and Elizabeth Charters. This estate was a favourite amongst both sides of the family, with shooting and fishing almost on the doorstep.

The property at Ambala was sold and Charters Ville became the family home, especially during the winter months, which in the north of India, is from November to March. Also in 1942 I was enrolled in the Auxiliary Force (India) having attained the age of sixteen. Each British school had its own contingent trained by regular officers from the British Army. Our Commanding Officer was Major Pearce Fleming with RSM Ken Wright.

We enjoyed the training, especially jungle warfare, in camps situated in the Siwaliks. In addition to a small annual payment I managed to win more money than the salary in various rifle shooting competitions. The biggest which comes to mind was the Aggregate Cup witnessed by Field Mashall Lord Wavell in 1944 at the Sixth Gurkha Regiment Rifle Ranges at Dehra Dun. I was pleased, the school as a whole appreciated the achievement, and above all Father was so pleased that he gave me a wonderful present – a double barrel 12-bore sidelock ejector made by W.J. Jeffery with 28 inch barrels. It was a peach of a shotgun, fitting me as if custom built. To follow was a 9.3 X 64 Mauser rifle to equip me to face any eventuality I might have to cope with in the future.

Ainsworth, who had been officer in charge of the Enternment Camp at Sabathu where German and Italian civilians were held, was transferred in September 1942 to Delhi, bringing him in contact with Viceregal Lodge, the Viceroy of India's residence; at that time this was Lord Linlithgow. In the course of his duties he came to know the Hon. Captain Andrew Elphinstone ADC to the Viceroy, and later to His Excellency Lord Linlithgow himself.

The Viceroy was a keen shooting enthusiast, and so was his ADC. Soon Ainsworth was introducing the ADC to some of our favourite spots off the beaten tracks which had to be approved of before taking the Viceroy to such places. There were two enormous jheels adjacent to each other, namely Ujinah and Kotla, about 55 miles south of Delhi, Kotla being at the base of the Alwar Hills. These hills extend to within 20 miles of Delhi to the suburbs of a town called Gurgeon where Father was posted during the years 1908-12. According to him, in those days these low lying hills were infested with panthers, so much so that the Government paid a reward of eight rupees per panther shot and produced before the Financial Assistant, at the time Malcolm Hailey who later became Sir Malcolm Hailey, Governor of the Punjab, then the United Provinces.

The ADC was impressed with both these jheels, fringed with millet crops, the deeper water overgrown with hyacinth. Ujinah had a "bund" (causeway) across it which was found most suitable for the Viceroy and his guests. Because of the size of the jheels, a number of guns were required on the outskirts to keep the duck on the move. This is where, after screening, a few people like myself were able to get a look in. And I really mean only a

Allen Memorial School, also known as Bala Hissar.

Charters Ville, a favourite amongst both sides of the family

look in.

On the 1st November 1942, the shoot took place. The Viceroy was positioned on the centre of the bund, flanked on either side by Captain Viscount Lord Ednan, Colonel Elliot and Colonel Toogood. On the other jheel, Kotla was the Hon. Capt. Andrew Elphinstone, two guests and Ainsworth. Security was tight. Reputable men were selected to act as flagmen to keep the duck on the move together with a few guns like myself.

According to arrangements, the first shot was fired at the prescribed time. The noise of hundreds of thousands of duck taking to flight was deafening. Shooting was brisk from both jheels, the duck comprising mostly pintail and teal, though numerous other species, apart from mallard, whizzed about but were not shot at. I was at the far end of Ujinah shooting pintail, quite rapidly at first, until I noticed a smoke screen surrounding the spot where I was shooting. The reason was a new Eley cartridge called Kyblack; cream coloured and contained in a buff coloured carton marked "War Packing", it was loaded with black powder!

According to schedule shooting stopped at 12.30 p.m. for lunch on the bund after which it commenced again, very lively at first, but easing off in the late afternoon, then with plenty of activity during evening flight which had to be cut short to keep to a time schedule. From all accounts the day's bag was very substantial.

To overcome the wartime cartridge shortage I used an 8-bore single barrel muzzle-loader which Father kept as a showpiece. This weapon was great fun, using black powder with heavy loads of shot to flight the wildfowl on the numerous jheels in the vicinity of Roorkee. One morning I bagged 29 pintail and one grey lag goose in one shot as they lifted off the water! These were all dead birds. Undoubtedly others must have died elsewhere.

Unfortunately this muzzle-loader had no housing for the ram-rod, so I had to carry it separately, all 45 inches of it. Often I let it remain in the 40 inch length of barrel, forgetting to remove it before firing a shot. Well, you can imagine the rod cart-wheeling off the gound with a loud zooming noise or the whistle it made if fired at overhead birds! Needless to say, once the rod was fired off accidently, that was the end of the shoot as far as I was concerned, though once I did use a thin bamboo as a substitute for a ram-rod. That shoot became a disaster, because the newspaper used as wadding ignited, setting the "sarpat" jungle on fire! I'm glad to say the fire was extinguished before it went out of control. This monstrosity of a muzzle-loader was never used when amongst elite circles!

Ainsworth spent a weekend at Charters Ville, taking me back with him to Delhi, the object being to witness another one of those Viceroy's shoots. This took place on 31st January 1943 at a place called Machera about 45 miles from Delhi off the Meerut Bareilly road in the United Provinces. This was a snipe shoot in a vast, very shallow jheel carpeted with short tufts of grass varying from a few inches to a couple of feet in height.

The Viceroy with his six guests had fixed butts for the first four drives, the first being from the north, followed by west, south and east. All they had to do was pivot 45 degrees to face each drive while the beaters advanced, then retraced their steps to change direction for the next drive and repeat the move until the circle had been completed.

The Hon. Captain Andrew Elphinstone and Ainsworth walked between the beaters who totalled about 25 including myself. Unlike most other beats when noise is encouraged, beaters driving snipe were instructed not to shout or talk loudly. The drive commenced about half a mile away from the standing guns (the Viceroy and his guests). Conditions for snipe shooting were perfect, no wind, warm with a blue cloudless sky.

The snipe were there in singles and in wisps but were reluctant to visit the V.I.Ps, until they were forced to do so by Andrew Elphinstone and Ainsworth blazing away, unable to load their shotguns fast enough to cope with the numbers. By now the jheel was ablaze with gunfire, particularly from the Viceroy and his guests.

As planned, each drive appeared to prove more successful than the former. In all, eight drives were completed in two different areas of this vast jheel. Though a painful experience for me to be an observer-cum-beater, I enjoyed the experience. The total snipe bagged, was, I believe, 750. According to Ainsworth who returned to Viceregal Lodge with the entourage, the Viceroy was so delighted that he summoned the official photographer that night to take photographs of the shooting party with this record bag of snipe.

I did well out of this snipe shoot, for Ainsworth gave me 500 cartridges, no.5 shot, made by J. Dickson of Edinburgh. These cartridges were part of a present of 12 bore cartridges to Ainsworth from Viceregal Lodge. In addition I was given a box of 25 no. 10 shot by the same maker. Size 10 is the smallest of lead shot, each catridge containing roughly 620 pellets weighing $1^{1}/8$ oz., ideal for snipe shooting, but I had other ideas for these high grade cartridges. I removed the minute pellets, replacing them with SG (nine pellets) because when shooting in many parts of India it was advisable to carry a few SG or LG, even though the shooting trip was planned for feathered game. One never knew when the unexpected would turn up, and it was better to be safe than sorry.

Chapter Two

Charles, who was posted to Amritsar, met me at the railway station and took me back to his bungalow, en route spinning the latest yarns. It was a question of a quick bath, dress, and off to a party where I was initiated to drinking in a big way as a result of which I was stoned out of my mind!

The next morning I remembered nothing of the plans for that day and was surprised to see Ainsworth's cook, namely Tufail, unloading baggage. Ainsworth arrived, took one look at me and mumbled something to the effect that he had seen dead people looking better than I did! He was certainly in a bad mood, bringing back recollections of my childhood days when he took charge to discipline me. His presence helped, but I was still unable to reason normally even when I heard Charles tell me to hurry up as it was nearing the time to leave! I was under the impression that it was another drinking session and this time I insisted I would not go, until Ainsworth, more or less appealed to me to join them. I obliged, presenting myself dressed up like the cat's whiskers. "Where the hell do you think you're going?" said Ainsworth, while Charles stood grinning. "To a party, of course." I replied!

When I'd sobered up I was embarrassed to know that according to plan, we were to set off on a trip into the hills which Charles had arranged some time ago and I had forgotten overnight! At last the penny dropped. It was 22nd October 1943.

Tufail, the cook, left by public transport, taking with him the heavy gear to await our arrival at Baijnath. Our departure was delayed for the usual last minute things. Baden Rector, who we expected to be ready further delayed the departure, but nevertheless, the foursome was completed and we headed north in good humour. On the way Charles suggested dropping in on a friend at Yol, a P.O.W. camp where this officer was head of N.A.A.F.I. The idea of visiting him was to purchase some liquid gold! Scotch was not available so we settled for Solan whisky, rum and beer. For a P.O.W. camp, the site chosen was beautiful with the northern slope leading up to snow-capped mountains while the rolling hills were clad with wild fig, medlar and pomegranate trees.

Back on the main road we headed for Palampur which was to be our night stop. The hill road, with continuous sharp bends, restricted making up lost time but we still estimated being at the rest house by 10 p.m. to order a meal.

After dark there is little or no traffic on these hill roads. Animals, yes. The common ones like jackals, foxes and deer aroused no interest until a

Himalayan black bear stepped on the road on a steep gradient, making no effort to move off or put a spurt on. At the sound of the horn it instantly stood up to face the challenge. Charles braked to avoid a collision and the bear stood its ground, moaning about the disturbance while we sat helpless, dumbfounded and frightfully uncomfortable. Charles switched the lights off. I cannot express the feelings of the others, but I almost wet myself! The lights were out for a few seconds only, yet it seemed too long for comfort. When switched on again the bear had gone. Charles drove off accelerating up the hill, hoping to encounter the bear around the corner and taking no notice of the abuse he was getting for not warning us before switching off the lights which was his idea of a joke!

At Palampur we awoke the resident cook who happily made available two rooms, but was unable to provide a dinner. However, after some persuasion he agreed to give us a snack while we sat down to a much deserved beer. He, himself made it obvious that a drink would do him the world of good while he cooked something! Giving him plenty of the hard stuff, he insisted on making his speciality... a chicken curry. Each of us was ravenous and looked forward to the meal. Some minutes later he came back to announce that he was unable to catch a chicken because they were roosting in the trees out of his reach, but eyeing the gun cases in the corner of the room he insinuated that there was an easy way to get the basic ingredients.

Charles immediately saw through his plan and asked him if he had ever used a shotgun. He gave himself great credit in the use of guns so much so that Charles told him to go ahead and select one. He did so and assembled it, meantime Charles went into the adjacent room and returned with a handful of cartridges, one of which he loaded into the right barrel. There was an immediate reaction to stop this irresponsible act, but Charles was determined to go through with it. Handing over the gun to the cook, barrels pointing upwards, he told him to get on with the job.

Ainsworth was annoyed and didn't mince his words. Charles took exception and very angrily retorted, "This is my affair. I've ordered the dinner, mind your own business or quit." The silence was broken by the loud bang of the gun being fired. "Bloody cruel to shoot a sleeping chicken." said Ainsworth. "Most unsportsmanlike." commented Baden. I was too terrified to say anything, even though I was a strong supporter of Charles. I was only hoping this business would not develop into a fight between brothers. Fortunately, before anything else could happen, the cook entered the room to announce he had missed the chicken! Charles told him not to worry, we all miss at some time or the other, and what's more there was plenty of ammunition. Taking the gun off him, he loaded another cartridge into the gun and told him to try again!

"Downright stupidity on your part." said Ainsworth.

"Listen.... when I want your comments, I'll call for them, until then leave this business to me." said Charles rather sarcastically.

In a polite and respectful tone I voiced my opinion for what it was worth. "If this affair is a taste of things to come, then we might as well abandon the trip right now." Charles had always treated me with kindness and understanding. He looked at me and smiled saying "Don't worry Mick, we'll be on our way shortly. These fireworks forecast great fun and games to follow." Just then there was another bang! Charles poured himself a large whisky and as master of ceremonies, toasted "The Chicken Curry!"

In walked the cook again, announcing with embarrassment that for the second time he had missed. This was due to having had words with a "cock-eyed" person which, according to superstition, brings bad luck for at least 24 hours! Calm and collected, Charles showed no signs of anger or stress. He really pampered the cook, gave him another drink, then advised him in the art of night shooting, offering him a further attempt with a more powerful cartridge to bring down a chicken. He declined the offer, pathetically stating that as a result of the second shot, all his roosting chickens had taken off and would be difficult to find by night, if they survived at all, considering cats, foxes and jackals would favour them. Once again Charles came under attack! Now you see what your irresponsible act has done to this poor chap's livestock." Ainsworth jibed in disgust. Charles replied sharply. "Your wisecracks are going to do no good in retrieving the chickens. Let's all go out and find them."

A combined effort helped recover the majority of the birds, much to the relief of the cook who was worrying about the financial loss he would otherwise have suffered – not that we would have let him incur such a loss. The chickens safely away the cook, now pleased as punch, was ready to oblige us with the speciality in a matter of half an hour. Charles, surprisingly, was now vehemently opposed to having a chicken for dinner. This was most odd, but he soon cleared up the mystery by telling us in his usual happy-go-lucky way that the entire stunt was staged as a practical joke. These cartridges he gave the cook to shoot a chicken were, in fact, blanks!! He had removed the lead shot!

The cook gave us a healthy breakfast and implored us that if we ever dropped in again we would be treated to his speciality, provided we sent him advance information.

The journey continued in good humour as we traversed gentle slopes carpeted with tea plantations. The motor journey was finally over when we arrived at Baijnath Rest House. Our cook was there to meet us along with a local, hired to act as guide. He had enlisted the services of prospective friends and relatives to act as porters on the pre-arranged expedition.

There was some final shopping to be done which Ainsworth entrusted to me, directing the cook to ensure the culinary necessities he required were pointed out to me.

With preparations complete, from here onwards it was going to be foot-slogging which called for a good rest before our planned shoot at the crack of dawn next morning. It was a well organised start. The Ghudhis (a hill tribe) set the pace and we soon ran out of steam trying to keep up with them, and the guide-cum-hunter was given strict instructions that under no circumstances were those carrying our gear to widen the gap between us and them.

The Ghudhis are a stocky, cheerful tribe, with pleasant features and easy to get on with. A traditional item worn by the men is yards of rope wrapped several times round the waist. Obviously it is of practical use for such people living in mountains, though I never saw them put the rope to use. After walking for some seven hours we were confronted with the first obstacle, a river. Fortunately it was not in spate, neither was it necessary to wade across because there was a place at which a crossing was possible by means of jumping from rock to rock. We then zig-zagged up through the pine forest, meeting a group of colourfully dressed men, women and children. They were heading in the same direction as us, and for a while we mingled freely.

On the road to Baijnath we had noted the beautiful women in this region. Well, those mingling with us now were real eye-openers. As a matter of fact I don't hesitate to say they were the prettiest I had ever seen in the country. On this point I must emphaise the word "seen", because in many parts of this sub-continent the women must wear a "burkah" (veil) not by choice, but by religious obligation.

These hill tribes absolutely adore jewellery, wearing it on their nose, neck, wrists, fingers, toes and ankles. Silver is the favourite, being indigenous to the country, though gold has no substitute for the very few rich. On this particular occasion these folk were in their finest clothes to attend a wedding.

In passing through the village where the wedding celebrations were well on the way, we were invited to the feast, but unfortunately were unable to accept the offer. However, we did partake of their illicitly distilled "zatt," guaranteed to grow hair on the chest! A drop of this potent stuff in our tanks certainly increased the pace.

In spite of the distance covered, the snow-clad mountains remained as remote as ever. This is an illusion experienced in this wilderness of mountains which stretch up and across, disappearing into eternity.

By late evening we were scanning across the lower ranges from where we had commenced the climb to see only a haze of smoke hanging over villages. We had cleared the inhabited areas and it was time to set up camp for the night. Selecting a spot sheltered from the wind, we pitched camp beneath an umbrella of fir trees. By coincidence, flocks of snow pigeon flighted in to roost in these tall trees. The Ghudis seeing that we showed no desire to shoot them, apparently thought that we were unaware they were edible birds, and had words with the guide to request us to supplement their dinner. The request was granted!

Our cook, Tufail was terribly worried about the thought of sleeping in these woods without any protection against the attack of bear or panther. Charles assured him that if he kept a log fire burning all night, no animal would dare come near let alone attack. To further put his mind at rest he was informed that it would only be this one night of inconvenience; thereafter he would be in the comfort and safety of a forest officer's bungalow!

Wood was freely available and used generously to keep two large fires burning furiously. Large stones were placed against these fires and when they got really hot, they were wrapped in cloth and offered as a substitute for hot water bottles.

One of these Ghadis picked up a rock about the size of a football, put it into a sack and gave it to Tufail who wanted to know as to why his was in a sack yet the others had been given their's wrapped in cloth. He was told politely that he should feel honoured to be one of the lucky ones to have a rock in a sack to serve a dual purpose, i.e. warmth and protection. He went on to explain how the rock placed in the sack could be wielded with force to defend one's self against the attack of panther or bear. To prove his point he gave a demonstration.

Swinging the sack around as though he was throwing the hammer, he struck the trunk of a tree with a tremendous blow. Tufail was highly impressed, his face aglow with admiration for this improvised weapon with which he was now armed to the teeth!

We lay awake for a while listening to the folk songs, softly sung against the background of penny whistles. This interlude was of short duration for the Ghudhis, no different from other villagers living in remote areas, are in the habit of getting to bed soon after dark and rising at dawn. By eight o'clock or so everyone, other than ourselves and the first watch, were asleep, including Tufail who lay between us and the Ghudhis, his hands clasping the wielding end of the loaded sack!

I was dozing off to sleep when I heard a whisper. For a moment I thought it may have been imagination, but then I heard it again and realised it was Charles whispering "Mick....Mick...."

"What's the matter?" I whispered back.

"Would you like to see some fun?"

"What do you intend doing?"

"Have a peep at Tufail. He's got the sack in his hands ready to use. All that we need do is to give him a start and he'll do the rest."

I don't think it's safe, he may injure one of us by mistake."

"Don't worry, we'll use a dummy for him to have a go at."

"What kind of dummy are you planning to use?"

"Well, the bloke on watch if you can recollect, is the rascal amongst the Ghudhis. We can enlist his services by divulging the plan to him, borrow his dark blanket which will be filled with cones etc., tie the four ends and pull the dummy towards Tufail while our accomplice shouts out the warning 'Bhaloo..Bhaloo'!"(a bear).

"It sounds great Charles, but I think someone is bound to get hurt in the panic to follow. Furthermore, Ainsworth and Baden will play hell when they find out we instigated the show."

"You're perfectly right." said Ainsworth in a tone slightly above that of a whisper. "Whenever you two buggers get together on a shooting trip there's bloody trouble. Now take my advice, leave Tufail alone, he's a timid chap, and this being his first experience of staying out in the wilds, God only knows what effect it will have on him."

"He will do one of two things. Either he'll wet himself or we can expect to witness a great show with the dummy!" said Charles.

"O.K., then go ahead with your plan, but please ensure that the guide's gun is unloaded just in case he lets fly a shot in the confusion and accidently shoots somebody."

Charles and I silently stepped across to the Ghudhi on watch, took him aside and disclosed our plan. He was certainly amused, consenting to give us the assistance desired. When all was set, the signal was given and he raised the alarm. There was instant panic. The dummy, an irregular black object advanced towards Tufail. In no manner did it resemble a bear, but in poor light the descriptive word "Bhaloo, Bhaloo, Bhaloo" was proof enough for Tufail to go on the war-path. Jumping to his feet, loaded suck in hand, he took a violent swing at the advancing dummy, missing it by yards and falling arse over tip and promptly leapt into our sector for protection!

Baden, who was dead to the world, hurried to his feet and hearing the words "Bhaloo, Bhaloo" grabbed his shotgun, loaded it and was poised for action: "Where is it, hurry up, tell me where it is?" he shouted. Charles, quick to grasp the opportunity, got Baden worked up by saying "There it is", pointing in the direction of tree trunks away from the congestion.

Baden was all set to kill. "Whereabouts in the tree?" He asked.

"What dark object."

"Which one, there are so many?"

"Damn it all, the one which is moving. Can't you see it?"

"Is it on the ground or up the tree?"

"Up the tree trunk."

"Which tree trunk are you referring to.?"

"The one with the moss on it!"

"I can barely see the tree trunks, let alone the moss!"

"OK Baden, I'll give you a good indication." Guiding the barrels of his shotgun until they were levelled at some imaginary object, Charles said "Do you see it now. Hurry up, I think it's about to come down and attack!"

"I think I've seen it Charles. Hang on." He took aim, then hesitated.

"Hurry up, it's on its way down. Quick, shoot the bloody thing."

There was dead silence as he took aim. All eyes were focused on him. Then came the anticipated blast which cracked the stillness of the night. An avalanche of branches came rustling down. Charles wasted no time to instruct Baden "Give it another shot, it's wounded!" Instantly the second barrel went off with more branches, bark and twigs coming down. "Good shooting." said Charles. "You've got it, but it's lodged between a thick branch and the trunk of the tree."

While Baden strained his eyes to locate the imaginary bear, Charles whispered in my ear. "Listen Mick. Get the dummy and throw it at the base of the tree."

I did so. The dummy fell short of the tree up which Baden was looking, but nevertheless, in poor light conditions, Baden was fooled into firing a snap shot. There was no further movement, and as far as Baden was concerned he had put an end to the bear! He stalked towards the spot where he had directed his fire, gradually disappearing into the darkness, his shotgun still held at the ready.

An embarrassing situation was averted, for the time being, by Charles tactfully telling Baden that a full-scale search would be carried out at first light to find the wounded bear. Fortunately we managed to remain serious until the Ghudhi to whom we had trusted, himself let the "bear out of the bag!" The giggling spread, but Tufail didn't think the business was anything to laugh about, ordering silence so that the sahibs should not be disturbed. Neither, Charles nor I could keep the secret any longer! Baden was told of the hoax, and while we screamed with laughter, Baden promised reprisals. Later though, when the others were asleep he started to chuckle! Delayed action humour.... not at all appreciated by the sahibs now trying to get some sleep!

A conversation started all over again. The Ghudhi's requested Tufail to provide a cup of tea, but as everthing was on ration after leaving the shopping area, Tufail adhered to our instructions by obtaining permission for a special serving of tea. Permission granted, he set about to make the tea, and at this stage told of the faked bear attack. He needed convincing and wanted confirmation from us as to the authenticity of the affair. With reluctance Ainsworth gave him the answer in the positive! The cook took a very dim view of the whole affair, telling us in no uncertain words that he was leaving us next morning. He frankly admitted that he was terrified and would not be able to stand up to the strain of things to come.

At the crack of dawn the clarion call of the Cheer pheasant in the vicinity helped to get us on the way earlier than scheduled. Tufail, had by now reconsidered his overnight decision to quit because no one was prepared to accompany him back to Baijnath.

We climbed out of the wooded zone, up a barren mountainside in seach of Cheer pheasants. Although we spotted a covey we failed to get them to flush. They are cunning birds, seldom taking to the wing; instead will run like hell in a crouched position until forced to sit tight. If you are lucky enough almost to stand on them or have a dog to flush them, only then will they fly.

By afternoon we had reached the snow-line. Tufail, for the first time in his life was trampling through it, the experience, we hoped, an ecstasy! Developing a spirit of exploration, he thought it fun to walk over virgin snow, looking back to see the pattern of his individual tracks, but ignoring advice to keep to the straight and narrow, it was not long before Tufail slipped, bounced once, twice, three or more times, gathered momentum on his behind and ended up with his more tender parts in violent collision with a Ghudhi's shins who stood in his path to break the fall. Thereafter Tufail's malingering paid off. He gained the sympathies of the Ghudhi's to the extent of being carried across obstacles!

With about three hours of daylight remaining, we began to get rather anxious about not having found a suitable place to set up camp. Our ideal was a sheltered valley with a stream or spring to provide a water supply, but contrast to what we had in mind, journeys end was, in fact, a couple of caves! Examining them, they were found to be dry with a low ceiling. A peculiar odour, however, indicated that some animal or animals were inhabiting these caves, but they were the most suitable spot we had come across to set up the camp for the duration of the expedition. It was considered necessary to kindle a fire to fumigate the caves. This was done by burning bundles of green leaves which belched yellowish smoke out of the cave mouths. The only things seen running out were rock lizards. After extinguishing the fire, the caves were cleaned out and made suitable for our dwelling. Tufail, however, was not happy with the choice, emphasising the fact that there was no water available to facilitate cooking, let alone washing and bathing. The Ghudhis immediately assured him that there was plenty of water. Taking him by the hand they led him to the side of the caves from where snow was shovelled into a bucket and Tufail told to melt it down over a fire, and of course, if he wanted more, well, mountains of snow surrounded him!

Having settled down comfortably, it was time to call for a celebration. Whisky topped up with snow for us, while rum and hot water was the choice of the others. After some time the atmosphere was just right to have some fun!

During the course of the journey the Ghudhis had watched me roll my cigarettes with interest. On the quiet I slit a cartridge, removed the gunpowder and placed a small quantity in the centre of a leaf of cigarette paper and rolled a cigarette, hemming the gunpowder in from both ends with tobacco.

This cigarette amongst others, was handed round to the Ghudgis to sample. They lit up, puffing at them while I mentally started a count down. Suddenly there was bright flash, and the chap who had the misfortune to

21

Left to right: Myself, Charles and Ainsworth

Ainsworth and Charles display the Western Horned Tregopan pheasants

Journey's end was, in fact, a couple of caves.

pick the explosive cigarette, reeled backwards in astonishment. The others were equally amazed until I could no longer remain serious. Explaining what I had done, the practical joke was accepted with laughter, even by the chap who had his moustache singed!

When retiring for the night, Ainsworth made sure that Charles and I were separated, placing Baden at the mouth of our cave, a place, in fact, I wanted for myself. I tried to convince Ainsworth I had weak kidneys, and would disturb them every time I wished to water the hillside! "If that is a genuine complaint, I suggest you keep an empty bottle near you, or better still, spray Baden when he starts to snore!"

The next morning while serving breakfast, Tufail complained of being in agony with pains and aches. he wasn't the only one! We were as stiff as pokers ourselves but had to put up with it if the camp was to enjoy meat meals. Tufail needed rest, as a cook he was based at camp where he could have plenty of it. However, when he saw everyone preparing to leave on a shooting trip, he wanted one of the Ghudhis to remain with him for protection.

"Protection from what?" enquired Ainsworth.

"Bears and panthers." Tufail replied.

"You won't find such animals at this altitude."

"But the Ghudhis tell me that these animals follow humans, furthermore we have occupied some kind of animal's caves to which they will return when they see you all leave."

"We are not leaving the area. Just going around the corner to try and shoot some game."

"Yes, but what say that while you all are around the corner a bear or panther visits these caves?"

"You have a catapult!"

"What good is a catapult against the likes of bear or panther?"

"Well, you are a good shot with it. Just wait until it's at arms length, hit it in the eye to partially blind it, then kill it with a loaded sack!"

Tufail was speechless, in fact, almost reduced to tears until Ainsworth deputed a Ghudhi to assist him gather as much firewood as possible. This made his day as moreover, the companion selected was one with whom Tufail had become friendly.

Within half an hour of leaving camp on a reconnaisance trip a covey of monal pheasants took off from a ridge and glided down the valley, across a stream to another mountain slope. This was our first encounter with these pheasants, but it did not take us long to learn their habits. The male pheasant gave a rather mellow whistle, at times resembling curlew. This whistle became frequent when they spotted us, others doing likewise, even though out of sight, indicating that the whistle was also an alarm call.

Our first two attempts to get within shooting range of them proved unsucessful, for they readily took wing before we were anywhere near them.

23

However, we soon came to terms with them by instructing the Ghudhis to walk along the tops of the mountains so as to drive the pheasants down to us. They certainly glided down fast and at first we missed them with every shot, but then later a few of these pheasants were bagged.

The reverberation caused in this particular area scattered the pheasants far and wide. We had banked on living off the land, yet what we had shot was not enough to feed the camp, so we had to do better on the days to follow by going further afield, not to mention improving the standard of our shooting.

The Ghudhis had a good knowledge of the habits of these pheasants, and recommended a scheme whereby they guaranteed to attract a large gathering of them into a small area. This bright idea involved everyone in the laborious task of clearing away snow from selected spots so as to expose the soil. Not having shovels, it was a question of having to get down to the task with bare hands. Collectively the job was done, frequently stopping to wonder if the effort was worth the trouble and bearing in mind that a heavy fall of snow would undo hours of hard work in a matter of minutes

The guide, pleased with the sterling job done, suggested another snow clearing operation where we first encountered the pheasants a short distance away from camp. The idea was to create two spots for the final shoot so as to lure the pheasants in the vicinity to scratch about in search of roots, cones, insects and grit.

Nearing camp the guide stopped, asking us to go ahead while he took the rest of his men on a snow clearing task. He instructed them to give him a 15 minute start, then putting his hand into a bag he carried, he took out a panther-skin mask, covering his head and shoulders. I asked the reason. "Well, it's like this" he said, "You Sahibs shoot on the wing. To hit or miss is of no consequence, but I cannot afford the expense of missing a shot, so I've made this mask which I use to shoot partridge, jungle fowl and pheasants. The art is in the stalking, preferably on all fours. As soon as birds see the mask, they fly up to the safety of the nearest tree, remaining stationary to provide a target I never miss."

The Ghudhis rose very early, made tea and sat around the fire talking in whispers so as not to disturb us. At first light they would be out answering the call of nature. One fellow on returning talked of seeing pug marks in the snow! This aroused our interest. We had a look at the prints above the caves where the animal had prowled about then come down to stop below the branch of a tree from which the monal pheasants were left hanging overnight. In most places the snow was far too deep to leave a clear impression. However, on a well trodden track, these prints were identified as being those of a snow leopard – much to the alarm of Tufail!

Because we never placed much importance on the snow leopard, Tufail tried to persuade the Ghudhis to track it down and have it killed by one of us. It was obvious that he was afraid of this animal returning to kill him while others were away from camp. He was assured by everyone that had the leopard wanted a human there was nothing to have stopped it from doing so when it prowled about during the night.

Each day we shot over new areas, improving both our stamina and the art of traversing the hazardous terrain where a careless step taken could lead to disaster. Apart from a few places monal pheasants were very scarce, and chasing them all day was a tiring business. To make matters worse there was never a certainty of a shot at them, let alone bagging any.

One particular dome-shaped mountain, fringed by conifers, looked extremely promising. The distance was a forbidding factor but the temptation was too great to resist, especially when food was in short supply. We had banked on feeding the Ghudhis on Thar, a large species of mountain goat which so far we hadn't encountered.

With a long distance trip in mind extra snacks were ordered just in case we were benighted. Leaving at dawn we climbed to the summit of our mountain, saw sunrise, then descended into darkness for a short while. Looking up, we saw the mountainsides sparkling like magnolia petals in the morning dew. Nearing our objective we were pleased to see a rather nice plateaux leading towards the dome from which a mantle of snow drifted down to the tree-line.

According to what had now become routine practice, the Ghudhis climbed to the tree-line while we spread out some 500 yards below them. No sooner had the guide fired the first shot than there was brisk firing from the other, though I saw nothing. There was then a lull, and before the Ghudhis joined us we heard an unfamiliar call of a bird somewhere below us. Imitating the call, the Ghudhis eventually identified it as a species of pheasant. The curvature of this dome-shaped mountain was vast, we were short of time, and so we decided to take the remaining area below us in a final sweep then head back to camp in daylight.

Leaving the guide to organise the beat, we hurried down about half a mile and positioned ourselves along the contour of the mountain. Shortly after the beat commenced a large bird resembling an owl zoomed past me, settling in a tree with a loud clap of wings. I walked stealthily towards the tree when another bird whizzed through at a terrific speed followed by more and more. They were definitely a species of pheasants, so I started to shoot at them, but missing left, right and centre! In fact, I shot so badly that at this particular time I couldn't have hit a cow's backside with a stick! My worst moment came when I failed to score an easy shot at one of these pheasants which resembled a fire-ball coming straight at me. I was embarrassed to think that if the expedition depended for food on my marksmanship, the lot of us would have given up the habit of living. I only hoped that the spasmodic banging along the line was more productive than mine.

A couple of the Ghudhis happened to come down to the spot where I had positioned myself. I frankly admitted to not having shot a pheasant in spite of a dozen shots fired. I did, however, mention that I had probably wounded one as they came turning and twisting past the tree trunks. One of them picked up a feather, showed it to the other chap, then hurried down the mountainside, returning later with a pheasant he called a "phoolgar" which meant a bouquet of flowers.

Soon we met up with Charles who proudly displayed a "Bout of Flowers". Yes, a cock Western Horned Tragopan pheasant which certainly lived up to the description of a flower. The head and upper part of the neck resembled a rhododendron, the rest of the plumage, a large red dahlia with each petal having a prominent white spot encircled in black.

When the rest of the Ghudhis assembled, a count of the bag was taken. Very disappointing indeed, just enough to keep body and soul together if it came to a question of survival! A final drive was agreed upon to augment the larder, but not without a warning that a bear had been seen moving down between the guns to disappear into the evergreen shrubs. With a bear in mind I wasn't very happy with the spot at which I positioned myself to intercept the pheasants. I had a walk around trying to find a more suitable place with better visibility. The only hope was to climb a large rhododendron tree and sit astride a fork, unable to turn my body towards the right, but at least comparatively safe.

Suddenly I heard a shuffling noise on my right-hand side. For a moment I thought it was a pheasant, but it turned out to be a huge bear, looking exceedingly aggravated. Every now and then it stood up to have a look round. Naturally, I gave it my undivided attention more through fear than choice. The Ghudhis shouted to each other to try and prevent the pheasants breaking back and this further irritated the Himalayan black bear which now frequently stood up to full height, exposing the big white 'V' on its chest.

I can't say whether it had spotted me when it stood motionless looking in my direction, but I became determined to take the initiative and have the first say in the matter. Changing cartridges from bird shot to solid ball and buck shot, I gradually manoeuvred the gun so as to use it off my left shoulder even though I'm not ambidextrous. It was going to be an awkward shot to fire with confidence from a distance of some 40 yards. The solid ball definitely went astray, and, instead of the bear running towards Charles who was equipped with a .375 Mannlicher rifle, it stood its ground, then uttered a series of growls, grunts and moans and hurriedly rushed away, avoiding every one!

Not having placed the gun firmly in my left shoulder I got rather a hefty recoil which caused a nose bleed. Naturally, blood had dripped to the ground before I could arrest the bleeding. All I now wanted to do was to get down and give an account of the episode to all those who were hurrying towards the spot where the isolated shot had been fired. Unfortunately I got entangled in branches and had to stay put, meanwhile one of the Ghudhis happened to pass below the tree and spotted the empty cartridge case and the blood. He immediately shouted, broadcasting the news of the find. Others made claims in the vicinity that they had seen my tracks, the bear's footprints and traces of blood!

The search was now on. My name was being shouted, but only echoes responded, strongly at first then rapidly being absorbed by the endless mountains. There was no doubt about it, things had got out of hand! I never intended to stage a puzzle, nor did I wish to make a practical joke of this incident which had now taken a very serious turn. I was just about to "surrender", knowing that the more I prolonged the agony, the worse Ainsworth's contempt would be for my stupidity. Yet I had the wind up and kept silent.

What baffled the Ghudhis was why there was blood, an empty cartridge and my boot prints, and yet no traces of the bear's track! The Ghudhis gave their theory which boiled down to superstition. The mysterious "Bhoot" (ghost) or the "Charail", which left no visible traces of their movements, had undoubtedly done away with me! Both Ainsworth and Charles though not believing in such superstitions, did show some alarm.

Another search was about to be commenced when I ended the misery by saying "Don't worry, I'm O.K." There was a startled look on their faces as they watched me climb down. The explanation over, I took the tongue-lashing of a lifetime for the inconsiderate act, not only from Ainsworth, but Charles and Baden as well.

We moved off, the guide and myself taking the lead. Within a few miles of the camp I pointed to a spinney, telling the guide it looked a likely spot for pheasants and to lend me his panther-skin mask to try out his method of shooting. He willingly obliged, so I instructed him to carry on with the others.

Keeping out of their view I made straight for the camp as fast as I could. Silently approaching the caves I saw our cook and his mate sitting side by side preparing the dinners. Putting on the mask I crept up on them, then rolled down a handful of pebbles to attract their attention and at the same time exposed the mask and imitated the growl of a panther. Both of them instantly dived into the caves from where they shouted like hell to the accompaniment of beating utensils. I made a quick getaway, climbing up to join the others as though approaching them from the rear.

As we got to within earshot of the camp our friends were still beating away with occasional shouting. When we arrived at the camp, the cook dashed out in hysterics, trying to describe how narrowly they had escaped from a panther. His version of the "attack" as he called it, was absurdly imaginative and exaggerated, giving every one except myself the impression that they had been, in fact, attacked, then besieged for no less

Homeward-bound

*The end of the trip at Baijnath Rest House: Monal
pheasants in the foreground; Tufail, the cook on extreme
right and the guide second from left.*

than three hours! If we hurried he said, there was every chance of seeing it somewhere above the caves.

Charles fell for the idea, persuading us to join him in an attempt to shoot the panther. We combed through a likely area which naturally proved futile, but for poor Charles it was a realistic business and he had hopes of laying a bead on a non-existant panther. My conscience would not allow this tomfoolery to go any further, so closing in on Charles I said "I have a confession to make."

"You're lucky, I have hundreds." said Charles. "Anyway, what's troubling you?"

"You won't tell Ainsworth, will you?"

"Of course not, you know that I always stand by you."

"Well, this cock and bull yarn about this panther affair is a lot of nonsense. All that the cook saw was the panther-skin mask over my face!"

"Rubbish!" said Charles. "The guide was with us all the time, and so were you."

"Admittedly, the guide was with you all, but if you remember I slipped away taking with me the panther skin mask which the guide leant me to try out on pheasants."

"And you mean to tell me that you came all the way to the camp, put the wind up the cook and returned to join us half way up the hill. I don't believe you."

"Fair enough Charles" I said "At least I've got it off my chest whether you believe it or not."

"What a blighter you are. I had contemplated doing something similar with your co-operation so that we could have involved everyone else. Now tell me all about it?" I did so and we shared a good laugh together.

We had come to the end of our stay in the caves. Just one more night and the next mornings' shoot to look forward to. In accordance with the plan laid out for the last day, the shoot started at the crack of dawn. The guide fired the first shot on the ridge, sending down a large covey of monal pheasants from which we had to pick out the male birds. The other spot where we had toiled hard clearing the snow paid off big dividends. Indeed, pheasants were there in plenty. The guide's scheme had worked wonders and our shooting did him justice. Sticking to our own rules for all game birds we tried to shoot cock pheasants only, though this was not adhered to by the guide who bagged a few hens with the aid of the panther-skin mask!

Homeward-bound, the rate of descent was augmented by the Ghudhis' desire to be with their respective families to celebrate the festival of Divali. This is a festival of lights in the simplest yet most effective of forms. Home-made clay crucibles, topped up with mustard oil with wicks placed in them to provide the illuminations. In addition, the entrance to the hut or house is decorated with laurels and the walls invariably form a surface on which the occupants paint designs and the most grotesque sketches of birds, snakes and animals. In every home on this occasion will be found a saucer of milk meant for snakes to drink before they finally hibernate. There is a superstition attached to this practice, namely that if a snake does enter a residence on this particular day, it has been provided for and therefore will not harm any member of the household during the year to follow. As in the case of our customary Christmas pudding so it is with the Hindu sect who must have puffed rice and hard perforated sweets specially prepared for the festival which they distribute to their friends and neighbours.

Our return to Baijnath was ahead of schedule and the guide and our friends the Ghudhis, were well rewarded for their stupendous services rendered throughout the memorable trip.

The experience gained on this expedition proved that the two species of pheasants we encounted at high altitude were not rare, neither do they face a serious threat of extermination. Admittedly, enthusiasts like we three Harrison brothers and a handful of others had thinned their population in one particular spot in an area covering thousands of square miles, but as long as these beautiful pheasants are not invaded by "civilization" they will continue to survive.

I returned to Delhi with Ainsworth, spending a week or so sightseeing and on one day was driven to Hissar and the surrounding desolate countryside to see herds of black buck and Chinkara (gazelle) literally resemble a moving carpet on the sun-baked plains or sand dunes. I was told that what I had seen was only a fraction of the number to be found in this area before the trigger-happy American Forces, based at Delhi, reduced their numbers by wholesale slaughter. Normally, these timid animals are not afraid of automobiles, but I found later that they certainly recognised danger at the sight of a jeep, a vehicle indirectly responsible for the near extermination of these fleet-footed animals.

I visited this same area and adjoining territory such as Sirsa, Rohtak and Hansi in November 1984 but never saw a single black buck or Chinkara. No, not even in the Central Provinces. A sad state of affairs.

30

Chapter Three

One moning in early January 1944 Father asked me to go along with him to give the dogs a day's sport and at the same time shoot a few partridges for the table. He took me to his favourite spot about six miles north of Roorkee to an aqueduct from where we walked east through pockets of tiger grass and bushland. Later, we stopped by the bank of a river to have a snack, and it was here that Father touched on the subject of my future. Expecting this topic to be brought up I had the answer ready.

My ambition was to be a Forest Officer, failing which my second choice was to join the RAF as a pilot. He approved of the former but vehemently opposed the latter on the grounds of safety and told me that I'd be much safer on my feet.

"You see Mick, I'm now an old man and need you to help manage our interests. Admittedly, it's landed property from which there is not much income, but just have a look at the countryside over which we have come. This crystal-clear river flowing through silver sand, the bushland fringed by the jungles of the Siwalik Range and in the background the snow-capped mountains of the Himalayas makes this area, in my opinion, a haven for outdoor people, and a stepping stone to the dense jungles for those interested in big game hunting. Suppose I purchased a fair slice of this land, built original but sophisticated thatched huts with modern interior decor, tapped the river to provide a series of lagoons for swimming and fishing, and above all created a game sanctuary? In addition, as you know I have 15 acres of land in the Dehra Dun Valley lying undeveloped, half of which merges with the dense jungles north of the Mohan Pass. In the hands of a trustworthy person with a live interest in the wilds, these places have the potential to be developed into a lucrative business. In short, a safari business, and the right person to take on this responsible job is obviously you."

Inspired by the trust Father placed in me and the wonderful opportunity to pioneer the first safari business in India I was overwhelmed with enthusiasm to get things moving. Of course, an undertaking of this scale was not possible overnight, nevertheless, with safaris on my mind I put the entire project on the drawing board and obtained the necessary estimates while Father put out feelers in connection with the availability and cost of the land in question. This was going to take time and to put my mind at ease Father suggested I took a trip somewhere, preferably Solan to make a surprise check on the workmen constructing the annex, in addition to which there was plenty of pheasant shooting to be had.

As much as I liked mountains I had only recently spent nine long months amongst them and instead decided to explore areas unknown to me. I had little to worry about, knowing the basic language of Urdu and able to differentiate by name alone a Hindu from a Muslim, and accordingly respect their customs and religious obligations. In any case, if I did run into any snags I would have Bulland Khan with me, an orphan whom Dad took under his wing, training him as a scout and general handyman. In 1940 he joined the army and served in the Middle East from where his regiment moved to the Burma front in 1942 where he was reported missing. However, he turned up very much alive and extremely fit in spite of all the battle scars inflicted in the Burma and North Africa campaigns.

His family name was Bulland Khan but he was nick-named Billinda by members of our family and knowing no better was quite proud of the name! Mind you, he was no weakling. He was, in fact, a very tough customer, extremely strong, brave and had a great sense of humour.

Accompanied by Billinda, who was as keen on shooting and exploring the unknown as myself, we boarded a bus and travelled about 10 miles in the direction of Meerut from where we trudged east with no fixed destination in mind. By-passing the village of Jogiwala we entered a vast depression and followed jeep tracks which lead to the edge of a "jheel" (lake) frequently shot by officers of the Royal Engineers based at Roorkee. It was a choice area from a shooting point of view and I'm sure the favoured few, with the versatile jeep and boats at their disposal, must have had some very pleasant sport.

Scouting around and avoiding the deep pools of water we eventually found a passage into the depths of this marsh which presumably in years gone by had been the old course of the river Ganges.

At times having to make long detours to avoid quicksand, we finally set foot on firm ground and managed to put many miles behind us until once again we were held up trying to find a place to ford the River Patri. However, once over so we were confronted with dense tiger grass jungle, the extent of which couldn't be fathomed, neither were there signs of habitation in this area. By now the evening was setting in, so it was not worth taking the risk of getting benighted in this wilderness of pampas grass or "Sarpat" as it was called in vernacular, so we chose to stay where we were.

Considering we had no equipment other than a blanket each, setting up camp was no problem at all! Billinda, being a resourceful chap, improvised a sarpat mattress for me, while I shot some black partridge in the vicinity which he immediately feathered, cleaned, sprinkled salt on and wrapped in lotus leaves. Then, covering them with a thick mud plaster he put them aside and set about putting down a large quantity of sarpat to burn during the night in place of wood which was not available. While he did this I discovered that leeches had penetrated my trousers at the ankle and lodged themselves on both legs. Though a pinch of common salt sprinkled on them is suffcent to guarantee a quick release of the suction pads, it isn't worth wasting salt when burning ember or cigarette end is as effective. Having "de-leeched" myself I gave Bellinda a helping hand to dig a shallow bowl-shaped cavity which was filled with sarpat and set alight.

The partridges in the mud plasters were then placed in specially prepared crevices at the edge of the fire, frequently turned and covered with embers. Billinda was no cook, but this primitive mud-baked dinner was something out of this world. Perhaps it was the lotus leaves that added the flavour.

The night was cold and sarpat failed to give a balanced heat unless continuously fed. Although Billinda periodically got up to keep the fire going, it not only kept him awake but me as well, because every time he added to the dwindling fire it burst into flames, leaping high into the air and the brittle stems exploded like gun-fire. There was always a lull between the "fireworks" and it was then that I knew we were miles away from civilization for usually one hears villagers on night shift, shouting to deter animals from destroying their crops.

Early next morning we threaded our way through the jungle, keeping as far as possible to narrow game tracks. Soon we were soaked to the skin by dew, but struggling on it was nice to hear the shrill call of the black partridge, a beautiful bird often kept as a pet, more for its unmistakable call than its plumage.

From an open spot within this jungle we observed a column of bluish smoke over the horizon, indicating perhaps the presence of a village. Entering a boggy area we ran into a herd of domesticated buffalo. Domesticated in the sense that they only recognised people in the local garb, but seeing a white face under a pith hat was enough to make them wild! Although they never attacked us, they were a source of worry by charging around, often forgetting our whereabouts and almost knocking us over.

Clear of the buffalo trouble we were out in the open, but at the outskirts of the village once again we were in a spot of difficulty with the pariah dogs who worked themselves into a frenzy. They were a vicious bunch, bent on tearing our pants off if they got half a chance, and they would have done so had not timely intervention come from villagers!

Getting rid of the dogs, the headman of the village invited us to a cup of tea. "Charpoys" were produced on which we were requested to make ouselves comfortable, thereafter a confabulation commenced. The two immediate topics discussed were the menace of a particular wild boar which ravaged their crops with impunity, while the other was fever, undoubtedly malaria.

I assured him that I would make every effort to eliminate the wild boar harrassment, but for the sickness, I made it quite clear that the medical profession was not my line. However, having some Aspro tablets with me I gave them to the needy ones, an act which placed me in an awkward position, for in a short time the demand exceeded the stock. I ran out of tablets and felt sorry to see parents walk away unhappily with their children, some of whom were naked, others wearing the bare minimum of clothing.

With the doctoring business over, the headman drew my attention to small elevated platforms constructed at the edges of wheat and sugar-cane crops. On these platforms they spent the long hours of night shouting their lungs out to prevent wild pig and deer from devouring the crops. From time immemorial this method had been used, in the last four months or so, according to them, a massive boar was ignoring all efforts made to keep him out. Their concern was not only limited to the damage to crops but the situation had become more serious from the boar having attacked a villager who ultimately died of the injuries. A youth showed me a terrible laceration on his thigh, the result of an attempt made by him to spear the boar. The dogs were no exception and they too had learnt to keep their distance from the wrath of this boar.

Continuing, the headman told of occasions when he had unsuccessfully discharged his muzzle-loading gun at the boar from an elevated position without having any effect on it. On the other hand he recounted an incident not long previously, when he fired and wounded the boar, as a result of which it charged, almost dislodging him from the elevated platform. Since then he had given up further attempts to kill it. The ill-repute of this boar was such that even a panther had attacked it in a very noisy encounter but had been beaten off.

While not happy about the accounts I had heard of this animal, I assured them that if they drove the animal into the open I would, in all probability, put and end to it but contrary to my expectations, they refused to oblige though offering every amenity in the village for as long as I desired. Accepting the offer to stay, a small thatched hut was put at my disposal, furnished with a charpoy, bedding and a crude table.

Next day, we set off with a few robust youngsters and had hardly gone a furlong when, crossing over a shallow stream over-run with rushes, a painted snipe flushed from almost under my feet. I shot it with the right barrel of the shotgun loaded with a No 6 cartridge and instantly there was a violent splashing amongst the reeds behind me, unmistakably that of an animal charging through water.

The psychological reaction of hearing the noise was to presume it was the boar. The locals lost control of their senses and ran while we stood our gound. The left barrel of my shotgun was loaded with an SG cartridge containing nine large pellets. I promptly swung around and fired at what was in fact a deer as it ran across an open space. It was a clean kill, and those who witnessed both the shots, one at the snipe and the other at the deer, commended my skill and depicted a similar end to the boar if it should appear before me. Try as I did to persuade these villagers to beat over likely spots which could harbour the boar, they refused point-blank, preferring to be spectators than beaters!

The hog deer was taken back to the village with instructions to the Muslims that it should be distributed evenly between themselves and the non-vegetarian Hindus to make a change in the normal diet of vegetables, millet, pulses and fish. Moving on with the braver ones along the fringes of the sarpat jungle, Billinda made some enquiries as to who had been camping at a place we were passing. "Sarsis" (a nomadic tribe) was the reply . Billinda followed up the topic by making several enquiries as to when they broke up camp, how many comprised the tribe, and in which direction they had gone.

On the way back to the village he requested permission to follow this tribe which he hoped to locate and bring back to solve the problem of getting beaters to shift this boar out of hiding. I allowed him to do so on a condition that he returned within 24 hours with or without the "Sarsis". He agreed and left in the afternoon to search for and bring back the nomads. In his absence I took a stroll where the sugar-cane plantations merged with the jungle. I was soon joined voluntarily by a number of folk presumably because I carried the rifle with me. Tracks of wild pig and hog deer were everywhere. Some wheat fields had been rooted to the extent that they resembled the work of a bulldozer. I selected one such field at the corner of which was an elevated hut on which I intended to position myself at sunset and spend a few hours in wait for the night marauders. Having satisfied myself with this site, I walked along the edge of the jungle on the off chance of meeting with the feared boar.

I was told that not far from where we were a jheel existed on which many wildfowl could be found but I would have to penetrate some distance into the sarpat before the place became visible. In spite of not having the shotgun with me I was curious to see the jheel and requested them to lead the way in. They declined to do so, but after assuring them that the boar would not stand a chance against the power of the rifle, they rather hesitatingly led the way to the marsh which was surrounded with extra tall sarpat, the tops of which formed an attractive silvery border to the horizon. A raft of red-crested pochard floated leisurely on an open patch of water, and further in, where reeds flourished, other duck, coote and herons were plentiful. Scanning the edges of this jheel I saw a sounder of wild pig, some feeding, others wallowing in the slush. I enquired from the Muslims as to whether they minded if I shot a pig for the Hindus. The Muslims, amongst the bystanders, were a sporting lot, encouraging me to go ahead and shoot, mentioning the fact that the pig couldn't care less whose crops they destroyed, Muslim or Hindu.

Up to now these fellows had not seen the 9.3mm Mauser rifle with a MV of 2250ft per sec put to use and I daresay they were surprised to notice that I intended firing from where I stood, about 200 yards away from the pigs. Selecting what appeared to be the largest, I fired and it collapsed on the spot, the 285 grain solid bullet doing a fine job.

The noise that followed was frightening. It was as though a sudden cyclone had struck the area. About 30 wild pig went helter-skelter through the boggy soil and thousands of wildfowl took to sudden flight, of which the majority were Ruddy Sheldrake which, in my opinion. are the noisiest of all wildfowl. However, within minutes they were pencil streaks across the sky and serene peacefulness returned to the wild.

As planned, I returned to the elevated platform to make myself comfortable in the hope that the wild boar on the wanted list would show up. At sundown the jackals howled, the village dogs barked in response, and later the whispering wings of flighting duck concluded the active period between dusk and darkness.

I spent three hours on vigil. Wild pig went to and fro, more often heard than seen. The problem was that they were shy of the flash light and hurried for the shelter of the sugar-cane field. I could have shot a few that braved the spotlight, but having the big one in mind I never bothered. Not being in a frantic hurry to get my sights on this boar, I saw no reason to overdo things, so returned to my hut for a nights rest.

Next morning I roamed around the edge of the jungle to shoot some partridges for the larder. When I returned to the village I witnessed the removal of a leech from the nostril of a buffalo. The parasite had been lodged there for a number of days. The buffalo had been kept thirsty, a neccessity before the parasite could be removed. This did not make sense to me but it was explained that a leech gets as thirsty as the animal. They tantalised the buffalo by placing a bucket of water just out of its reach, at times pulling the bucket away as soon as its mouth touched the water. I observed that when the buffalo tried to mouth the water, the leech would do likewise by cautiously protruding an inch or so out of the nostril. No doubt, both of them were desperate to quench their thirst, meanwhile amongst a group of villagers, one chap was having his thumb and finger bandaged with thin strips of cloth. When he was ready, the bucket of water was placed within reach of the buffalo, but before the animal was actually allowed to drink its fill, the man with his fingers bandaged, submerged his hand in the bucket. The buffalo commenced to drink, the leech protruded out and with thumb and fingers he jerked the leech out of the nostril. I had seen scores of leeches in the past, but this one was enormous, measuring at least nine inches in length and two inches in circumferences. As tough as leather, it took some killing and the amount of blood which oozed out of it was cause for alarm. I was told that if this parasite is not removed from an animal's nostril, it will stay there until the beast gradually emaciates and death ensues.

At noon, the dogs heralded Billinda's return. He brought good news, having contacted the Sarsi tribe, and, in fact, had induced to return. They had been left a short distance away at a place where they had chosen to set up their dwellings. This tribe is, unfortunately, not welcome to stay in either a Muslim or Hindu community. Of course, they are fully aware of their status as outcasts. They are notorious thieves and branded as frauds, never taking up any form of employment. Naturally, as a nomadic tribe their diet is strange and varied with a special partiality for hare and jackal meat. They travel far and wide accompanied by livestock such as donkeys, goats, chickens, parrots, quails, snakes and a variety of hunting dogs, including the popular greyhound. When passing the outskirts of towns, they usually stage some form of entertainment with the help of a monkey, birds, or snakes. By doing this, they manage to raise money and if the audience is keenly involved in the performance, a member of the tribe will often get the chance to ransack houses!

The following morning they gathered near the village, armed with spears and "lathis" (a stave with one end weighted with metal.) Some carried drums while others held savage looking bull terriers on leads, their white coats blood-stained, some showing fresh and old battle scars. The potential danger of the boar in question was explained to them after which we moved on to start the first beat.

I postioned myself about 500 yards ahead to intercept the boar should he break cover. The beaters set about the job of driving out the wildlife. The timid foxes, jackals, caracal (large wild cat) and peafowl came out first followed by hog deer then sows with sucklings. I held my fire, anticipating the appearance of the large boar, but he failed to show up on this beat or on several others which followed.

I then changed direction to beat through a much denser jungle. By now the Sarsis had begun to doubt my ability to shoot, considering they had driven out numerous animals without my firing a single shot. Of course, they were unaware that Billinda had already warned me not to kill anything until the boar had been accounted for otherwise they would help themselves to the dead animals and that would be the last we would see of them!

In the new drive the dogs appeared to have worked themselves into a frenzy, the tom-toms beat louder and faster and the shouting was blood-curdling as it homed in on one particular spot. Above all this noise I could distinctly hear the loud abrupt grunts of a boar. This was short-lived and the sudden outburst stopped as suddenly as it started. I was perplexed to know what could have happened, though I suspected that the boar had broken back. Leaving my position, I advanced towards where the dogs still occasionally barked and reaching the spot I saw the Sarsis bunched together. Straightaway I thought that one of them had been killed. Much to my relief, death had not struck, though a few of them, including dogs, had been injured by the boar. One Sarsi in particular was in a bad way. His thigh was ripped all the way to the buttock. There was no question of getting him to a hospital or a district dispensary. Such amenties don't exist around the corner, neither do these people care. They have their own remedies and cures for wounds which, in fact, are frequent occurrences in their somewhat hazardous existance.

I insisted that further beats be called off, but the Sarsis would have nothing of the sort. The chap who was seriously wounded was taken back to camp by one of his colleagues, leaving the remainder to continue with the effort to get the boar shot. According to Billinda's description of the boar, it was undoubtedly a huge brute, fearless, aggressive and very powerful. When cornered he saw it fight back, tossing dogs and Sarsis alike out of its way in spite of being speared and belaboured with the weighted lathis. I asked Billinda how he remained unscratched in the encounter? He gave the sensible reply that he used his head and eyes to keep out of its way!

The chances of beating this boar out before me was very remote and I was requested to accompany the beat in the hope that a similar incident would occur in which case I would be in a position to use the rifle. I did so without having any success. The Sarsis suggested the ultimate .... set fire to the jungle! I explained to them that not only was that an offence, but a thoughtless and outrageous act to commit, pointing out the dangers of the fire spreading across the entire countryside.

It was agreed that we would head back towards our respective dwellings, selecting en route a few more places over which to beat. In the process of doing so, once again a pandemonium broke out. This time the case was directed towards me. Rather than stand where I was, I moved forward in case of a repetition of the previous incident. To my surprise I saw a Sarsi climb up a solitary dry tree from where he directed the beat. It was within a matter of minutes that he pointed below, shouting "woh jattah hai" (meaning there it goes). The sarpat where I stood was sparse, enabling me to get a glimpse of a boar dashing through at which I took a snap-shot. The bullet found its mark and the boar somersaulted two or three times, then, getting up attacked the dogs which were in hot pursuit. By doing this he provided me with an opportunity to finish him off. A large boar indeed, yet after a close examination we agreed it was not the wanted boar. There was no fresh spear wounds, and it was not as black, nor as big as the one that played havoc with them.

With about 400lb of pork in hand, the Sarsis lost interest in everything other than having a feast. I cannot blame them, they had worked tremendously hard and deserved every bit of that boar.

The area having been considerably disturbed during the day, I was not keen to sit up that night but instead decided on an early night despite which I remained restless, pondering over the day's events and planning various tactics by which to get even with an animal that so far I had not even seen.

In the morning we set off for the Sarsi camp although Billinda was certain that they must have slipped away at dawn. On the contrary, they were very much at home. The fellow who had been ripped by the boar was laid up, though cheerful. The wound was covered over with a paste prepared from garlic and turmeric which acts as a repellent for flies, and is alleged to be a most effective cure for injuries. What intrigued me was the method they devised to keep the gaping wound together. A mesh-like frame made from the sarpat was placed around the thigh and tightened so as to hold the flesh firmly, yet to allow ventilation, thus helping the paste to dehydrate and heal the laceration.

I intended sitting up at night if we failed to encounter the boar in the beats to follow, so we concentrated on areas furthest from the village so that in the event of him being disturbed there would be a chance of him remaining in the jungle surrounding the cultivation. I used the same strategy as on the previous day by not shooting at any and every animal that appeared before me. Only before packing up for lunch did I account for a hog deer, a sow and a few jackals. Billinda took away the deer for the Muslim population of the village and with his own interest in mind as well.

During the afternoon I had a chat with the headman of the village and explained to him that my intention was to sit up all night for the boar , but required a few of his men to dig a pit for me in the centre of a harvested paddy field adjoining the jungle. I had noticed that this field had been frequently visited and rooted by wild pig. The advantage of this spot was that being out in the open I would have a wide field of vision.

The scheme met with mixed speculation and comments. A safety device was suggested which was to construct a protective ring made of thick sharpened sticks embedded in the ground, pointing outwards at an angle of 30' so as to pierce a charging boar! I disagreed with what they had in mind for two reasons. Firstly, the boar would be suspicious of the new construction, and secondly, it would obstruct my vision or even deflect a bullet.

The headman, along with a few others, accompanied me to the spot in question where they commenced to dig the pit to specified dimensions. While they did this, I looked for likely places from which to expect the boar to enter the field. I found two well used game tracks which I kept in mind. I came back and sat down, watching the pit being dug. The headman advised me that when I returned in the evening to the pit, I should not use the insect repellent which I was in the habit of using during the night. I was interested to know why he should have mentioned this. His reasoning was quite logical, explaining that the odour would be alien to the boar, making him suspicious.

The pit dug, I gave instructions for the finishing touches to be carried out. This was to spread the soil of earth evenly over the field after which I jumped in to test whether the height factor was to my satisfaction. It was, and as far as I was concerned, everything now depended on luck.

At dusk, escorted by Billinda, I entered the pit with rifle, shotgun and flashlight. A crude stool was put in as an afterthought. I would have liked faithful Billinda to remain with me, but knowing he coughed a lot, he would be a handicap rather than an asset. I sent him back to the village with orders to join me only if I fired a shot.

Since the days of my childhood I had been fascinated by the howl of jackals, but on this particular occasion the noise appeared to be amplified and made my blood run cold. No doubt, this sensation was due to a fear which is pronounced when alone in an area where danger lurks by night.

In the fading light I saw jackal, fox, caracal and, later, a lonely hyena amble by. None were aware of my presence or perhaps they just couldn't bother about the two eyes and a tuft of hair at ground level.

However, after a while a porcupine walked straight onto me and was astonished at the size of the "earth worm" it saw! Uttering a horified grunt-cum-scream, it spread out its quille to resemble a pin cusion and bolted in top gear.

At about seven o'clock I watched the dim lights being carried by those who must sacrifice their nightly sleep to reap a harvest. Separating, they headed for their respective elevated huts whence the shouting would commence they indicated the positions of the night watchmen.

A sow accompained by her large family of sucklings made a general nuisance of themselves for what seemed to be hours. Finally they came within a stones throw of the pit and became vaguely visible. I forced a subdued cough at which the sow immediately responded with a grunt and the sucklings rallied around her after which the entire family raced across the field creating a hell of a noise. They apparently entered a sugar-cane field, because not only did one of the watchman create a devil of a shindy, but also rattled large tin cans placed within the field by tugging at a rope attached to the cans.

By about 2 a.m. the waning moon had reached its zenith slightly improving the visibility. I was half way through a cup of tea when a loud grunt startled the life out of me. Unfortunately, I was unable to locate the exact direction and had to scan my immediate surroundings. Spotting a dark object I gave it my undivided attention and the more I concentrated on it, the more convinced I became that it was the boar. When trying to fix a bead on it, it would miraculously vanish. This illusion occasionally arises when one is suffering from eye strain as I undoubtedly was. However, some minutes later, another more raucous grunt was uttered which frightened me so much that I nearly leapt out of the pit. This time there was no mistaking its whereabouts. I focused my eyes in the direction and soon saw its outline. The boar standing still, then advanced towards me sniffing violently, a sign that it was aware of my presence. To my immense relief it came no further and began to root, occasionally giving a snort or grunt to convince me beyond all doubt it was a boar.

As I watched I began to lose confidence in myself. The thought of wounding it and then having to deal with an animal of such ill-repute, perhaps ending up in the pit with me would be a horrifying experience. It was too late to consider changing my position or for wishful thinking. Seconds ticked by, chills ran up and down my spine and my heart thumped louder as if demanding to be set free from this tense drama.

It would be a question of a split second, the time taken to squeeze the trigger and the expulsion of the bullet which would end the suspense one way or the other. Would it be a success or tragedy, a clear miss or the wrath of a wounded boar? The answer to these questions stood about 50 yards away, unconcerned about the grave situation I'd placed myself in.

I made an effort to relax, reassuring myself that a well placed bullet would kill the boar instantly. I prepared myself for the crucial moment but found I couldn't see the sights sufficiently clearly to place the bullet on a vital spot, so held my fire hoping the boar would approach to within spitting distance to ensure a clean kill, though it would increase the odds against me if I should wound it when so close.

The boar suddenly stopped rooting and walked menacingly towards the pit. I had the sights on it as it came, but dare not fire because this was one type of shot I'd never take a chance with unless forced to do so. A boar's facial structure is solid, long and pointed, so a bullet splinters on impact and there is every likelihood of the animal withstanding the shock. Furthermore, it will inevitably charge in the direction it faces, having seen the adversary or not. Under the circumstances I decided to leave it alone rather than take a chance shot and have the boar sharing the pit with me!

As luck would have it, it stopped midway to root again, gradually turning to give me a broadside view. Somehow, it sensed or perhaps saw me because it suddenly began to grunt violently. I held my breath and squeezed the trigger. The flash temporarily blinded me, nevertheless, I dropped the rifle and picked up the shotgun. In fact, nothing moved in front of me, but I could hear heavy stertorous breathing coming from the boar which lay motionless on the spot where it had stood a few moments ago. I got out of the pit and as I took a few paces forward, to my surprise the boar struggled to its feet and bolted in the direction it faced which, to my good fortune, was towards the jungle I gave it two barrels of buck shot as a parting present which upset his course and appeared to bring it swinging back at me! I hurriedly reloaded and followed its movements by sound which was appallingly loud.

Billinda, accompanied by some of the watchmen, arrived on the scene to be given an account of what had happened. When we walked over to where the boar crashed into the jungle, we met an unwelcome reception, for the boar, presumably in a state of stupor, made repeated attacks at random, failing each time to find a way out into the open and have a go at us. It was not worth taking further chances with this animal in the darkness so, speaking in a whisper, I called the business off until daylight. We had hardly gone 50 yards when the boar rushed about in the jungle grunting like fury. Naturally, I turned around and while I was pre-occupied with covering its movements, I had not noticed the immediate dispersal of the villagers until I heard Billinda shout "Bhagoo, bhagoo.... soohar peecha purgiah" (meaning run for it, the pig is after you.) Somewhat puzzled at the command given by Billinda, I spun around to see our friends already going like the clappers, hearing this sentence must have added fuel to fire. In the frantic race for survival, one of the men's hurricane lamp had failed to stand up to the trial and had caught fire, in spite of which he trailed it, leaving a flame behind him!

Next morning the Sarsis were summoned and were told about having a wounded boar on our hands. They straightaway volunteered to beat it out into the open, but I foresaw too great a risk involved with this brute of a boar which would be more dangerous than ever. My plan which was to cordon off a small area of the sarpat jungle where we knew the boar to be and go after him with just one Sarsi, Billinda and myself. The plan met with approval, except that a bull terrier was to be included in the party, preferably on a lead, to warn us of the presence of the boar.

Returning to the spot where I had fired at it, I found a pool of coagulated light coloured blood, which proved to me that the boar had been hit in a vital part, probably somewhere in the upper region of the abdomen. Following its tracks which took the shape of a circle, then cut across at a tangent, we located the spot where it had entered the jungle. Penetrating the grass, we noted that the boar had left a blood trail on one side of the grass only, indicating that the wound was high up and the bullet had not passed through. Tracking was easy as far as the blood trail was concerned, but penetrating further into the razor sharp sarpat was most unpleasant, especially when it became matted and we had to crawl through tunnels on all fours.

Some distance inside we found a spot where the boar had fallen or sat down and lost quite a bit of blood. From this point it had back-tracked in a ziz-zag manner towards the direction from which it had entered. This rather complicated matters, making the task an increasingly nerve-racking affair. I knew that during the night it had charged about in this area, but this did not mean that we should take chances and crash around. We had to move stealthily, visibility being a couple of yards at the most. Our best bet was to rely on our sense of hearing to detect the slightest noise or movement.

I tried to re-establish our bearing in relation to the last occasion when I heard the boar run and cause a panic amongst the villagers. If I was right then the next hundred yards or so along the track we were following could be crucial. Either we would find the boar dead, or we were in for an ordeal with the odds against us. Moving on, we came to yet another place where it had fallen and mowed down about ten feet in diameter of sarpat, the stems of which it had chewed to shreds in anger and pain. What worried me after seeing this spot, was the lack of blood compared to the amount it had been losing elsewhere. Now I had to face reality, the tide had changed, and circumstantial evidence pointed to the fact that time had helped to resuscitate the boar, and being on home ground it had everything in its favour. I was fully aware that disaster could strike at any moment without even a shot being fired in self-defence. Sweat trickled into my eyes, the discomfort of miscroscopic splinter shed by the sarpat down my neck and a feeling of claustrophobia, reduced me to a state of lassitude. All that remained was will power and the principle drilled into me by Dad, "Never leave a wounded animal".

It's terribly hard to go on and on in a state of tension with nothing happening and I was approaching breaking point when the dog began to show signs of interest and had to be held back by shortening the lead. Obviously it had picked up the scent of an animal, becoming more excited the further we advanced until the Sarsi was finding it difficult to hold it back. The dog commenced to whine, then barked. Instantly the boar responded with an angry grunt.

I located its position and immediately moved ahead of the dog in order to get a shot at the boar unimpeded by the Sarsi or the dog. Resting one elbow on my knee I sat broadside to the dog with my rifle held firm and ready to fire. The dog continued to bark savagely and I knew that if the boar charged, it would home in on the dog and endanger both Billinda and the Sarsi, perhaps even myself if it went slightly off course.

The dogs accompanying the other Sarsis who had formed a cordon in the area also started to bark and this brought the boar charging at us. Its approach was fast and within seconds it was going to be on the dog. I anticipated its paths and followed it by sound as the brittle sarpat stems were smashed. There was no time to take careful aim as I had done by night, neither was it necessary at point-blank range. I swung the rifle and pulled the trigger. The dog jumped aside, Billinda and the Sarsi dived face down towards me, while the boar rumbled past and collapsed about 10 yards beyond. I knew I had nailed it, nevertheless, I was not prepared to take any chances with this unpredicitable animal. The bull-terrier had almost dragged the Sarsi towards where the boar remained silent and out of view.

I cautiously took a few paces in its direction then peered through the grass. Advancing still further I saw a black mass lying flat on its side. Getting a better view of it I found it was still breathing and placed another bullet into its neck.

The Sarsi was so thrilled that he lifted me onto his shoulders, shouting "shahbash gorah sahib" (well done Englishman) and commenced to dance about much to the amusement of Billinda. The other Sarsis soon arrived and after the formalities of congratulating me were over, the boar was dragged out into the open, taken to the village and put on display. We were given a tremendous ovation after which many of the youths of the village danced around the boar, every now and again striking it with staves.

When skinning this boar, some facts about its past career were uncovered. Prominent on its hide, surrounding the neck and shoulders, were deep lacerations believed to be those caused by the panther. Its ears were torn to shreds, one tusk was fractured and foreign bodies such as lead pellets of various shapes and sizes, together with the deep spear wounds, accounted for some of its battle scars. Most of the lead shot had only been responsible for superficial injuries, but must have been a sore point for many years. No wonder it had been driven to detest the human race, seeking revenge whenever an opportunity arose.

The only lead which failed to remain within the boar were the two final bullets, one of which stopped it in its last abortive charge. The bullet with which it was wounded in the first instance had broken one leg at the shoulder from where it splintered, causing havoc in the abdomen. How it managed to survive for so many hours and still had the stamina to launch that final charge was unbelievable, yet typical of the courage of a wild boar, one of the most dangerous animals when wounded.

The one time formidable mass of strength and the indisputable master of the territory, now lay butchered to await a share out especially amongst those who had a bone to pick with it! Sarsis are never content, and asked for a further supply of meat to help them along on their never ending travels. They had done a magnificent job, so I willingly agreed to provide them with their needs. Plans were soon drawn up to commence beats. I was surprised to observe that villagers who had previously refrained from participating in the beats were now enthusiastically joining in.

Previously I had been hesitant to fire a shot other than at the boar on the wanted list, but now I promised to give them a treat of a lifetime, including a much sought after delicacy, the porcupine.

Content in every respect the Sarsis pulled down their shabby tents and loaded them onto their horses and donkeys on the top of which poultry found suitable spots to ride to the next destination. On one of the horses a dispute arose between a monkey and a beautiful game cock. I was very amused with the game cock's determination to settle the argument arising presumably over squatting rights!!

My interest in the game cock caught the eye of the leader of the Sarsis who presented me with a broody hen and a solitary egg which when incubated would, if properly trained , he assured me, become a champion fighter.

Chapter Four

Influenced by heavy rainfall, especially during the monsoon, the Siwalik Range of hills, stretching along the base of the western Himalaya, contains vast dense jungles with an abundance of big game, including herds of wild elephant. The landscape varies from undulating terrain to steep jagged peaks while numerous streams and rivers flow through the hills to form ideal conditions for both big and small game to flourish. And flourish they did until World War II converted the birds' and animals' paradise into practice battlefields, driving the timid wildlife from the protected interior to the slaughter of the accessible exterior.

The elusive tiger and panther continued to avoid the onslaught, though they too fell victim to unlawful shooting from autombiles by night. V-J day brought peace to the world and to the wildlife when the various jungle training units ceased fire and withdrew, leaving the jungle as it had been before the invasion of camouflaged men and mechanism. Admittedly, sportsman like myself and others would soon be bringing back old memories of gun-fire, but this would be child's play compared with the din of artillery, mortar and machine-guns.

Norman Mahaffy and I had on previous occasions visited the neighbourhood where I had now been granted a permit to shoot. In fact, I selected this area because the inhabitants of a small settlement were well acquainted with us. Coming to know these people was by chance. We were cycling back along a narrow country footpath which forked into this settlement at the edge of the dense jungle. At this spot Norman suddenly jumped off his cycle and shot a hyena dead in the fading light. Neither of us had identified what it was carrying in its mouth before being shot. To our astonishment the object turned out to be a year-old-baby carried away from outside a hut and killed by this wretched hyena. In spite of having failed to save the life of the infant, the inhabitants were more than grateful to us for shooting the scavanger, and the babe would have a grave instead of being devoured. This incident led to a standing invitation to be their guests at any time. We took advantage of the offer and dropped in quite frequently, shooting over their land which adjoined the Forest Reserves. Naturally, our visits became a source of financial income to the entire population, comprising some four or five families and in addition, venison was usually on the menu for this village called Asifnagar.

With a valid permit to shoot in the Reserve, Father, Norman and I set off for the village, and no sooner had we arrived than a passer-by exchanged news with the locals as was the general custom. Something

45

sensational had happened! A tiger had been trapped in a net near the village of Daloowala. Our friend, guide and headman of the village, namely Agayru swiftly had us on the move to the place in question. On arrival he wasted no time with the customary protocol of introducing the Sahibs to the gentry of the village and having a cup of tea. Instead he obtained the exact location where the tiger was to be found and took us to the spot.

A Sikh farmer met and gave us an eye-witness account of the incident and the evidence to authenticate his story lay before us – the charred carcase of not only the tiger, but a wild boar as well!

According to this farmer, he often erected a long strong net measuring about four feet in height and placed it along one side of the potato field. The purpose of the net was to trap wild pig by allowing them to enter the field, then manoeuvre around so that when he disturbed them they would be forced to run into the net.

In this case a solitary boar entered the field, but before the farmer could move, a tiger beat him to it by roaring and immediately bounding across the field in pursuit of the boar. In a matter of seconds both tiger and boar were entangled in the net, and the more they tried to free themselves, the worse became their plight. The farmer terrified of the outcome of his catch, dare not go anywhere near them. He said that the noise the two animals made was indescribable. Seeing that they were unable to escape from the net which had formed a ball around them, he hurried off to the village from where he borrowed a muzzle-loading gun and returned with it to shoot the animals.

At the sight of a human, these two animals went raving mad, making an extra effort to escape. They had been able to reach a thicket in a series of jumps and tumbles. It was here that the farmer got his chance to sneak up to them and fire the gun. Then, as he put it, there was great "tamasha" (meaning fun). After discharging the muzzle-loader he was convinced that both the animals started to fight and in doing so they created such bedlam that the earth vibrated! Then to add to the confusion, a fire ignited in the grass and the entire thicket was burnt to the ground. In this small, but fierce fire, perished two of the most feared animals of the Indian jungle.

Rather than allow the farmer to spread a story that these animals committed suicide by setting fire to themselves, we convinced him that the muzzle-loading gun, primed with black powder, had been the cause of the fire. The explanation was simple. The paper used as wadding must have caught fire when leaving the muzzle of the gun. I should know. I'd done it myself! His version, on the other hand was rather absurd, namely, that the ultimate of these animals was certainly death, therefore to end their suffering quickly, the boar struck his hoof against a stone to spark off a fire in the thicket to put a quick end to the terrible ordeal.

Leaving the farmer with the barbequed quarry, we set off back towards

A fine Cheetal stag shot by Norman Mahaffy in the vicinity of Asifnagar.

The huts at Asifnagar village where many a night was spent.

the village of Asifnagar, shooting jungle fowl en route. In crossing a dry river bed we observed numerous footprints; prominent amongst which were the pug marks of a tiger. Following its tracks for a furlong or so, we noticed they abruptly changed direction to track those of a camel. It became clear that the camel had increased the length of its strides and then commenced to run. The tiger had done likewise, but after a short distance deviated from those of the camel to head for a "sal and banyan" tree jungle.

With some hesitation we continued to follow the tiger's track and no sooner had we entered the jungle than we noted that the tiger, instead of penetrating into the jungle, had hugged the fringe of the jungle to out-flank the camel. The pug marks suddenly vanished after taking a sharp right turn and in their place were the irregular tracks of the camel, obviously in a state of panic due to the tiger having sprung onto it. A short distance away the camel lay dead in a rather open space, its long neck twisted backwards showing deep claw wounds and the throat pierced by the tiger's fangs. A very small portion of the camel's hind quarters had been eaten. Rigor mortis had not yet set in, proving it had been recently killed, and most probably our approach disturbed the tiger from its feed.

With the chance to shoot this tiger, we decided not to pursue any more partridges or jungle fowl which were very plentiful in the area. Agayru, with the assistance of his mate Kalu, set about constructing a "machan" (hide built in a tree) overlooking the carcase. They finished the job, complete with an improvised ladder within an hour.

Norman was due back in town that evening, and had to leave us to handle the tiger while he, along with the two men, would return to our headquarters, picking up what game they could en route. We agreed, requesting Norman to send the men back by evening. Father and I climbed into the machan after which the ladder was removed and concealed some distance away by the departing party.

We waited all day in the hope of the tiger returning to the kill, but it failed to show up. In the evening our two men arrived with our dinner which we ate straightaway, then we directed them to return to the nearest village and rest until morning.

It was interesting to watch the abundance of bird life preparing to retire for the night. Each species congregated in separate trees. Jungle-cocks crowed everywhere and soon pied hornbills arrived to roost in a nearby banyan tree where they restlessly hopped about, making a terrible noise. We did not appreciate these enormous birds so close to us for the simple reason that, in the event of a shot being fired, they would take to their wings, producing a din similar to an express train passing over a railway bridge. A disturbance of this nature is something to be avoided after firing at a tiger, so I got down from the tree to get rid of them. I was surprised to find that their unrest was due to the presence of a python sharing the same tree. Having got rid of the hornbills, I watched the python slenderly disappear into the higher branches of the tree. As much as I would liked to have shot it, I had to refrain from doing so least I disturbed the tiger.

Where there's a "kill", it's as sure as darkness follows daylight, the jackals will be there! A pack of them arrived, and so did the cunning rare wild dogs. The relationship between them was far from amicable. They rushed about snarling and growling at each other for a considerable time, trying to establish superiority over each other. A hyena joined in to settle the issue, attacking these fidgety animals after which, irrespective of their torments, he settled down to dine. I asked Dad whether we should shoo them away, but he quite approved of their presence because if they suddenly bolted, it would signal the arrival of the tiger.

The moon had risen and light penetrated through the trees to form strange patterns on the ground below us. It was past nine o'clock, the hyena was still gluttonously feeding while the jackals hung around at a safe distance, spasmodically trying to get a mouthful of flesh from the carcase. The novelty of the affair wore off as time advanced. Somewhere in the interior a "Kakar" (barking deer) started to bark until he ran out of steam. I noticed that Father was nodding off to sleep and it was not long before I did likewise. Suddenly the loud bell-like call of a sambur cracked the silence of the jungle, and both Dad and I almost stood up with a start. In a matter of seconds the jungle rang with the alarm calls of cheetal, sambur and peacock. Father whispered a warning to be on the alert as this could mean the tiger was in the vicinity.

It was one thirty when the forest reverberated to the roar of the tiger. Instantly the deer uttered their alarm calls, the peacock followed suit, resenting the disturbance caused by the animal's resonant roaring in the dead of night. Having announced his arrival, the scavengers went helter-skelter from the scene after which there followed an ominous silence.

I glanced at Father; he was concentrating on the kill which was quite well illuminated by moonlight. A cracking of a twig somewhere behind us tempted me cautiously to take a look. There I saw the tiger stealthily walking away to my left, every now and then stopping to sniff the ground. I nudged Father and whispered in his ear that I had seen the tiger, but he never as much as blinked an eyelid, neither did he bother to have a look for himself.

Judging from Father's unconcerned attitude I could see there was to be no change in plan. The tiger was to be allowed to commence feeding before we did anything. Then Father was to take the first shot and if necessary, I was to cover further eventualities. There were no two ways about it. He intended to stick rigidly to the agreement and I should have known better than to have tried to distract him.

I could do nothing about the tiger, other than admire its magnificence as it suspiciously manoeuvred around in the scanty cover. At one time it appeared to have made up its mind to walk over to the kill, but half way across stopped by the side of a tree trunk and sat down in perfect view for me to have taken a crippling shot. As a matter of fact, my trigger finger had never been subjected to such a torture before. Undoubtedly, it had sensed the presence of man, or at least was aware of them having been around and remained seated to scrutinize its immediate surroundings.

Having decided not to come any further, it walked away into the thicker jungle and disappeared for about half an hour, then returned, its stomach, no doubt, getting the better of its will power. This time it didn't stop to procrastinate, but re-enacted a kill by springing onto the camel resting its forepaws on the carcase and staring into the dark jungle. Finding there was no danger about, it lay down at right angles to the kill and started to lick the flesh. Judging by its enormous size I'd say it was a male.

The climax to this spectacle came all too soon. The tiger was no more than 15 yards from us, so a shotgun was the more suitable weapon to use at this short range. Accordingly, in the process of changing weapons, the tiger must have seen the movement and instantly leapt away with a terrific roar. Father immediately looked at me and rather angrily said, "Oh Mick ... why did you move so hastily. I warned you to let it settle down to eat. Didn't you see that I hadn't even as much as raised my gun?"

I was a bit annoyed myself and replied, "My interest was in the tiger and not in your gun. The trouble with you is, if I may say so, you're far too slow." There was silence, then Father continued, "You can't teach an old dog new tricks. You're still a novice at the game and too damn excitable."

"Maybe you're right Father but you have brought me up with a gun and need no proof of my ability when it comes to the question of using it. I tell you the tiger would have been lying dead if it was left to me. You must face the fact, your eyesight is not as good as it used to be, neither is your hearing nor your reflexes. I'm not asking you to concede to your lifetime hobby, but be proud of having a son who can do what you did in your youth."

Father remained speechless while I meditated over the unpleasant remarks I had passed. He was then 73 years of age and I wondered if I'd live to that age, let alone brave the hardships of the wild as he was still doing with zest. Amongst the vicissitudes of his great shooting career, this incident was a bitter disappointment. No doubt, he was regretting the lost opportunity, which after all, was a gift for him in his old age, but mishandled and sent astray by me. This episode in late February 1945, has since been of profound sadness to me because, although not aware of it then, it was in fact, my first and his last time to share a machan in the solitude of a jungle with a tiger at our feet.

We spent the rest of the night in silence, hoping that the unpredicatable animal would return to the kill. He never did, so we vacated the machan at sunrise and returned to the village where we debated the pros and cons of the tiger paying a further visit to the kill during the day or night. It was unfair to keep father out indefinitely, so I suggested we return home, but he was determined that one of us should hang on and try our luck with the tiger, preferably as he put it, "you, with the keener eyes and youth in your favour." Rather than offend him, I agreed provided he went home straightaway to rest after having spent a sleepless night.

Accompanying him for a fair distance we parted and he wished me good hunting. Placing his hand on my shoulder he said, "Son, the spirit is willing, but the flesh is weak. I wish I was your age again." He had taken me under his wing ever since I was a little toddler, guiding and teaching me the tricks of the game, and now, when I was man enough to take care of myself and Father as well, I felt guilty of having deserted him. As he walked away down a lonely track I watched a man who, when in his prime, was a pillar of strength, now white haired, weather beaten, rather frail and gradually being overcome by the cruelty of old age. Seeing the lonely figure disappear out of view I was engulfed by emotion and soon rejoined him, much to his surprise, but against his wishes.

Norman was very disappointed to hear that we hadn't shot the tiger, and being of a restless nature as far as shooting was concerned, it was not long before we were back again in the hope of meeting up with this tiger. I enjoyed Norman's company for his complete disregard for comforts or lavish arrangements and we got on famously together, accepting our lot in a sportsmanlike manner.

As a novice he was a good shooter, but a bad hitter, nevertheless, over the years I admired his determination to learn the language, tolerate the many discomforts of the wild, eat what was put before him, drink whatever I drank and, above all, he remedied his habit of missing everything that flushed before him. He eventually won over the affections of my sister Clare whom he married and became a popular member of the family.

Having carried out our primary duty by shooting a deer for the inhabitants and a few jungle fowl for ourselves , we had a few drinks and retired to the thatched hut, then in the early dawn set off for tigerland. There was no guarantee of seeing tiger or panther in these jungles by daylight or even by night. Pug marks, however, were always to be found, and if fresh were well worth following. On this occasion, while walking along a dry "nullah" (stream) we picked up fresh tracks of tigress with two cubs. Then, a little further on we saw a spot where she had answered the call of nature, so fresh that it was almost steaming! The pug marks led out of the nullah to our relief because we did not want to harm her unless in self-defence.

We continued along this nullah which was about eight feet wide. Trees, shrubs and sarpat with its silver plumes grew profusely on either side of the banks. After some distance the nullah widened eventually to form what must have been an island where it forked and re-joined again. At this spot the distance between us increased. The island was well covered in bushes and pampas grass and we could distinctly hear a shuffling noise. Our reactions coincided – down in a crouch, gun at the ready for any eventuality. Nothing happened for quite some time, meanwhile I was trembling with excitement not knowing what to expect. Then Norman attracted my attention with a hand signal, pointing to a spot between us, then directing me to go forward which I did but still unable to see a thing. Keeping an eye on him and what lay in front increased the tension, especially when Norman raised his gun to take aim then put it down again. He did this several times without firing a shot. Suddenly he lay down, took aim yet not a shot was fired! All this added to my suspense, not knowing the outcome if and when he did fire.

Eventually he fired, and all hell was let loose. The ground trembled as animals and birds, especially peafowl, took sudden flight, the tall grass began to give way, then from beneath the embankment came a very ill-mannered herd of wild pigs, panic stricken to say the least. My nerves already on edge, I hadn't the courage to face the "charge of the Light Brigade"! Hurriedly I placed my gun against a bush then leapt up to hang onto an overhanging branch, lifting my legs clear of the ground and watched about 40 wild pigs go whizzing through, some directly below me. It wasn't funny at the time, yet when calm returned I had to chuckle.

Norman was convinced that he had "knocked a big boar for a six". Indeed he had, but we couldn't find it! However, a short distance away we found a blood trail. Worse luck, it meant following up a wounded boar, which was not a comforting thought. The blood trail led up and out of the nullah, across scanty grassland and at the end of which we heard a youngester crying. His story was that soon after a shot was fired a boar came running towards where he sat keeping watch on his grazing buffalo.

Being in imminent danger he ran and jumped onto the buffalo's back but the boar followed, collided with the buffalo and fell over, at the same time the buffalo butted the boar and ran, and he fell off as it increased speed. Taking the youngster with us we soon found his buffalo to his immense delight though it was still looking infuriated.

Finding the spot where the incident occurred, once again we followed the blood trail back into the jungle until we found the boar lying dead at the bottom of a steep nullah, perhaps the indirect cause of death being its fall from a height of some 15 feet. Pulling it up with an improvised rope, we managed, with the help of the buffalo, to haul the boar back to the youngster's village to provide his family and the Hindu community with a real treat.

Early that evening Norman and I took a stroll through grassland encircled by small hillocks when I experienced a sensation of being watched. Looking back I viewed the landscape, then walked on continuing a conversation, but once again felt uneasy, and when I looked back for the second time I saw a tiger sitting on the crest of a hillock watching us.

Excitedly I pointed it out to Norman and both of us crouched in a nearby hedgerow watched with interest by the tiger. Naturally it was intrigued by our behaviour, especially having lost sight of us when we hid behind the scanty hedgerow. It raised its head and looked in all directions, then presumably having spotted us, it gradually began to lower its head until all we could see was its forehead and ears. The distance was some 70 yards.

It was doubtful what the big cat intended to do, but we took the initiative after a quick decision to take advantage of the cover provided by the hedgerow, move in opposite directions and close in on the quarry at the top of the hillock.

Stealthily crawling up the hillock, at any moment we expected to go into action. Fortunately, neither of us were trigger-happy because instead of being confronted by the tiger, Norman and I came almost face to face! The tiger's cunning was more than a match for our pincer movement, leaving us completely bewildered as to its escape route.

I mentioned to Agayru having seen a tiger in the nearby hillocks. He got quite excited and was optimistic that I would shoot it that very night, provided we were prepared to leave straightaway for a place where it would probably be found. Norman was tired and suffering with a nasty headache, so declined to go after the tiger, but was in favour of me going ahead.

I had a snack after which I set off with Agayru to a salt lick situated in a dense part of the jungle. We reached the spot when it was pitch dark, however, according to Agayru it was not late as far as the tiger was concerned. Deer were frequent visitors to the salt deposits, and if a panther or tiger was in the area, then they often lay in wait for them. The presence of a tiger in the area was established, so a visit to this spot was highly probable.

He briefed me as to the direction from which the tiger would approach tha salt lick and recommended a spot where I would intercept the tiger if it obliged me with a visit. I was under the impression that he would construct a crude machan but when I suggested it, he looked rather amazed, then said "what... at this hour! You're not afraid, are you?"

I sat down under a bush, resting my back against a tree to face a small glade through which a game track cut across to the salt lick. Innumerable caracal, mongoose, civet cats, foxes and deer passed by within spitting distance. Two cheetal stags faced each other in rivalry, providing me with some facinating entertainment. I wish I could have seen all this in better light, nevertheless, the noise from the clash of antlers was as thrilling to hear as it would have been to see. In a flurry of fierce fighting, the issue was decided, the defeated ran like fury chased by the victor, and the curtains were drawn for the next act.

Part two entailed a long wait. This happened to be very unpleasant for me. The profound silence was broken by some carnivorous animal crunching bones not far behind. The situation became increasingly tense, not knowing what the animal was, and to add to the dilemma I was not sitting in the safety of a tree. I tried consoling myself with the fact, that, whatever the animal was, it was busy eating, so was unlikely to fancy me for its dinner! But, when the crunching ceased I wondered whether it had detected my presence and was in the act of stalking me? To add to my already nervous frame of mind, parrots suddenly started to screech in the trees above.

My thoughts ran riot; I saw myself faced with a two pronged attack, one from ground level, the other from overhead. I visualised a silent python on its way down and a hyena wondering whether I was sufficiently disabled for it to finish me off. Well, my bravery came to an end, I was reduced to a defenceless object at the mercy of anything wishing to attack me. I only remained where I was because my limbs wouldn't respond. As much as I tried to remain calm I realised I was hopelessly ineffective, petrified and foolhardy to continue bluffing myself that I was not afraid.

Stubbornly I sat tight, thinking the situation would change in my favour. It took a timid little hare which appeared a few feet away to convince me that I was unable to defend myself. I couldn't even lift the gun to my shoulder! This was it. No longer could I stand the agony of being alone, sitting on the ground in a dense jungle and convinced I was surrounded by hidden danger. Eventually I stood up to make a hasty retreat only to find my legs had gone numb! What a terrible fiasco this would have been in the event of an emergency! However, in due course my legs obliged, but had only gone a few paces in top gear when my jacket got caught up in overhanging thorny creepers, and the "jungle boy" was arrested for attempting to escape in a disgraceful manner! Jerking myself free, I disturbed a roosting dove which took off loudly , colliding into twigs, leaves and branches to give me the most dreadful shock imaginable. I ran for what I believed to be a wide open plain, but in fact, it turned out to be tall tiger grass into which I barged face forward. Once again I disturbed a roosting partridge from under my feet. The noise was enough to make me reel backwards, missing some heart-beats in the process. However, I found my way out and then came across a narrow, well-used path. I hadn't a clue where this would lead me. I just ran and ran, hoping to clear the jungle, but it wasn't my night. This path took me deeper into the jungle until it became a cul-de-sac!

By now I was quite desperate and on the verge of a breakdown, unable to think clearly or do anything to my advantage. Panic stricken, I turned about, and the jungle had me running a marathon. As I jogged along, there were times when I had visions of a tiger catching me up, and I was forced to burn up my already fading energy to escape from the animal I originally set off to ambush. From time to time I had awful hallucinations, not only of the tiger, but panthers, wild dogs, hyenas, bears and everything else on four legs, taking immense pleasure in chasing me out of their domain!

I was soon too exhausted to run any further, so I decided it was high time

I put my best friend to use. It was the easiest way out of this predicament, for a coward I'd proved myself to be. I stopped, turned around and fired two shots into the trees! Straightaway there was a general disturbance. Peacocks uttered their characteristic "payoo" call, birds of all kinds fluttered out of the trees, monkeys stormed angrily through the branches in disarray, while other beasts skedaddled away in all directions. I reloaded the gun and the smell of cordite reassured me that I was in command of my senses. I now pulled myself together to regain the confidence I had lost in myself.

Had I not started off by running wild in the first instance, I could have homed in on the village by just listening to the crop-scarers shouting. However, having calmed down I had no further trouble in finding my way back to the hut.

Even though the summer was fast approaching and the shooting season closed, I continued to roam the jungles to study wildlife, plentiful as it was, but shy and hard to find. During the course of these trips I was struck down by malaria which lingered on for months, sapping my energy and ultimately responsible for a loss of physique. I was really miserable and all the recognised treatments failed to cure the fever. However, a local homoeopath was summoned and under his treatment – bitter liquids taken regularly for a couple of months – I was fit once again. He recommended swimming as the best form of exercise after recovering from the illness, and considering the day temperatures rose as high as 115 degrees I was delighted to spend hours in swimming pools or in the Ganges Canal, building up muscles which had lain dormant.

Owing to my illness Father had postponed his departure for his summer headquarters at Solan, but I now insisted that he went and took Mother with him while I looked after the harvesting of the mango crop and any other matters needing attention before joining them at Marjorie Ville, Solan where I'd spent many years of my childhood.

With the start of the monsoon, the humidity of the plains was a new experience for I had never spent any length of time in such weather conditions before. However, I tolerated the prickly heat, the invasion of frogs and every insect which could fly or crawl, including snakes, now more difficult to detect in the uncontrollable vegetation. The frogs, harmless as they were, had a habit of entering the house in search of insects which were attracted to the electric lights. Similarly, snakes occasionally did likewise in the search of frogs and so this circle of predatory instinct continued, despite my efforts to eradicate the menace. It didn't bother me all that much, for I was accustomed to these creatures and knew whether they were harmful or not.

Content with life, I supervised all that was entrusted to me and the thought of joining Mother and Father did not enter my mind, in fact, I was quite prepared to stay where I was until their return in autumn.

Chapter Five

I never looked forward to the delivery of mail as I wasn't in the market for receiving letters except from Mother or Father, or the occasional one from Ainsworth and Charles giving advance notice of a winter fixture to get away from it all. To my surprise, out of the blue, came a letter from Ainsworth enclosing a copy of a letter which is reproduced below.

D.O. No. 4788/19-21
Office of Supdt. Police
Simla. Dated 8th Aug.'46.

Dear Mr. Scroggie,

Kindly refer to your remarks on my Weekly Crime Diary for the week ending Saturday the 27th of July, 1946.

As already reported, the Police party were not successful in killing the animal in the Sabathu Area. A large number of villagers turned out to help, on some days as many as 500 were present and a large area was beaten, but I have come to the conclusion that beating is not the correct method to use now that the grass is so thick when large areas cannot be penetrated on account of prickly bushes and cactus covered with creepers. However, this might be successful in January or February. I think the only way to deal with the animal at the moment is to wait until it kills some cow, buffalo or human and then to sit up over the kill. I have made arrangements for immediate information when it kills to be telegraphed to Simla, and for a machan to be built immediately and I will go out on receipt of such information or send an Inspector if I am unable to go myself.

If we have no success by October I would like to take out another police party, this time placing them in machans at various places over a tied up cow or buffalo. I think I know fairly well where the animal normally lives to within half a mile, therefore, this method might be successful unless the animal has been disturbed by our visit.

There were some conflicting stories regarding the animal, its habits, whereabouts, and it was not until we had been there 4 or 5 days that I got some idea where it might be. After we had one day's beat in the area, the animal again made an appearance, entering a small cowshed in the middle of the night and dragged away a half grown cow several yards down the hillside. I wanted to sit up at night over the kill but it was such an inaccessible place that it was impossible to see the kill from any side due to the thick undergrowth, so I had this area closely beaten but without success.

I think there is no doubt that this is the animal responsible for the killing of human beings in the area, but it will now have to confine its activities to cattle, as all the inhabitants sleep behind locked doors and very rarely go out after dark, in which case it will be driven to make daylight attacks on human beings. I think the animal must be very old and is most probably a panther. I saw pug marks but was unable to tell whether they were those of panther, leopard or tiger.

Even if the animal had appeared in the beat I rather doubt whether we would have killed it with .303 rifles as the men are unable to resist the temptation of shooting at anything from porcupine to deer. And as the beaters would not walk in a straight line there was the risk of accidents amongst the beaters and those who sat amongst the bushes at the end of the beat.

I would be very grateful if anyone could be found to help in this matter. The most important thing we require is a person with some experience of big game shooting, man-eaters in particular, otherwise it may also be possible to find some keen 'shikaris' who may like to help.

Another interesting thing about this animal is that it has seldom come to notice or made a kill, either human or beast except during the moonless nights of the month.

Yours sincerely.
Sd. S.P. Fisk

J.A. Scroggie Esq. O.B.E., I.P.
Deputy Inspector General of Police
Ambala Range. Ambala.

Copy forwarded to the District Magistrate, Simla, for information and any suggestions he may have regarding further action.

Sd. S.P. Fisk
Supdt: Police. Simla.

Copy to Inspector who will come to Sabathu from Delhi to be sent urgently to him through S.H.O. Sabathu.

I think the most likely place is on the Sabathu side of the river which runs between Chansa an Delgi, about one mile downstream, from there a further distance of a mile to a mile and a half.

Don't worry about going into State Territory and ask S.H.O. Sabathu for any help you require. Good Shooting.

Sd. S.P. Fisk."

Having read this letter and Ainsworth's request to join him on this official assignment, I jumped at the opportunity to be with him as a brother and shikari.

Meeting at Ambala, we travelled up to Solan where we talked about this unidentified animal with Father. He was prepared to accompany us on the mission in spite of being unwell. Mother made sure he didn't and both of us supported her reasoning. Though disappointed he understood the situation and gave us valuable advice as we left for neighbouring Sabathu.

Branching off the main Kalka Simla Road at Dharampur we were soon at Sabathu, a very small township, familiar to Ainsworth who had been posted there in 1941 as Officer in Charge of Sabathu Internment Camp. The S.H.O. (Station House Officer) of the Police Station gave us up-to-date information about the animal's latest activities.

Moving out of Sabathu we headquartered ourselves in a village from where operations would be central and most convenient. Walking over these hills during the monsoon is rather tough going. The entire countryside is overgrown with foliage and everthing is wet, damp and humid, conditions under which mosquitoes, flies and fleas thrive. Indeed they were pests we could have done without, but generally they never got a second thought once our primary mission of finding the whereabouts of the animal began to be planned. The inhabitants of the villages we visited gave us similar stories about this animal believed to be a panther, and a very cunning and elusive one at that. Its victims, if human, were always women. In the most recent case it entered a hut, crossed over sleeping male members of the family and attacked a woman, carrying her away in its jaws in leaps and bounds while the inmates watched panic-stricken and helpless.

At another village we were told that it attempted to dislodge a chain holding together a partially open door. This it did by using its paw by trying to get the chain off the hinge. The man in the house who was watching the act, though terrified, picked up a stave and struck a severe blow at the animal's paw which was immediately withdrawn to the sound of roars. This incident occurred at dusk. By daylight however, he found short white hairs stuck to the woodwork and on the floor, providing evidence that he had hit the paw.

Most of the information gathered so far was feasible, but visiting another area, the accounts given about this animal were astonishing and, in some cases, we were inclined to consider them the height of imagination. Nonetheless, irrespective of our findings, these people were in the grip of the most terrible despair, neglecting their cattle and their crops. All that mattered was self-preservation.

After listening to two fates of a similar nature, we saw the reason why every man, woman and child was the subject of hallucinations and terror.

In the first incident, two women were busy washing their laundry in the stream when they saw a man walking towards them. There was nothing extraordinary or peculiar about this person, but next time they glanced at him he had miraculously become a panther. Amidst the confusion a young woman was struck down by the panther, mauled in the stream in the presence of her friend, then dragged up the hillside into the jungle. The girl narrating this incident broke down and became hysterical, depriving us of the chance of further questioning.

The second episode was equally absurd. In the story a group of women returning from the popular spring with the day's supply of drinking water were passing a bull which was grazing alongside the narrow winding path leading to the village. Suddenly, what was originally a bull, became a panther and in a gruesome attack took a woman out of the column, carrying her into the nearby lantana bushes.

These two reports told us that by sheer coincidence a panther, in each case was already in the act of stalking the women washing their laundry, or in the second case was preparing to attack the bull when the group of women passed by; having a preference for a woman as a meal, it selected one of them instead of the bull. Another possibility which could not be ruled out was that a maniac was masquerading as a panther and taking advantage of the situation caused by the activities of a man-eater in the area to get away with murder.

Our suspicions were quenched when a woman was killed next morning while cutting grass. We managed to find the corpse and noted her stomach and breasts had been devoured, proving beyond all doubt that a panther was responsible for the killing. Its pug marks were beside the corpse and lead away from the scene. An interesting feature about the pug marks of this panther was that one set appeared somewhat deformed because only the heel left impressions on the soft soil. This of course, could have been the direct result of the blow it was alleged to have got when attempting to dislodge the chain holding the door together.

Our desire to have the corpse removed to a spot near a tree and to have a machan built over it on which we could sit, was vehemently opposed. The reaction was understandable, but we did miss a reasonable chance of shooting at or at least seeing, this animal. The next of kin, did, however, agree to place the corpse on the ground at intervals so as to leave a trail passing a medlar tree. The objective was to sit in this tree and hope that the panther would follow the trail, providing us with a chance to kill it. We spent all night in this medlar tree being bitten to hell by mosquitoes and soaked to the skin by a steady prolonged drizzle. A disappointing night indeed.

It was unlikely that the panther would kill again next day, so we organised a beat which turned out to be a hopeless effort. For one thing the lantana jungle was too dense to penetrate, furthermore, the beaters followed each other in large groups, leaving wide areas of the jungle untouched. Only one valley was heavily bombarded with boulders which flushed a covey of Kaleej pheasants and a Kakar (barking deer).

So far all our combined efforts proved useless. We had sat up by day at strategic points over a large area, spent a couple of nights out and organised a beat. What we hadn't tried as yet was the most common dodge of all. The use of live bait such as a buffalo calf or a dog. At last we tried this method, keeping vigilance over some animals, and on one occasion I observed a colony of monkeys feeding at the edge of a maize field. Suddenly they panicked, but found their way to the pine trees which they climbed hurriedly, then commenced to raise their alarm calls while leaping from branch to branch and tree to tree until they finally disappeared over the hill.

This behaviour of the monkeys was conclusive evidence that they had seen a panther. Naturally, I became very keenly absorbed in the immediate surroundings from where the monkeys bolted, expecting to see the panther appear in some open spot below the trees. But, typical of the big cat in India, it preferred to be unsociable and remain unseen.

News reached us that same afternoon, of another victim of the panther. We hurried downstream to be met by the bereaved family of the missing lass. Falling at our feet they implored us to recover the body, but try as we did, and though picking up a trace of blood, our efforts were in vain.

I had a bright idea which I mentioned to Ainsworth. This was to use a human as bait. He scorned the preposterous suggestion and jokingly said "You'll have to go a hell of a long way to find a lunatic asylum from where you may, with a bit of luck, get a volunteer to oblige you in this game!" I was serious and replied "The person to act as bait is right here." Ainsworth looked at me in dismay, then enquired "You mean Illum Din, the orderly?" "Of course not," I replied. "I shall personally take the prerogative as hunter-cum-bait and you will cover me from a vantage point to make sure the panther dosn't sneak up on me."

Although Ainsworth opposed the scheme, he had no other choice than to give me the protection I requested. After having borrowed a colourful "ghugaree" (woman's long flared dress) and an equally bright shawl, the "Belle of the Himalayas" was escorted away by big brother to a picturesque stream where the illusive panther was to be seduced. Selecting a wide part of the stream, I sat conspicuously on a rock while Ainsworth, assisted by Illum Din, climbed a tree from where they had a bird's eye view of the immediate surroundings.

The visibility on either side was about 30 yards, enough to protect myself against a surprise attack. Ainsworth, on the other hand was covering the rear, so I wasn't all that badly off, in fact, felt quite at ease. However, at sunset, I must admit I got cold feet and didn't fancy remaining disguised as a woman any longer, neither did I relish the idea of being on a rock a few feet off the ground.

We spent the best part of eight hours on constant vigilance and while I was prepared to have an affair with the panther by daylight, I had no inclination whatsoever of him cuddling me by night! My plan proved a failure, I just wasn't his kind of girl!

Next on the known list of kills was a goat, but we failed to find the carcase because of heavy and incessant rain causing the stream to resemble a roaring river so making it impossible to ford. However, by evening the rain subsided and the sun came out to add a glitter to the glorious countryside, highlighting the miniature waterfalls which are a characteristic feature seen in these hills during the monsoon.

Repeating our usual procedure we spent hours every day sitting up at different places in the neighbourhood of villages, hoping that for once the panther would behave like a gentleman and show itself in the open. Of course, it remained in hiding until ready to strike, and that it did usually in some area we had already covered. The time came when we needed a break from this frustrating mission and we returned to the Police Station at Sabathu. Ainsworth sent a telegraphic message to the boss informing him of his intention to abort the assignment. The unexpected reply was to continue the effort to destroy the man-eater. This was bad news because both of us had done our best and were not ashamed of admitting failure.

Still undecided what further tactics we should try, the S.H.O. told us that a runner had just brought news of a bull having been killed by a panther near his hut some three hours walk away, we had experienced disappointments before, another one would be of no consequence.

Arriving at the spot in late afternoon we found the carcase lying on a hillside where the grass was some two feet tall. The bull was rather large which probably prevented the panther from dragging it across to the adjacent lantana jungle, or perhaps it became suspicious and left the kill.

This was a factor to our advantage, for the bull had not been fed on at all, but at the same time there was no tree in the close vicinity on which to have a machan built. This meant we had to lie in wait for the panther on the ground or make do with a scanty cactus plant. It was not a pleasant thought considering the grass was about two feet tall, through which the panther could creep undetected. Nevertheless, we were determined not to lose this opportunity, being optimistic that the animal would return to the kill.

Leaving Ainsworth to keep an eye open for the panther, I, along with Illum Din and a local inhabitant, set out to improve the hide by cutting down other cacti and neatly arranging it against the one already there. The thorny tentacles of this species of cacti are easily broken or cut, but we had to do this very carefully because the plant excretes a milky fluid in large discharges from the slightest wound inflicted upon it. Fortunately these wounds heal rather quickly, yet the white fluid remains visible and unless hidden would give the panther cause for suspicion.

When I sat down to cut one of these plants from the base, I realised my backside was resting on something soft, and what is more .... it wriggled! I had a strong idea what it was, and without any hesitiation dived forward from the "cushion". Checking the spot I thought perhaps I'd find a dazed grass snake, but to my horror, when parting the grass with the muzzle of the shotgun, a Russell's viper hissed and struck frequently as it took evasive action. Whilst swiftly striking at the muzzle of the shotgun, it somehow managed to bite itself and could not release its fangs. Unable to free itself from the self inflicted bite I left it to die of its own venom if suicide by such means was possible. There was no getting away from the fact that, had it injected me with venom I would have died there and then because, in the listing of poisonous snakes in India, the Russell's viper is second to the notorious cobra. Just to be on the safe side and not to have the viper on my mind during the hours of nightfall, I ran the muzzle of my shotgun through the viper coil and deposited it in a valley a few furlongs away.

Putting the finishing touches to the hide, it blended quite well with the landscape and as we were higher than the carcase we were able to see the horns and a portion of the bloated stomach showing just above the grass. This, of course, at the approach of darkness would gradually be absorbed into the hillside. To have the grass flat all around the carcase would have been a help, yet such interference would certainly make the panther suspicious.

Illum Din and the local inhabitants were directed to return to the village while Ainsworth and I prepared ourselves for a night of uncertainty. The latana jungle was the most likely place from which the panther would approach, but we decided not to take any chances and sat back to back in order to gain all round protection with minimum of movement. Until sunset it was comparatively safe, but our optimism began to fade with the light, and henceforth the advantage was to be with the wily animal. There was no evading the thought that the hunters might very well be the hunted!

A large eagle owl persistently hooted somewhere above us, causing cold shudders to run through my body. It was a question of mind over matter; there is a superstition that this owl hoots where generally death is the outcome. This was a bad omen and despite not being superstitious I could not help but take a pessimistic view. The ugly thought of the man-eater creeping up through the grass was something I could not get off my mind. I cannot express Ainsworth's feelings at the time, but speaking for myself, I was regretting having put foot in this area.

We sat like statues, whispering to each other only when it was essential, otherwise it was a question of moving our eyes rather than our heads. How long this business would go on for, was anybody's guess, yet we just had to sit there and put up with it, trusting in each other implicitly for protection in the event of the man-eater deciding to pick one of us rather than settle for the bull it had already killed.

We had previously agreed upon the use of two signals to warn each other of the presence of the man-eater. One nudge indicated a strong suspicion while two nudges meant the panther was at the kill and I was cautiously to turn around, then focus the flash-light on the kill, allowing Ainsworth to fire the shot. In any other eventuality we were to exercise our discretion and do what was most appropriate to avoid a catastrophe. As to be expected, the use of one nudge was somewhat abused, but then, better safe than sorry. The jackals arrived, a welcome sight, because they would leave if the panther was close.

The mental torture was bad enough without having to put up with mass attacks by mosquitoes which bit us with impunity, and after satisfying their appetites must have hurried away to pass the word around that there were two extremely accommodating meals confined to the isolated cactus. The only friendly sight on this dismal night was a blaze of fire-flies which had gathered at a particular spot resembling an over-illuminated Christmas tree.

Suddenly there was a simultaneous exchange of one nudge, in fact, there was no necessity to wait for the pre-arranged two nudges. The jackals rushed off, I started to inch myself around noiselessly until we both faced the kill. It was too dark to make head or tail of what was licking and tearing the flesh of the carcase, nevertheless, the noise helped to pin-point the objective.

I slowly raised the flash-light and held it parallel to Ainsworth's shotgun, then whispered ... "ready?" Ainsworth replied "OK". I switched on and straightaway two eyes, bright as headlights of a car gleamed, even though I was not spot on target. In a split second I had the beam focused on these brilliant eyes. It was an unforgettable sight, a snarling face, ears folded back and unquestionably a panther. Its body was in a crouched position, somewhat obscured by the bull, but one thing was certain, it was poised to spring either at or away from the spot-light. Before it had chance Ainsworth fired two barrels of buck-shot, causing the cat to leap in the air, after which it plummeted down the hillside with the most terrifying roars. These were short lived and the only noise was that of an alarmed peacock and a dog barking in the distance. The waiting game was over in literally a flash, a five second exposure would not be an over-estimation.

We walked over to the carcase of the bull to find that the panther had eaten quite a bit of flesh in a very short space of time, though some may have been eaten by the jackals.

It is unwise to go in search of the panther because a beam of light would reveal nothing which might lie in wait beneath the grass. I paced the distance back to the hide. It was about 18 to 20 yards, close enough to have crippled the panther. With this thought in mind we settled for a celebration and opened the last bottle of beer in the haversack. It exchanged hands twice and the celebration was over, and so was the strain and stress. We were now at liberty to smoke, talk, laugh and above all, retaliate with vengence against the mosquitoes.

The first sign of dawn was heralded by the beautiful whistling of the Kastura, a bird slightly larger but similar to the blackbird, later the Kaleej pheasants screeched, followed by the peacock, the drongo, the golden oriole and numerous other birds, until the entire valley appeared to be celebrating the end of the man-eater.

The scarlet horizon soon showed the silhouettes of humans coming over a ridge. Undoubtedly the gun shots must have echoed throughout the hills in the profound silence of the night, waking up the inhabitants, some of whom were now on their way to us. Illum Din headed the column, marching quite smartly through the grass and when he came near enough to halt and salute, he tripped, lost his balance and with it his desire to give his usual impressive salute. Picking his turban up, he sprang to attention and paid the compliment smartly enough, in spite of which Ainsworth sternly told him to be prepared for a refresher course in square bashing. He saluted again, acknowledging the award, then asked the all important question, the answer to which was a disappointment to him, havng taken a side bet that the panther would be found dead.

We scrutinised the spot where the panther crouched at the time the shots were fired. Two pellets out of 18 had hit the bull, surely a bigger percentage must have been on the target, the panther. Going down the hillside a blood trail was picked up some 40 yards or so away from the kill. Illum Din was delighted. His winnings were as good as in his pocket, a rather too confident statement made at this early stage. To a hunter's way of thinking, where there is a blood trail, there is hope of finding the quarry dead or putting a finish to it. We did neither of these two things; the panther had, to our bitter disappointment, entered the lantana jungle, so ending the immediate pursuit.

Illum Din produced a flask of tea and some hard-boiled eggs while discussing our next move. A unanimous decision was to send the inhabitants who accompanied Illum Din back to the surrounding villages to spread the news that the man-eater had been wounded, and that all able-bodied men should unite to find this animal, dead or alive. To assemble enough manpower would take some time, and we took some much deserved sleep. We were gingerly awoken by Illum Din announcing that lunch was ready, and that the beaters had also arrived, enthusiastic to get started.

In a matter of half-an-hour we were off, followed by a retinue of beaters and no doubt, onlookers, well wishers and advisers! Stopping at the crest of a hill, a whirling mass of vultures arose from the carcase of the bull. On reaching the kill we found quite a few people already standing beside the bull and hundreds of vultures sitting close by, impatiently waiting for the humans to leave. This took some time because Illum Din had been briefed to give the beaters rigid instructions, emphasising the fact that though we presumed the panther was mortally wounded, a guarantee could not be given that the animal was dead, so when combing through the jungle it was imperative to be cautious.

We moved down the slope to the spot where the panther had entered the jungle. Once again Illum Din took charge, deploying the beaters almost shoulder to shoulder in preparation for the search.

From past experience with wounded animals, we had believed that the panther would follow a course which would offer the least resistance, that is, downhill. Ainsworth followed the blood trail, and was going to stick to it as best he could, while I was to be some 20 yards below him and below me was the "Lambadar" (headman of a village) who carried an antique muzzle-loader, grossly neglected and resembling a rusted piece of piping rather than a fire-arm.

Penetrating the lantana jungle was terribly difficult and painfully slow. Beaters broke formation and bunching together they followed those carrying guns. This was to be expected, but it served no purpose in finding the panther. It was almost impossible to walk upright; at times it was on all-fours and our progress was in a crouched position, struggling to keep the shotguns free from obstruction. Fortunately, here and there, we had some relief, finding areas where we could stand erect with fairly good visibility.

A pariah dog which previously had been running about uncontrolled, rather surprisingly attached itself to our group, but was reluctant to go forward. At times it was so close to my legs that it almost tripped me. When it persisted in this manner it brought back memories of a fox-terrier which did the same thing when a panther was in the vicinity. I immediately shouted a warning to Ainsworth that I suspected the panther was close.

My presentiment was correct. Within minutes pandemonium broke out just below me, where the panther uttered a loud growl, followed by a series of even louder ones. The situation became a bit chaotic, nevertheless, Illum Din's raucous Sergeant Major-like voice came over loud and clear in his pidgin english, "Panta jump on head.... all blood". What he meant was a puzzle, however, it seemed that he had been mauled and both Ainsworth and I made a frantic effort to come to his aid. After forcing our way through the thorny barricade we arrived by his side to find the beggar unhurt! Normally he was as black as the ace of spades, but something had frightened the life out of him. His complexion was stone grey and he had become speechless which was most unusual. When he returned to reality he rattled away in a mixture of languages from which we understood that the panther had jumped past his head and was covered in blood. Probably it had been lying amongst a landslide of rocks from where it must have lunged forward either to attack or escape from his path.

Building up a further picture of the incident, supported by circumstantial evidence, it was quite clear the panther was incapable of swift movement. We could see that it had dragged iself down the hillside, affording the "lambadar" an opportunity of killing it at close range, but unfortunately his gun failed to fire! Asked if his muzzle-loader was primed, he answered in the affirmative and to prove his point he used another percussion cap and pulled the trigger. This caught us off guard. The gun went off with a rumbling boom bringing down leaves and branches. The smoke remained trapped below the umbrella of lantana and the odour of crude gun-powder hung in the air.

To follow the panther's track was fairly easy because in going downhill it had left the foliage and mud clearly disturbed. Furthermore, a fresh blood trail had started which was a great boost to our morale. There was now no need for all the people to follow the trail. We gave them the option of returning to their respective villages or stay put and await the outome of our effort. The majority were pessimistic and were quite eager to return to the comfort of their villages before being overcome by darkness. Above all, there was superstition which was rife amongst these hill tribes. One fellow spoke of having to cross a small stream in a gorge, where soon after sunset a Chirrail existed. A Chirrail according to these people, is an abominable creature resembling a human, but walks with its toes facing backwards and has finger and toe nails as long as bull's horns! To add to the bizzare description it has enormous fangs and yet it only requires physical contact to kill, if it so desired. Escapees were left with an evil spirit within them which eventually killed them, or it had to be thrashed out by a competent "Sadhu" (witch-doctor). To avoid this creature it was imperative to have in one's possession some form of metal, preferably an iron bangle, or a naked flame.

Illum Din was once again changing colour for the better and needed no second invitation to take our advice and move out of the jungle with the rest of the villagers, not without saluting even though he was in a crouched position!

We had moved some distance down to the steep part of the slope where, under some fig trees we found the dry remnants of a goat's skeleton, presumably a victim of a panther. After searching the area around these trees without any success, we rested in a peaceful atmosphere; the flow of water, the distant call of a cow and the solitary music of the lark eased the tension. In a matter of minutes we had glimpses of the river and the lantana jungle was being broken up by massive rocks, yet the trail appeared to lead straight on to the river's edge. It did, leaving smudges of blood on the smooth surface of river stones, indicating the stomach and rear legs were being dragged. This trail of blood disappeared on contact with water from which it seemed obvious that the panther had crossed the river. We did likewise, the depth of the water being between 18 inches and two feet but flowing rather fast.

A thorough search of the opposite bank revealed no signs of the panther having crossed, so it must have been washed down river or deliberately floated down.

We walked up river on opposite sides for a short distance, then went down river for a good mile or so. The effort was most disappointing and due to dusk it was a matter of common sense to concede defeat after a hopeful start.

Neither of us shared the view that the panther was indestructible, yet it had to be displayed dead to convince the people of its elimination. This now depended entirely on what support we would get next morning for another search of both banks of the river. For a start, a message was sent to the police station to relay instructions to the adjoining police station to send out search parties on both sides of the river just in case the carcase was found, or a mortally wounded panther was seen.

To augment the search we were joined by a squad of riflemen from the police station at Sabathu. Fanning out some 200 yards on each side of the valley, accompanied by a vast number of inhabitants and their dogs, we moved down river very slowly, hoping that with disciplined policemen the search would be thorough. To dampen our spirits, the heavens opened and it bucketed down with a typical monsoon deluge. Within an hour the river was in spate, washing away any traces of blood the panther may have left on the river bank or elsewhere

A ray of hope at last. A dog barked again and again but remained stationary, an indication of a find, perhaps the panther! This was encouraging as it was ahead and just above the river. It was on my side of the bank beneath a cluster of trees for which I headed as fast as I could. Getting there I saw the dog still barking and looking down at the base of some huge boulders. As I approached I visualised the panther lying dead or incapable of protecting itself. To my disappointment, and no doubt everyone else's, the dog had apparently chased a fox or porcupine into its shelter.

It is difficult to judge distances over rough terrain, but at a guess I'd say we had covered at least 10 miles from where the panther was known to have come to the water's edge. On the return journey we closed ranks and came up river until back to square one. Linking hands to form a chain, my party crosssed the narrow river and joined up with the other. We decided on a final effort, concentrating on a half mile radius. Moreover, to avoid the monotony of the areas already covered, we exchanged sides and a further search was systematically carried out yet we found no trace of the wounded panther and much against our sporting principles, we aborted the search to return to the village in despair.

As there had been no overnight rain Ainsworth and I once again searched the valley for perhaps a fresh trail of blood or a gathering of irritable birds or circling vultures. No such signs existed, it became a puzzle to know what had happended to the mortally wounded panther. The most obvious conclusion was that the panther had drowned and presumably lay trapped between rocks over which murky water flowed.

Meanwhile we left for Solan where Ainsworth spent the night then returned to Delhi. No sooner had he resumed work than news was conveyed to him from the Police Station at Sabathu that the panther had been found dead in a decomposed condition. According to Ainsworth, who returned to Sabathu shortly after receiving the information, the panther had been found wedged between rocks at a bend of the river, not far from where we gave up the search.

The man-eater never struck again, proving beyond all doubt that the panther recovered from the river was the culprit. In fact, by virtue of its victims, the panther should never have been called a man-eater. It was really the woman-eater of Sabathu!

Chapter Six

There had been no family gathering for quite some years, and a family as large as ours was not easily assembled, as they were scattered across the Punjab, North West Frontier and Baluchistan, all serving in the Essential Services.

I got in touch with everyone and leave was coincided so that a convenient date was fixed to assemble at Charters Ville to take Mother and Father by surprise. Normally they expected a few members of the family to spend the festive season with them, but on this particular occasion, the 22nd of December 1946, my parents were overcome with joy to find the entire family with husbands, wives and grandchildren turning up at short intervals throughout the day. Accommodation was no problem, but the old cook was having hysterics at this sudden influx of people without having been given prior warning of their arrival. However, he was given orders to engage temporary staff to help out during our stay.

By evening everyone had arrived and settled down. Soon bottles began to appear and the large hall once again came to life, the piano took a bashing from the girls while the men got together and exchanged yarns. The dinner gong put an end to the hilarity and the conversation became more sober. It was not long before a discussion on the country's political situation was dropped in favour of the prospects of a shooting trip. A unanimous decision was reached that we leave town and spend Christmas week somewhere in the wilds.

The necessary arrangements were made and next day the cars were loaded and away we went down the Meerut Road for six miles, then turned onto a bullock-cart track. The next six or seven miles were no joy ride and, frankly, it was quicker on foot. While jogging along, a black buck was spotted tearing across a vast plain. Charles promptly stopped his car, loaded his .375 Mannlicher rifle and we witnessed a spectacular shot from 200 yards or more. Shortly after, we crossed through a narrow ridge which was densely clad with thorny bushes. On our left was the village of Mandlana and from there, as far as the eye could see, was an ocean of tiger grass, marsh and jheels. An open sandy spot at the base of the ridge was selected as being the most appropriate place to set up camp.

There were no tents, nevertheless, provision had been made to improvise shelters with tarpaulins, ground sheets and blankets. The weather was perfect, and the men were happy to rough it, while the women were given far better facilities to keep them happy. When everything was organised we shooters slipped away to tackle the snipe and partridges. The sound of shots soon brought visitors from the village and from amongst those who showed an interest in the sport we engaged beaters for the length of our stay in the area.

The evening set in, the air was crisp and the aroma of barbequed buck worked up healthy appetites. The bright light from the Petromax lamps created a wonderful atmosphere in the peaceful wilderness where the only lights seen are the stars and the moon. Jackals lost no time announcing their arrival at the spot where the buck was carved but our dogs gave them a hot reception until they were tied up.

Something had to be done to solve the barking and howling so I silently crept away with shotgun and flash-light to quell the trouble. To my surprise I found I had company. It was Charles who had a similar idea. When I flashed the torch on the spot where the buck had been gralloched, the eyes that sparkled were quite fantastic, a bizarre kaleidoscope of "traffic lights" which appeared to switch on and off.

Four shots dispersed the pack of jackals, but caused terrible confusion in the camp where the excitable labradors tied to the poles supporting the improvised tent, jerked themselves free to retrieve the kill! Not expecting stormy weather, the poles had not been very securely pegged down, so the dogs came bounding across, trailing the tents with them! Meanwhile in the camp there was screeching and shouting, laughter and abuse all mingled together. Lights were lit and from where we stood we realised what havoc had been caused!

The majority of us were up at dawn for a duck shoot in the nearby Paddy fields and jheel. We picked a mixed bag and by nine o'clock the shooting had ceased. Wading out of the water I tried to negotiate a short cut and in doing so found myself in deeper water, then I suddenly sank lower into a bog. In fact, I was up to my waist, struggling along with shotgun and ammo held high. Leeches added to my worries, for though I had no objection to them attaching themselves below the knee, I did resent them trying to take advantage of reserved areas!

I had almost overcome the obstacle when, to my horror, I saw a submerged mugger (marsh crocodile) lying motionless on the sponge-like weeds at the bottom of the water. It was a few yards in front and facing me. Neither of us moved, I was too petrified to think clearly – a shot would not penetrate to the depth where it lay and I couldn't outrun a mugger in water. We stared at each other, the crocodile calm and confident, and when it emitted a bubble I was not prepared to find out exactly what it had in mind. I beat it to the draw by firing two shots into the water just above where it lay, sending up columns of water high in the air, then desperately struggled to make a quick getaway, aware that the mugger might be hot on my heels! I didn't stop splashing through the water and the slush until I was clear of the danger zone.

Those who heard the two shots, followed by the awful splashing immediately took cover thinking it was a wounded wild boar approaching them through the rushes in a devil of a temper. Fortunately there were no inexperienced hands at the end of the rushes awaiting the "wild boar" otherwise I might have found myself at the receiving end of a charge of buck-shot!

After breakfast the beaters were lined up and we set off across the swamps. Billinda kept strict discipline over the beaters despite which they frequently broke formation to pick up empty shells when shots were fired. He was a hard taskmaster, and became highly unpopular with a couple of beaters who eventually threatened to withdraw unless Billinda controlled his language and spoke to them more respectfully. The altercation was amicably settled, and we continued with the full complement of beaters.

The further we advanced, the more exciting events became. Black partridges and snipe , wild pig and hog deer were often moving at the same time, and the choice of cartridges became quite a headache. The marsh was deceptive and it was not uncommon to see someone stagger and fall or find yourself with one leg anchored in bog up to the thigh and the other leg stretched forward to complete the splits. This is not the best posture when you have an infuriated wild boar on the rampage! I was caught thus by a massive wild boar which proved more than a match for the combined efforts of the dogs to handle. In fact, one of the dogs decided that discretion was the better part of valour and ran towards me for protection pursued by the boar. To my relief, the dog peeled off when about 10 yards away, giving me a chance to fire at the pursuer without hitting the dog. The two shots had no effect on the boar; he belted past as though still after the dog, but collected more lead from most of the guns until Charles finished him off with a rifle.

The marsh was becoming unbearably boggy, particularly for Father who was feeling the strain, so we wheeled around and headed for easier terrain. Here, a solitary cow was found resting, miles from anywhere in a place more suitable for a buffalo than a cow. Ainsworth became inquisitive and changed course to find out the reason. As he neared the cow, she struggled to get up but after making several attempts, gave up. It was apparent that she was bogged down. Just then a snipe took to the air at which Ainsworth fired, causing the cow to erupt and, after battling against the mud, she finally bolted, holding her head and tail up high and looking as wild as the countryside itself. For some unknown reason she turned and headed briskly straight for Father, who was at first unconcerned, but then sensed he was undoubtedly a target. He faced her with courage, putting up a defence while the rest of us chuckled. The boggy nature of the ground did not give Father a fair chance to defend himself successfully, and he went down flat on his back. I was the closest and realised this was no laughing matter. I grabbed a stave from a beater and went to his aid, helping him to his feet. He was covered with slush from head to foot quivering with anger and in no frame of mind to appreciate the humourous side of the incident. The reason for the cow in the wilderness was presumably due to the Hindu owner finding her barren, and rather than sell her to be butchered, left her there to fend for herself.

During a short break Billinda mentioned he had overheard a conversation about the presence of muggers in a small but deep jheel somewhere in the locality, and if we were interested he would find out more about them. Charles was the only one with a rifle, so he suggested we visit the spot and told Billinda to obtain more information. His report was favourable, and by making a slight detour we would establish whether there was any truth in the statement regarding the muggers. Within half a mile of the spot we were told not to fire any more shots lest we disturb the crocodiles.

The jheel was tucked amongst tall rushes and at the far end was a tiny island on which three muggers lay basking. A raft of spotbill ducks soon became suspicious and took off to join some red crested pochard floating close to the island.

While the rest of us watched from concealed positions, Charles manoeuvred himself into a shallow watercourse from where he fired. Two muggers instantly dashed into the water, while the third and largest remained motionless. Straightaway Charles gave it another shot.

The mugger was as dead as a door-nail, but now arose the question of its recovery. There was no boat available and the beaters emphatically refused to enter the water, let alone swim in it. It was very deep and treacherous owing to an overgrowth of plant life which formed a carpet below the surface. Under the circumstances it was considered best to abandon the task of recovering the mugger, but Billinda decided to trigger off trouble by calling two of the beaters cowards. These men, already bearing antagonism towards him defied Billinda to swim out and retrieve the mugger himself. Billinda immediately commenced to strip. We vehemently opposed the foolhardy idea, but Billinda was not the kind of man to be ridiculed without doing something about it. Though he was prepared to obey the order to refrain from swimming out for the mugger, he frankly told us that he would return later when he was off duty. Knowing he would do just that, it seemed proper to let him swim out whilst we stood by to give him covering fire. Having tied his turban around his waist into which he housed a dagger, he walked to the shortest point between himself and the mugger. We told him to shout if he had the slightest indication of being attacked by muggers so that we could plaster the surface of the water around him with shots. In fact, we did this before he commenced his hazardous swim.

Being a strong man and a powerful swimmer, he started off as though he was competing in a race, but then he slowed down revealing the resistance of the underwater plants. However, he reached his objective safely, watched all the time in silence and suspence. Then there came a triuphant moment when he stood alongside the mugger, to be applauded by everyone except the two men who had dared him to do what he had now accomplished. Beaten by jealousy, they adopted an indifferent attitude, reminding their colleagues that there was still the return journey to be completed.

Using one end of the turban to tie up the mugger's mouth, Billinda tied the other end to his waist into which he lodged the dagger, then dragged the mugger into the water and started back. Towing a heavy crocodile through such dangerous water demanded skill, courage and strength, and this he was out to prove he had plenty of by the magnificent way in which he handled the situation.

Suddenly his progress slowed, he swung around, reached for his dagger and lashed out into the water underneath him. A rifle bullet fired by Charles struck the water about a foot away, sending up a column of water resembling a depth-charge, while the rest of us emptied our guns across the water at a safe distance on either side of him.

All was well with Billinda. Nevertheless, we watched each stroke with anxiety until he stepped onto land, hauling the mugger clear of the water. Although exhausted, he immediately grabbed the more belligerent and despicable of the two beaters, bodily lifted him off the ground and pitched him into the water, then looked for the other one to give him the same treatment, but he had taken to his heels, never to be seen again.

After Billinda had cooled down he warned the rest of the beaters not to underestimate him as he would not tolerate their nonsense. There was, however, no need to give this warning because he was already being hero-worshipped.

We asked Billinda if he had been attacked by a mugger. He modestly admitted that he was attacked, but when he turned around to defend himself and jabbed at the back of a mugger, it turned out to be the one he was towing! The water must have helped revive the paralysed nervous system for just a moment, flicking the tail and propelling the mugger forward to collide with Billinda. He was not ashamed to confess that with the burden tied to him, he stood little chance if he had been attacked and was afraid. Who can blame him?

The marshland had provided enough thrills for the day. We decided to return to camp along the base of the ridge, shooting grey partridges as we went. Intrigued by a white object balancing in mid-air about four feet off the ground, Ainsworth and I went to investigate. On coming closer it began to flutter and we indentified it as a white pigeon suspended in the centre of an almost invisible net, held up by two thin iron rods. Our immediate reaction was to set it free but just then a fellow appeared out of a bush and asked us to leave it alone as he had placed it there to trap a falcon. Telling the rest of the party to carry on without us, we hid to watch proceedings.

After a long while this man pointed out a falcon circling the top of the ridge. He threw a stone towards the pigeon to make it flutter. The falcon was a good distance away and appeared disinterested, but gaining height after circling, it suddenly headed towards the pigeon and then from an angle of about 45 degress, it dived at terrific speed, finally folding its wings to resemble a three inch mortar shell on its way to its target. The next moment the net, pigeon and the peregrine falcon were lying yards away in a tangled mess. Hurriedly, the falcon was removed from the net, hooded and placed in a bag, the pigeon was injured yet when released took off, whizzing low along the ground to settle in a sacred pipal tree.

At sundown we had a few snifters, kindled the camp fire and relaxed with a well stocked bar to see Christmas in. Some of the days outstanding incidents were re-enacted to bring lots of laughter from the ladies and were equally enjoyed by those of us who, in one way or another, were directly or indirectly involved with each episode.

We didn't rise to the sound of church bells or the familiar sight of an illuminated Christmas tree, nor the customary exchange of presents wrapped in colourful paper. In contrast, but befitting the occasion, nature's naked beauty was there to be praised. A wealth of bird life chorused the music, the prolific wild-plum studded with red, yellow and green fruit, substituted the Christmas tree, and the grandeur of the marshes painted with green, gold and silver, the little hills, the date palms and a blue sky was an authentic picture, not an artists impression on a Christmas card.

The entire adult population of this village had turned out to see us, the interest being more in the women than the men, the reason being that our women were rarely, if ever seen before. There were numerous invites by individual families to honour them by taking a cup of tea in their humble dwellings. Of course, to accept the offer of one, and refuse another would certainly lead to some form of animosity, therefore to be fair to all, we begged their leave extending an offer to them to drop by our camp if any of them were interested in availing themselves of venison or pork of which we had plenty from the previous days shooting.

When we broke up camp that year in December 1946, none of us then realised it was the very last of such trips undertaken as a united family. Charters Ville saw in the year 1947 with the family wishing each other a very happy New Year. It was not to be so, and the house never saw the family reunite again. It became a very lonely place, especially for my Mother and Father who later witnessed the end of the "Jewel of the British Empire". Yet they would not quit, hoping that I would stand by them to set up a safari enterprise.

The consensus of opinion amongst members of the family was that such an enterprise managed by myself, with all due respect, would be very risky, bearing in mind that the country was on the threshold of independence.

The dreaded wild boar

The finest catch of "Mahseer", including the record
hooked by Bobby Harrison

With no knowledge of what the future was going to be for the British community, it would be unwise to embark on the business until we knew exactly how we stood once a new Government held the reins. After all, we had been the landlords, and shortly we would be the tenants.

Naturally I was heartbroken that my ambition was in shambles. I went to Dehra Dun with two objectives in mind. To apply for a Forest Officer's job, or a commission in the army. The Royal Military Academy, the Sandhurst of India, became my choice. I was interviewed later, sat for the competitive entrance examination and was selected to attend the next couse with joining instructions to follow nearer the time for training to commence.

The news was exhilarating, more so to my parents than myself, knowing that I would be close to them, a matter of 45 miles from Roorkee. I did, however, miss the companionship of my brother-in-law Norman who obtained a good job in the Anglo Iranian Oil Company at Abadan (later to be nationalised by Moddediq Hussain and the British work-force were obliged to leave shortly after to return to the U.K.).

Nevertheless my sporting activities continued and I added fishing to my outdoor interests after witnessing the terrific fight put up by a Mahseer (a fish known as the tiger of the river) before it was eventually landed, over an hour after hooking. When weighed it was 76lb. I was surprised to see the size of its main scales which were as big as saucers.

The Mahseer is found in the upper regions of the large rivers, especially where they enter the plains below the Himalayas. In addition to the rivers, Mahseer are found in the canals, but once again only in high regions where the water is cold. At one time my uncle Bobby Harrison, a very keen angler, held the record for the largest Mahseer hooked. I believe it was sometime in October 1909 at a place called Tangrot on the river Jhelum where he had the finest day's fishing of his life with a catch of 13 Mahseer, including the record one of 101 lb.

I must admit that I never had much success with the sport and caught nothing worth shouting about, though a big Mahseer did get away, because I did not have the experience to play it. The tiger of the river is a befitting name for the Mahseer; strong, fast and courageous, breaking a line as if it was a length of cotton thread. There were plenty of Mahseer in the Ganges Canal which flowed past within 200 yards of Charters Ville but I never did catch a Mahseer weighing more than a couple of lb! (When visiting a friend in November 1984 at Rishikesh, about 15 miles north of Hardwar, holy city of the Brahman community, I was told that to catch a Mashseer weighing more than 10 lb on the river Ganges itself, or on the canal which commences from Hardwar, could be considered a record! The reason was over-netting and, sadly, the use of explosives which though illegal, is rife in the valley separating the Siwaliks from the Himalayas.)

I made a comparison between fishing and shooting. One rarely sees a fish, especially the big ones moving about freely in their natural habitat, whereas in shooting, the quarry is generally seen, with a few exceptions. Weighing up the two sports, personally I preferred the gun to the rod.

Chapter Seven

It was my policy to shoot where I was welcome or in areas where the inhabitants took an indifferent attitude towards the sport. Naturally, I occasionally wandered into zones where the people objected to shooting and, rather than violate their principles, I kept away from any such place influenced by the Brahman community who are strictly vegetarians and firm believers in live and let live. Some take this religious obligation so seriously that they take precautions not to step on ants when going about their normal work!

It happened that I inadvertently shot a deer in one such area where the Brahman caste was in full command, and as a result I was ridiculed, abused and told never to put foot on their land again. Fair enough, I now knew where I stood and refrained from shooting in that neighbourhood, but before leaving the vociferous agitators I advised them to cordon off their sacred jurisdiction to ensure that predatory birds and animals should have no access to it!

To the misfortune of the inhabitants of this area, a tiger became a man-eater! They couldn't get rid of it as easily as they got rid of me. Life was precious, killing was condemned, but how could they enforce this religious function on a tiger! Guns were only possessed by a chosen few, usually for services rendered to the Government, and it was unlikely that the heads of departments would recommend a firearm to any individual resident in a territory where its possession or use would be apt to stir up communal unrest. Admittedly, in the adjoining areas, a few Lambadars (headmen) possessed muzzle-loading guns but they carried them as a symbol of their status in the village and could hardly be considered competent to use them with proficiency. My remarks refer to villages in the United Provinces where, from personal experience, I found the peasant class more versatile with words than weapons. Of course, there is always the exception to the rule, but sadly not in this case. The village where this man-eater took up residence lay about 15 miles north-east of Roorkee towards Lakhsar junction.

Bearing in mind that a man-eater was at large amongst a passive, non-violent community they were naturally in a devil of a quandary. On the one hand they were against the sportsman who indulged in shooting, on the other the man-eater was at liberty to pick them off as and when it wished. There was no solution to the problem except solicit the help of those they despised.

Ashamed to approach a hunter themselves they used the back-door method by contacting Razak, a man from a neighbouring village with whom I stayed whenever I shot in that particular area. Of course, Razak had nothing in common with these people and was not prepared to do their dirty work unless one of them accompanied him as spokesman personally to invite me to a place I had been told to avoid.

Razak spoke first, then invited his companion to continue with the subject which affected his village, the name of which immediately rang a bell. Remembering my maltreatment, I told him to return to the village where everything had the right to live, including the man-eater. He was lost for words. I asked him a straightforward question. "Are you inviting me on behalf of the village to kill the tiger?" His answer was yes. "But is not this against your custom and preachings?" I asked. He replied "Yes". "If that is the case, why am I now being requested to kill in the very same area where last year you all almost lynched me for shooting a deer?" He found a feeble excuse by conveniently tellling me he was away when the incident took place!

Actually, from the very moment I heard of the man-eater I was prepared to go after it, but I was just taking pleasure in driving home the fact that the human race must live at all cost; irrespective of whether he eats flesh or vegetable, it is still a matter of destroying some form of life.

With me at the time was my good friend Sandy Rollo, a keen angler, hunter and professional photographer who accompanied me to the village where the man-eater was operating. Under normal circumstances our entry into the village with firearms would have been most unacceptable, but now we were looked upon as angels of mercy and the rifles a Godsend. Sandy, a gentle, soft-spoken personality certainly fell into the category of angel, immediately becoming terribly popular, whereas I was probably recognised as the devil by a small minority with whom I'd had a brush and was given the cold shoulder.

Getting down to our business we obtained the relevant facts pertaining to the man-eater and set off for the jungle, taking with us a goat as bait. Two machans were contructed on separate trees overlooking a glade and the goat was tied to a peg equidistant from both positions after which the work party returned to the village. Before climbing into our respective machans I noticed Sandy taking aim at something on the far side of the glade. When he lowered his rifle I enquired what it was. "Nothing at all, just testing the telescopic sight."

"You don't mean to tell me you're going to shoot with a telescopic sight at such close range if the tiger should show up?"

In his usual innocent manner he replied "Of course I"m going to use it, otherwise I won't be able to differentiate between goat and tiger, and in all probability shoot the poor goat by mistake!"

"Knowing you, you'll shoot the goat in any case to ensure you get meat for dinner in this strictly vegetarian village!"

The man-eater could pick them off as and when it liked

A dense jungle is a wonderful place to be in, especially when perched in the safety of a tree. There is so much to observe and hear provided the golden rule is adhered to .... silence and stillness. The privacy of wildlife is absolute, the presence of man is resented or to be more exact, feared. Perhaps only the man-eater knows better, that man is not omnipotent.

A pair of ribbon-tailed fly-catchers detected my presence and irritably flew to and fro, shy at first but in time becoming more sociable. The male bird was always more conspicuous, more so when he occasionally put on a display by fanning out his long white tail feathers to resemble a minature fountain. The female, dressed in red and white with a much shorter tail, hopped about at the very end of a branch until she settled down on her nest. A golden oriole which flew across the glade towards the tree received a hot reception from the fly-catcher and was forced to change its course. No matter what bird tried to settle on this tree, inluding a large owl, it was beaten off by the courageous little bird with an 18 inch tail.

Contrary to expectations, the goat remained unconcerned at having been left exposed to night marauders. It was certainly playing it cool, and perhaps instinct had warned it that under the circumstances silence was golden. Many hours had elapsed, very boring ones at that because the jungle appeared lifeless.

Not a thing moved. Not even the goat.I had reason to believe it had passed out from the shock of being separated from the herd and left out to the mercy of panther or tiger. Shining a torch, there it was sitting down and leisurely chewing the cud! Incredible!

Shortly before dawn the goat suddenly began to prance about, bleating for the first time. Within seconds beams of light searched the glade. A cowardly hyena trotted away from the goat offering a tempting shot caught between two spot-lights. But fortunately for it the tiger had priority and we held our fire.

We remained on our machans until sunrise, then keeping watch over each other we got down just in case the man-eater caught us unprepared. Keeping to the open fields we walked back to the village, the goat following at the end of a rope, now ceaselessly letting off steam, which is what it should have done in the jungle! I suppose it had reason to rejoice having survived a night in the jungle!

After sleeping soundly till three o'clock in the afternoon we were ready for another night out, but this time didn't leave the selection of a goat to the choice of the owner. Viewing a herd of grazing goats we picked out one which was already blowing its top! Taking it along to the same spot we made sure it didn't see us climb into our machans. When we had settled down a signal was given to Sandy's servant to remove a sheet off the goat's head after which our companions returned to the village leaving the goat alone, or so it must have imagined.

This goat was a champ, because as soon as they left, he really bleated and continued non-stop, surely an irresistible attraction to a panther or tiger, provided of course, they were in earshot of the bleating.

In spite of being very alert, the tiger took us by complete surprise! It was far from dark and I later learnt from Sandy that only a few minutes before he had taken a photograph of the goat from his machan. Everything happened in a flash.

One moment there was a lonely goat in the glade, the next a tiger was standing on its hind legs twisting backwards as though having received a hard kick, whilst the goat was in the middle of a buck jump. Before I could raise the rifle to my shoulder there was an unexpected change of scene. The tiger became scared of the goat and in a couple of bounds had vanished into the undergrowth, while the goat, having uprooted the peg to which it was tied when the attack was launched, stood petrified facing the opposite diretion, then suddenly came to its senses, realised it had had a lucky escape and dashed across the glade, the rope and peg still attached to its neck and being swung about like a yoyo.

What really puzzled us was why the tiger jinked, roared and sprang off in the opposite direction without as much as touching the goat. The only logical explanation for the extraordinary occurrence was that when the goat gave a frantic jump, the peg to which it was tied shot up and struck the tiger's fangs. Being terribly suspicious animals, an object of this nature striking it could have upset it.

The goat having vanished did not solve our problem. We had no proof whether the tiger was the man-eater or not, but one thing was certain, a tiger was in the vicinty and we had to decide whether to climb back into our machans for the rest of the night or return to the village, haunted all the way by the thought of being ambushed by a man-eater.

However, as there were two of us we considered it reasonably safe to leave the jungle by way of a short cut rather than follow the winding track along which it was more likely the man-eater would prowl. It wasn't a casual stroll in a park, each step could be the last for either of us at any time. Sandy led the way and I followed close behind taking crab-like steps so as to keep a watch on the rear. A shrub amongst the undergrowth suddenly shook quite violently bringing us to a stop, our rifles swinging in the direction ready to fire, but nothing appeared, neither did the shrub or anything else move. The indefinite wait for something to happen increased the tension on our already highly strung reflexes and furthermore the light was gradually fading.

A tiger normally moves very stealthily, so it was unlike one to have caused the shrub to shake so violently, yet it was possible as we heard no movement after the sudden disturbance. Rather than continue the journey in fear of being cornered by the tiger, we thought it better to check this spot first to establish whether the tiger had been there, or whether some large bird like a peafowl had jumped off a branch.

Taking no chances we very carefully advanced keeping an all round watch. Creeping up on the shrub surrounded by tallish grass we nearly jumped out of our skins when our friend the goat leapt forward, pulling the branches of the shrub to the level of the ground. It took a few minutes to recover from the shock before I thought of unravelling the rope and peg which were lodged in the branches and responsible for trapping the goat after its encounter with the tiger. As I stepped forward it made another bid for freedom without any success, then it suspiciously watched me fiddle with the entangled rope and peg. The ungrateful beast, not appreciating that I was doing it for its own good, caught me with my back to it and gave me a devil of a butt, almost sending me head-first into the shrub!

As the villagers have no public conveniences, the inhabitants make free use of the countryside to answer the call of nature. I mention this fact because soon after dawn next morning two men were doing exactly that when the man-eater caught them with their pants down. The fellow who was fortunate to escape ran into the hut we occupied yelling "Sheer....Sheer!" (meaning tiger). He tried to say something more, but collapsed before he could do so. When he regained consciousness, he gave us a vivid account of the catastrophe as to how the tiger suddenly appeared from behind a heap of cow-dung and sprang onto his colleague. There was a cry of terror, he looked back while running and saw the tiger carrying away the limp body of his friend.

The tragic news spread like wild-fire in this small village and the death of another of their brethren who had fallen victim to the man-eater was mourned.

Taken to the spot which was about a furlong from the village, we picked up the blood trail across a fallow field, through a crop of wheat to a belt of thorny bushes fringing the dense jungle. A "dhoti" (cotton shawl) caught in the thorns of the wild-plum bush dangled like a flag flown at half-mast on a very still day. It was blood stained. A little further, a stream about 10 feet wide had been leapt across with the corpse; the impact on landing had left deep impressions in the soft soil in addition to which a pool of blood indicated the tiger had dropped the body to rest a while. The apex of the dense jungle lay within a stones throw of this spot, the most logical place one would imagine the tiger to head for, but the tiger out-skirted this place and entered a scanty jungle of trees and tiger grass. It penetrated quite far then turned sharply into a basin of creeping evergreens.

Sooner than expected we found the corpse, a gruesome sight as the tiger had already fed on one thigh and the stomach. I had previously seen many a revolting scene without any adverse effects, but now I felt sick at the sight of this victim. Fortunately we had none of the villagers with us who would have insisted on removing the corpse for a cremation ceremony, ruining our chances of getting even with the man-eater.

There was not much of a choice of trees on which to construct a machan, furthermore, we would have to do the job ourselves without readily available ropes and cushioning. However, rather than disturb the area by cutting thick branches for the purpose, we did this some distance away where a banyan tree substituted its long tentacles for rope.

The chopped branches, lashed into a framework about six feet by four feet, were carried back to where the corpse lay and hauled up a tree of our choice. Fastening the structure firmly between the branches of the tree and padding it with green leaves provided a platform to accommodate Sandy and myself. The machan was complete, the camouflage effective and all that was left was to escort Sandy's servant a short way out of the jungle to return to the village.

By two o'clock the scene was set. We had divided the area to our front into two sections in order that we knew exactly who was going to fire first, thus eliminating the chances of one trying to outdo the other, the result of such hasty actions often leading to everyone missing. A prominent tree-trunk was agreed upon as the dividing line; the left of it was under Sandy's jurisdiction while to right was mine. Below us lay the mutilated body, a sight we would rather not look at; the atmosphere was morbid and made our stay on the machan unpleasant.

During the afternoon a herd of wild pig arrived in the vicinity to arouse our interest. They kept to the undergrowth for quite some time, then gradually covered ground until they were roaming about below us. A group of three stood watching the corpse very inquistively. They were suspicious and grunted as though inviting the rest of the party to have a look at what they had seen. Others came along after which they rushed about in circles round the corpse. Their antics were quite amusing but then an average size boar fearlessly walked up to the corpse and began to eat the flesh which encouraged others to join him. This was an intolerable invasion. I loudly mimicked the growl of a tiger which had the desired effect. Whether they thought it was a tiger or not, they rumbled away in a disgraceful retreat!

Shortly after the wild pig had gone a crow-pheasant uttered a series of hooting noises followed by the cackling of a jungle-fowl, indicating the probable presence of a carnivorous animal. It was too early to expect the man-eater, nevertheless, we kept a careful watch on our respective sections. Within five minutes of the alarm calls a tiger appeared on Sandy's side of the tree-trunk.

I was terribly envious, watching this masterpiece in nature's camouflage, manoeuvre its supple body through the undergrowth noiselessly. Sandy's rifle was already at his shoulder covering the tiger on its way to the corpse. I thought it better not to lift a finger in case the movement was detected.

The tiger was standing beside the corpse when Sandy squeezed the trigger. Instantly the tiger roared and sprang into the air to fall heavily to the ground, curling up like a striped prawn and growling as it gasped for

The goat which beat off the tiger.

The victim of the man-eater which led to its downfall.

breath. Then came the last kicks, the final gasp, the twitching of the nerves followed by the stillness of death alongside its last victim.

The sound of a .375 Mannlicher rifle shot must have been heard by the villagers who had been praying for this shot to be fired. I can imagine the instant reaction of the people to leave what they were doing, forgetting for the time being the misery which surrounded them. Those who had the ability to run did so, arriving on the outskirts of the jungle, to shout and enquire if it was safe to join us.

Giving them the all clear, about 20 of them arrived headed by Sandy's servant. The centre of attraction was not the man-eater, but their dead comrade. In silence they stood, pathetically looking at the victim until someone took off a sheet which he had thrown over his shoulder and screened the corpse. He was, I learnt later, the eldest brother who, by custom, was required to have his head shaved as a mark of respect for the death of a close relative.

The machan was taken down on which the corpse was placed and the slow journey back to the village commenced with the usual rhythmic chanting of a funeral procession at the rear of which was carried the man-eater. Those who remained at the village met us with mixed feelings of both joy and bereavement; the occasion demanded a tactful overture of condolence for the irreplaceable loss to the family and the villagers in general, rather than to stand proudly on ceremony with the man-eater. These "live and let lives" were eccentric people who showed no visible signs of appreciation for what we had done, but deep down in their hearts there must have been unquestionable relief for the freedom willed to them by Sandy.

Chapter Eight

Boarding a train on the 9th May 1947 for a 36 hour journey, I left behind the prosperous provinces and was soon chewing sand as I travelled across desert and barren mountains to enter the province of Baluchistan. Suddenly, the desolate sun-baked wilderness burst into an emerald basin and for a moment I thought it was just another mirage, but this was no deception. Admist this green belt was the city and cantonment of Quetta, re-built after being razed to the ground by a disastrous earthquake on 31st May 1931.

Despite having taken no part in athletics for some time, I was, nevertheless, in good shape and managed to live up to my former reputation. During the course of the prize distribution, the Chief of Police Mr. H.D.M. Scott.IP. asked me to call at his office for an informal chat. I did so and the topic involved sports in general together with a few references to Charles who had served under him with much popularity. He then touched on the subject which usually embarrassed me, and had developed into a complex.

Placing a monocle to his eye and looking as serious as a judge he said,

"Now then young man, what is your profession?"

"Honorary Secretary, Walkers and Gazers Association!"

"In other words you're without a job."

"At the moment yes, but I'll soon be in the army as an officer."

"Have you actually committed yourself as yet? Well, have you?"

"I've been selected to attend the next course at the Royal Military Academy at Dehra Dun.

"Then you are still free to change you mind. Here, complete this form, I'm offering you the post of an officer in the Baluchistan Police Force."

"Thanks very much, but I'm not interested."

"Not interested, eh! Well, in that case you give me no choice other than to enlist you under the Emergency Powers Act, or detain you under the Vagrancy Act as being a person not having any substantial means of livelihood."

More in fear than by choice, I filled in the form and signed it.

"Good lad, I'll issue a letter confirming your appointment, meanwhile you can run off and get yourself medically examined by the Police Surgeon. I'm sure everything will be alright and you will find work interesting after your training; at the same time I want you to take charge of the sporting activities within the force."

Fitted out with a fine uniform, a couple of pips on each shoulder and a .455 revolver attached to the Sam-Brown made me feel that at last I was someone responsible and no longer dependent on others for their generosity.

In this province I was faced for the first time with a language problem which really shattered my hope of pusuing my sport. I was obliged to depend entirely on interpreters and missed the pleasure of being able to converse with the local tribes, share their humour or become alert to any ulterior motives in untrustworthy company. From all the information I had gathered from various souces it was clear that duck shooting was the favourite sport during the winter season at a lake known as Bund Khustal Khan or another spot called Malazai. This was no consolation to me, as I preferred a variety of game, both big and small. I admired the splendid display of mounted trophies at the military Staff College, common amongst which were those of Urial and Markhaur, species of wild ram and large goat respectively. This collection was, no doubt, from the good old days when fine specimens were shot by officers based at small outposts such as Fort Sandeman, Loralai, Hindubagh, Mach and Chamman. In spite of the fact that these animals must have been plentiful in those days, it must be remembered that the sportsmen had to cover vast distances on foot or horseback to reach areas where these animals were to be encountered, and I assure you such places are not easily accessible.

As time advanced, my own experiences confirmed the reports of my informants that there was a lack of fauna in the areas transversed by lines of communication, but the prospects of Chickor and Si-Si partridge shooting looked good if one was prepared to walk long distances over rugged terrain. I was like a fish out of water, knowing I could overcome the geographical conditions, but the language barrier remained unsloved and I deferred trips into the interior.

I had no choice other than to concentrate on athletics, swimming, football and hockey. This brought me closer to social activities which hitherto I had been avoiding. Naturally, I was soon involved with wine, women and song, each day, each week, drifting further and further from the sport I had enjoyed so much in the past. I attended the majority of dances in town, took to the floor rarely, but stood my ground at the bar drinking steadily, and when the time was right I'd move over to join the fair sex and have the last dance. I never went steady with any girl though I had my favourite and left it at that, knowing well that this was a phase of life we all go through without plunging into the serious aspects of matrimony.

This hectic spree was great while it lasted, but then came a saviour, namely Harbab Khan to whom I was introduced as having a reputation of being one of the most skilful hunters of this province of Baluchistan.

Harbab spoke English which helped us to get to know each other and freely discuss the prospects of shooting and, above all, he knew what he was talking about. He had all the answers relevant to wildlife found in his part of the world. He very frankly told me that to shoot with him was a difficult task, especially if I wished to go after the Markhaur which demanded a tremendous amount of climbing, a lot of stamina, a bottle of water and no luxuries such as juicy meals, drinks and beverages, furthermore, no camp beds or tents, lights or bedding!

After having played his cards and finding I remained undettered, he drove me up to Hannah Resevoir from where he pointed out the more significant mountain peaks. "That one", he said,"is Murdad which means death. I will not take you there as nothing exists on it. And that one is the Queen of Quetta, on which in years gone by there was quite good hunting. Now, see this one here, this is Takatoo, the highest of the mountains on which I assure you there is plenty of Markhaur to shoot provided you can face the challenge of reaching them. There is one more place not visible from here but I will show it to you when you climb Takatoo, that is, of course, if you are prepared to come with me and climb as high as that!" I was no chicken and replied "Look Harbarb, if you have climbed these mountains then I will do the same." "Good", he said, "but many other Sahibs have said the same thing and turned back half way. Never mind, you tell me when you are ready to undertake the trip and I will be pleased to take you."

Harbarb opened the boot of his car and produced his .270 Holland & Holland rifle, loaded it and invited me to empty the magazine at a demarcation sign painted in white some 200 yards away. He was out to test my skill with a rifle and I was equally bent on proving to him I was no novice. I asked him if the rifle was accurate to which he promptly replied "I don't keep inaccurate weapons!" That was a fair enough reply and I got down to business by splintering the stone with each shot. He gave me credit for the way I shot, then himself did the same and said "We should shoot well together, but you may have to fire at a moving target which is very much harder to hit."

On the appointed day I joined him, taking with me as directed two bottles of water, a blanket, rifle and ammunition, while he and his two bodyguards took their own rations. This consisted of wheat flour, sliced dehydrated lamb, dates and a few "sardas" (large oblong melons). After travelling along a gravel covered road on which the car skidded as though being driven by a crazy drunk, we diverted on to something which could hardly be referred to as a dirt track; in fact, it was an imaginary road used perhaps only by camel caravans. However, we crawled along over the stones and boulders, jarring the chassis, flattening the exhaust pipe and puncturing the fuel tank which was fortunately detected before we lost all the petrol. The small hole in the tank was sealed with ordianry soap mashed into a dough like substance by adding a drop of water. Surprisingly this improvised adhesive stuck firmly to the tank and got us to our intended parking spot.

We commenced the assault on this inhospitable mountain at about eight o'clock in the morning. At times I thought of Harbarb's words about many

Sahibs turning back when only half way up the moutain! To tell you the truth I felt like doing just that when I found there was nothing to see other than the monotonuous rock formation. The ascent went on and on, getting more boring each hour in spite of Harbarb's encouraging words that any moment we would encounter the illusive Markhaur. But the Markhaur was nowhere to be seem, whereas the summit of the mountain was as large as life above us. Here I saw the difference between a mountaineer and a hunter. One can see his objective, the other can't. The mountaineer gets a kick out of his achievement when he reaches the summit, whereas the hunter, doing the same thing, may look down with disgust!!

Although I, like every sportsman, always expected something to shoot at, this was one occasion when I thought the whole trip was planned to test my endurance so that Harbarb could add another name to his list of absconders. I was out to see, if not shoot, a Markhaur, but as far as I could see the only living creatures on this mountain were ourselves.

A solitary juniper tree, a landmark and a promise of life, was the spot where Harbarb chose to call a halt and set up camp. While we rested a lamaguer eagle glided majestically over us, the rays of the evening sun highlighting its golden chest. It kept its distance, contemptuously looking down at us foot-sloggers in the hope that we would "give up the habit of living" and provide it with an abundant supply of meat and marrow! Harbarb said something in Baloochi (his dialect) to his two men then told me that perhaps I was a lucky person, as a visit by this eagle indicates for sure that an animal is going to be shot.

Leaving the two men at camp, Harbarb led me to the edge of a precipice from where he scanned the far side of the george with binoculars. "Look", he said, "a white Markhaur". I could see the white object with the naked eye; to me it looked like marble embedded in the orange and black rock formation, but a look through the binoculars left no doubt that the object seen was a white goat, an albino Markhaur.

Concealing ourselves I was assured that before dusk this rare freak of nature would be feeding below us. How right he was because in a short time the animal was on its way down, slowly but surely along the edges of the wall-like cliff. Soon others were seen leaving the crags to descend to where a few blades of grass or shrubs could be found to feed on. When they had gathered in the wide gorge below us, Harbarb told me to take my pick, emphasising the albino, although there was a bigger head amongst them.

I selected the albino, but found it a difficult shot to take as it was immediately below me. However, I fired the first shot and was not too surprised to find I had missed. All the Markhaur scattered, some coming up towards us, others including the albino racing up the opposite cliff at which I continued to fire until I emptied the magazines without any success. While I was in the act of reloading my rifle, Harbarb whistled very loudly, at the sound of which most of the Markhaur stopped instantly affording him enough time to fire a shot and bring one crashing down the precipitous mountainside, a spectacle which took my breath away.

"Good shot Mick!" said Harbarb. I was puzzled by this remark and emphatically denied having fired the crippling shot, but he insisted we both fired simultaneously and that my bullet found its mark. To prove the point I showed him the cartridges in my hand which I was in the act of loading into the magazine. He smiled, saying "I remember an officer who did not hesitate to claim a Markhaur under exactly the same circumstances."

Harbarb requested me to return to camp which was only a short way off and send his two men over to him to help recover the dead Markhaur. They pushed off while I relaxed, cursing myself for having missed all those shots. It was just after dusk when they returned with the carcase. Every bone in its body was broken, resulting from the terrific height from which it fell, its flesh was pulverised and only the stumps of the horns remained attached to the head.

A fire was lit between two stones across which another flat stone was placed and allowed to get extremely hot. On this stone chapattis were baked and eaten with slices of barbequed meat, a humble yet tasty meal followed up by dates and a slice of sarda each. Harbarb apologised for not being in a position to extend renowned Baloochi hospitality in this God forsaken place, but promised he would lay on the traditional feast on a day when it would be suitable to me. We got our heads down for the night, utilising half the blanket to lie on and the other half to cover ourselves. There was no soft earth, no grass nor a fire, so this was the most cold, uncomfortable and silent night I had ever spent under an open sky. I lay awake for the better part of the night trying to gather out the reason why the Almighty had neglected this Suleiman Range of mountains, yet favoured the Himalayas with a wealth of everything.

In the morning we were unsuccessful in finding the Markhaur despite a hellish walk to the north-west side of the mountain. However, from here Harbarb pointed out what he referred to as the best and most picturesque shooting spot in the whole province, this being the Zargoon Mountain, heavily clad with juniper forests. "Someday I will take you there but you must have more time on your hands. You must also be prepared to face the off chance of meeting up with the unpredictable outlaws who shoot first and talk later." He went on to tell me about an incident when his shooting party came under fire, wounding one of his men and after a day-long sniping duel they finally beat off the trigger-happy opposition. I considered this a rather exciting invitation from which I would not like to be dropped, irrespective of the risk involved. Maybe, I'd get the chance to add an outlaw to my list of trophies! Perhaps everything happened for the best, for this trip never did materialize and neither did I ever get the chance to visit this reputed beauty spot.

We failed to shoot any more Markhaur although we spotted a fine specimen resting under the shade of a protruding rock. To get near it was quite out of the question no matter which route we took, but Harbarb was determined to try one of his tactics by firing a shot in the hope that the Markhaur might panic and run into us. I watched through the binoculars as Harbarb fired. The Markhaur sprang to its feet and elegantly traversed the wall-like cliff with the greatest of ease, at times jumping down from ledge to ledge, the distance between each appearing to be no less than 15 to 20 feet, below which were sheer drops of thousands of feet. The plan never worked, nevertheless, the sight was more thrilling than shooting the animal.

On our descent towards where the car was parked I shot a fair sized Urial, the first of its kind on my list which somewhat compensated the missing of the albino Markhaur. The experience gained on this trip was of immense value to me, which I was later to use to my advantage in equally rugged terrain around Fort Munro and the Salt Range.

I persuaded Harbarb to take me out more often, but he was of an eccentric nature, sometimes only too willing to oblige, at other times putting forward frivolous excuses or was otherwise indisposed. I was far from ready to venture forth by myself due to the language problem, though I frequently went out pigeon shooting but this was only to pass the time away. In my frustration for a more adventurous life which was not forthcoming, I was once more tempted to give up shooting in favour of a hectic social life. I was back as a "bird watcher", having to make up for lost opportunities which created unpleasent situations arising out of treading on other cockerel's grounds!

It was a Saturday night, the 16th of August 1947 at 9pm, while in the midst of a dance that the music stopped and an announcement was made that all police and army personnel should immediately report back to their respective headquarters. Outside the club, sporadic rifle-fire could be heard coming from the city, the sky was aglow with fire and smoke, and jeep and lorries loaded with steel helmeted troops came belting down from the Cantonment area. The communial rioting following Independence had finally spread to Quetta, and for the second time this ill-fated city was reduced to shambles.

During the first part of the night the situation was really grave, the city area was ablaze, and as the majority of businessmen were Hindus, their property became the prime targets for looting and arson. There was exchange of fire between Sikhs and Muslims, the weapons used being rifles and shotguns. The police and army were given orders to shoot to kill anyone seen looting or committing an act of arson. A curfew was imposed, which meant nothing at the time for there was complete chaos; the streets became highly dangerous with high velocity rifle and machine-gun fire being directed at people committing arson, but unfortunately police and army personnel came into the cross-fire. By the early hours of the morning the Brewei tribesmen had entered the outskirts of the city, but fortunately they were beaten back. Though sporadic firing continued, the use of the knife by Baloochis, Achakzais and resident Breweis became quite serious.

An assistant Superintendant of Police, Mr Henry Olliver tried to break up a demonstration in the course of which he was struck down by a hatchet despite firing two .38 revolver bullets into his assailant. My brother Theo was soon by his side to remove him by jeep to hospital. The news spread fast that a police officer had been seriously injured and taken to hospital. I immediately went to the hospital, as I also had with me a Sikh I had rescued from a smouldering shop who had been stabbed 18 times and left for dead. Miraculously, with timely medical attention he survived. After having him admitted I saw Mr Olliver in the process of being stitched up. He was really lucky to have escaped death. The hatchet missed the skull, but opened up a gaping wound from his forehead to a point below his ear. Later, however, he was flown home for professional treatment to save the sight of the badly injured eye.

Lines of communications between Quetta and its distant outposts were, at the best of times, bad. The Post and Telegraph Departments were manned by Hindus, many of whom had been killed, while others left their posts to join refuge camps or special trains to take them across hundreds of miles through hostile territory to India. Many got through, others didn't.

I was given an assignment, accompanied by three police constables armed with .303 No 4 Enfield rifles. The job was to proceed by jeep to Fort Sandeman and Loralai to deliver urgent mail from Sir Aubrey Dundas, Agent to the Governor General, to the Commanding Officer, Zhob Militia and the Superintendent of Police Mr R. Blong at Loralai. In addition a V.H.F. wireless set had also to be delivered to the Superintendent of Police. I received a very good reception at the Officers' Mess at Fort Sandeman where I personally delivered the urgent mail to Col L. Barrett who was commanding the Zhob Militia.

On arriving at the residence of the Supertintendent of Police late in the evening, I knocked at the door to a very unwelcome reception. Loud and clear rang out a short sentence "You bastard". Never having met the officer, I was stunned to hear the abusive language. The sentence was repeated again! To hell with the likes of this officer I thought, I'm off, and was about to go when the door opened and a person appeared in uniform. Regulations demanded I salute a uniform of higher rank, which I did but with contempt for the person wearing it. In the next breath he said. "I don't think we have met before, come in." As I stepped in a voice spoke "Hello, hello." I looked in the direction to acknowledge the greeting. "Take no notice of that bastard" said the Supertintendent. It was his Assam Mynah, one of the finest of talking birds, which had been responsible for causing the embarrassment!

My mission complete, I thought it was now in order to put the shotgun to use on the way back to Quetta. The road from Loralai to Ziarat was very scenic, ascending to a height of some 10,000 feet above sea level.

During the descent from Ziarat to Quetta, an Urial was spotted. Not a good pair of horns, but with a food shortage expected in the Province I was prepared to shoot game, in or out of season! Taking the .303 rifle from a constable I moved a short distance away to take a shot at the Urial when there was shout of "allikah" followed by a further sentence. I knew the word meant man. I stopped in my tracks keeping the rifle in the "trail arms" position. A couple of tribesmen appeared, armed with .303 MK II rifles, muttering something in their Baloochi language. In a matter of a minute or so they dropped their rifles to the command of my men. "Outlaws." I was told. "Shoot them or take them back?" they asked. I ordered the confiscation of the rifle bolts, and departed giving shotgun shooting a miss just in case I ran into further trouble.

There was a general state of depression throughout the entire country, and Baluchistan was no exception considering it depended mainly on exports of grapes, peaches and nuts, much of it coming from Kandahar via Chamman, then transported by road and rail to Sind and the Punjab. This lucrative business came to a standstill owing to Sind, and especially the Punjab, being in a turmoil.

A clean-up operation commenced in Quetta as soon as the situation returned to normal. There was nothing to fight over for the Hindus who survived, the majority, had gone to their new country which was India, re-named Bharat. This name caused too much confusion in the rest of the world, especially amongst those involved in business who could not find this country shown on the globe. Soon the name India was reinstated, replacing Bharat on all letter heads and addresses.

West and East Pakistan also created some problems and only time explained their geographical position. Much the same happened some years later in Africa and other parts of the former Empire.

Quetta was taking shape again. During this period I met the Nawab of Bugti State, Akbar Khan and his younger brother Ahmed. They were both fine men, particulary the Nawab himself who was educated in the Chiefs' College at Lahore; he had a good knowledge of English, and a dynamic personality coupled with the ability to possess both Eastern and Western culture. While in Quetta he dressed emaculately in Western style, but when I accompanied him to his territory he wore his Chieftain's regalia so as not to offend his tribesmen.

Travel through the rugged territory was very tedious as there were no proper roads, the jeep , however got us there after an unforgettable journey. The approaching vehicle must have been seen from afar, for we were met and escorted by his tribesmen on horseback who joined the cavalcade from every nook of this torrid land. Many of his lieutenants were soon by his side as he entered his palatial residence in his kingdom at Sui. (Some years later, natural gas was discovered in the area, nationalised and known as Sui Gas, bringing in a highway followed by the development of industry to ravage this once almost inaccessible territory.)

His palace was modest yet attractive, more befitting the taste of his people than himself. Outsiders rarely, if ever, entered the territory which had little or nothing to offer to leisure loving people.

After having spent the night in comfort we set off for a pre-arranged shoot. Overnight preparations had already been made for the favourite sport, a bustard shoot. I gathered from the Nawab that beaters on horseback were in position some miles away awaiting a shot to be fired to signal the advance across a plain covered with a sage-like plant, sand dunes, narrow dried seasonal streams and veins of rock.

A rifle shot was fired out in the distance. Shortly after horses appeared on the horizon in a semi-circular formation, the riders waving white flags. The Nawab, myself and a few of his chosen tribesmen had positioned ourselves in a dry sun-baked stream, about three feet below ground level and some 100 yards apart. Between each gun a flagman was hidden to divert a bustard heading directly towards him by suddenly standing up and waving a flag. The bustard would immediately jink and fly across to the right or left, bringing it into range of one of the guns on either side of him.

The bustard, at times can be as foolish as the ostrich. It delays taking to flight, preferring to run rather than fly. Eventually it takes to flight, but is very deceptive and in spite of being a big bird is often missed.

As the horses with riders approached, the bustard, flew towards us, generally in singles, ziz-zagging as they came, to provide a very exciting shoot. We hardly moved from our positions. The horsemen did all the running about, driving the bustards on to us.

A feast was laid on that evening in my honour which consisted of a whole barbequed "Dhumba" (fat tail sheep) filled with fried rice and quails, enormous chapattis to go with it and an array of grapes, peaches, sardas and large red pomegrantes. The guests were the tribal chiefs and a few other notable gentry of the State. There wasn't a single woman as a guest, neither dancing girls, nor maid servants. This was a man's party in a man's country where only the tough can survive.

Everyone sat down on their haunches on a thick carpeted floor with velvet bolsters to recline on. The large room was dimly lit and in the far corner the guests had placed their rifles and sten-gun, while at the threshold lay their gold embroidered sandals. By religious custom, alcohol is forbidden, so the problem of whetting ones' appetite before diving into the exotic spread was easily resolved!

I was certainly a misfit at this gathering, unable to converse with anyone other than the Nawab and unable to join in the feast-making of these wild people. I must have given the guests the impression that I was a misfit who had no business encroaching upon the hospitality of their ruler. I made my feelings known to the Nawab but he was very understanding, telling me to relax and assuring me that I was his guest and that was all that mattered. Furthermore, he pointed out that I was a stranger in a very strange land, where the white man was never seen, except on one previous occasion when a R.A.F. pilot had baled out from a fighter after developing engine trouble.

In spite of having tucked into the delicious food I was told by the Nawab that the guests commented on my poor appetite, remarking that their women folk ate far more than I did! Of course, I could have made a pig of myself, but I wished to remain dignified amongst these treacherous looking people who kept me under constant watch. Of all the tribes I had met up with, these undoubtedly were the most unfriendly. They were fierce in appearance, well built, ebony black with long hair and beards forming natural ringlets.

After dinner, green tea was served, which is drunk without any milk being added. It was very tasty, in addition to which it acts as a digestive. As the small cups and saucers were being passed round I accepted one from the tray unaware of the custom that followed! Once the cup is empty, you do one of two things. If you want more, leave the cup as it is and it will be filled up again, or, if no more is required, then the cup must be turned up-side-down on the saucer, leaving no doubt in the mind of the servant as to what he should do. Ignorant of this custom, I appreciated the second cup of tea, but then, despite shaking my head to denote I wanted no more, the wretched servant went on filling my cup not taking the slightest notice of my sign language. I believe he thought I was suffering with chronic attacks of indigestion or else he was just being plain awkward!

The Nawab was extremely popular amongst his subjects and he made no fuss about mingling with the poorest of them. Before our departure he was asked to participate in a tent-pegging contest, a sport in which he took a keen interest. I was highly impressed by the superb horsemanship and there were few occasions when the riders failed to have a tent-peg at the end of a lance.

After a prolonged handshaking session we hopped into the jeep and left for Quetta. An escort of horsemen galloped alongside, firing their rifles in the air, to make it a very impressive farewell.

In the evenings I found it relaxing to do a bit of pigeon shooting amongst the "Karaizes" found in the suburbs of Quetta, especially along the road between Billaili and Kuchlak. "Karaizes" are a serious of wells dug at short intervals and linked by a tunnel to form a subterranean canal, a characteristic irrigation system in this arid land.

It was at one of these Karaizes that my performance was watched as I shot the pigeons which rocked out of the wells. When there were no more pigeon to shoot, the onlooker from the car walked over to me and said in

English "You are a very good shot" and introduced himself as Khair Mohammed. He then invited me to join him in a similar shoot a few miles ahead to which I agreed and both of us walked back to his car. With him was a bodyguard of three riflemen who courteously bowed as I entered the car. I noted the side of the car facing me was riddled with bullet holes.

A short distance away he pulled up, opened the boot of the car and took out a gun case containing a pair of Purdey's. The possession of such expensive guns indicated he was a keen sportsman and was a symbol of his status. It didn't take him long to convince me that these guns were not show-pieces – he shot as well as I did, perhaps better. In a matter of a few hours our common interest lead to a lasting friendship. He was the son of the Chief of the Tahreen Tribe whose domain was the rich district of Pishin.

Khairo, as he liked to be called, was a character one does not easily forget, tall, dark and handsome with a striking personality, his generosity towards the poor and his fine scruples were amongst his commendable qualities.

In this part of the world where the tribes live dangerously, wealth or popularity create jealousy, and breach of promise or dishonesty cause hatred. Jealousy and hatred is a damnable part of human nature to which these hot-headed people can find no answer, other than violence, the outome often resulting in death. This leads to revenge, the root cause of feudism in which Khairo was unfortunately alleged to have been currently involved. The bullet holes in his car were proof of at least one attempt having been made on his life.

With Khario I had the opportunity of visiting many remote tribal areas which would otherwise have been impossible. I appreciated the precautions he took for my safety, for when a journey involved passing through the jurisdiction of an adversary, he didn't use his car to avoid recognition and perhaps jeopardise an innocent life. I jokingly told Khairo on one occasion that his travelling incognito was for self-preservation and not for my benefit. He took this remark seriously and said "Micky, to die upholding the pride and prestige of the Taheern tribe is the greatest honour that I can be worthy of. I am not afraid of anyone other than Allah."

I witnessed a punishment inflicted by Khairo on one of his subjects for petty theft. It happened at a duck-shoot when a wounded sheldrake was picked up by an onlooker and concealed in a blanket worn around his body. He was questioned about the duck, but denied having seen it much to Khairo's annoyance who searched his person and found it hidden under the blanket. Turning to me he said "Micky, here's your duck. I must teach this man a lesson not to steal."

After what appeared to be a severe reprimand folowed by a kick in the pants, the offender ran like hell in a ziz-zag manner and I thought that was the end of the matter, but suddenly Khairo's shotgun swung to the shoulder with the barrels pointing at the moving target. I immediately intervened, but it was too late to prevent him letting fly both barrels at the man on the run, who ran on rubbing his behind and legs vigorously! While agreeing with Khairo, that No.8 pellets could not cause grievious injury at 50 yards, I did not approve of the use of a firearm to administer punishment. Khairo upheld his action as being appropriate on the grounds that these thick-skinned men only understand physical punishment. However, there was no malignancy created by this incident, proof of which came when both of them met later to shake hands, exchanging a good laugh together as though nothing had happened. Khairo gave him a couple of duck which the fellow accepted with gratitude, commenting on the sheldrake as the one being responsible for the "hornet stings!"

Of the many trips undertaken with Khairo there was one which I found very enjoyable. We had a night stop at his house at Pishin and set off at dawn by weapon carrier across the Gulistan plain towards the Afghan border. The mobile journey ended at a small settlement where we were given a very friendly welcome, after which it was foot-slogging, mile after mile over rough terrain, occasionally putting our shotguns to use on chickor or bustard. The bodyguards must have found this walk terribly monotonous until they spotted a Chinkara (ravine gazelle) and were given permission to open fire. I was amused to see they didn't bother to stalk within range of the antelope, instead just knelt down and blazed away from about 500 yards and ceased firing when it was completely out of sight. The animal was way out of range and running so there wasn't a hope of hitting it. I told Khairo to tell them that in my opinion they were unfit to hold the coveted job of bodyguards and should revert back to being in charge of donkeys! Khairo interpreted my remark in all seriousness to which these fellows took exception and challenged me to a duel!

We arrived at the base of a range of barren mountains close to a crystal clear river which I was told was the Lora. Though only a stream compared to the smallest rivers of the Punjab, it did, nevertheless, have beauty, and above all guaranteed an unlimited supply of fresh water. We selected a suitable spot to camp at a wide part of the river-bed where the sand was dry and the large boulders afforded protection in the event of attack by outlaws.

During the night a perishingly cold wind, known to the locals as the "kozzac", almost froze us to death. Because of the bitter conditions no one was prepared to brave the weather for an early start as planned. The unscheduled delay did however provide me with the unexpected sight of swarming grouse. I had on many occasions seem Imperial sand grouse arriving punctually at 8 o'clock in the morning at a water hole. At this particular spot these brids came flocking in by hundreds of thousands, literally obliterating the sun for a matter of some 15 minutes or so. There is music in their call while they are in flight, but once they settle to drink, their thirst is quenched quickly and in silence. The departure from the water, once again fills the sky with music.

Rifle shooting was on the agenda for Urial or Markhaur, depending on the altitude climbed. The bodyguards were detailed for the dirty work and were sent to climb high to give protection from tribal activity, namely trigger-happy outlaws keeping intruders out, and to drive down Markhaur which inhabit the higher altitudes. But our attempts to bag an animal proved fruitless and we gave up further efforts, having met with a hospitable tribe residing in the area; the chances now of finding these animals was very remote indeed as these tribesmen are born hunters and travel vast distances in pursuit of the wild goat.

I stopped at a graveyard in the precinct of this village. There were approximately 20 graves covered with piles of rocks. There were no tomb-stones, no flowers, no trees, no boundary wall and no inscriptions whatsoever to indicate to future generations who lay there. However, as a memento to great hunters their graves were indicated with tall poles embedded into the rocks on which were suspended mangificent Urial and Markhaur's horns. When I saw this, it gave me food for thought. Could this be a source from which some record heads had found their way to Officers' Messes throughout the North West Frontier and Baluchistan!

We were later taken on a conducted tour of this fortress like settlement which I found comparatively clean compared to those I had visited in the fertile plains. I watched with facination the women weaving colourful carpets in the most exquisite designs. This was the only place I had been to where Muslim women did not observe the customary practice of wearing a veil in the presence of men other than immediate relations. I must confess the girls got my undivided attention. Some were dark-skinned, others fair with blue eyes and jet black hair. They were all very attractive, but one in particular was an eye opener, a Cleopatra in fact, but poor Caesar couldn't do a thing about it lest he got a knife stuck in his back!

On our way to a house where a night stop was scheduled, I casually asked Khairo whether the women of his tribe were as pretty as the ones we had just seen. He replied in the affirmative, then went on to explain the origin of many of the fair-skinned tribes who inhabit this natural rugged mountainous barrier, separating Eastern Europe from the East. He told me that the majority of the tribes are tall, tough, rugged and sometimes as inhospitable as the mountains themselves. Orginally they were believed to be decendants of deserters from Alexander The Great's Army which crossed over the North West Frontier to conquer as far as the Punjab. These deserters were well aware of the consequences of their act, since they commenced a new life in these impenetrable mountains, marrying into the local tribes yet always suspicious of intruders who might be agents attempting to bring them to justice.

Our guide had made an error by leading us away rather than towards our destination and this was only discovered when we found ourselves in a situation from which there was no easy way out except to turn about. Confronted by a ring of mountains with perpendicular cliffs was a spectacular sight, but we had been led to the mouth of a death trap by mistake because in such places are invariably found the most notorious outlaws. Before making a hasty retreat Khairo exchanged a few words with his men so that they separated, forming a cordon around us. If we were pursued and fired at, these men would be in a position to out-flank the enemy or engage them, providing us with an escape route. For a moment I thought Khairo was staging an act to put the wind up me, so I played it cool until I noticed he became quite irritable at my unconcerned attitude, this convinced me that the situation must be serious. When we were a good distance away Khairo asked me if I had ever seen a cat lying in wait for its prey, how it conceals itself to the very last then suddenly pounces to make certain of a kill. Outlaws adopt the same strategy which was the reason for the precautionary measures taken when retreating from this area.

I couldn't work out why an outlaw should bother about attacking us without provocation. Khairo's explanation was that a rifle is an outlaw's most treasured possession, rated higher than a wife! As he put it "He can exist without a wife, but not without a rifle. A wife is a burden who cannot be sold, whereas a rifle is worth its weight in gold!" They don't normally kill a person to obtain his rifle; the usual practice is to steal it, or capture people like us and deprive us of our weapons. Only if they meet resistance will they shoot to kill and our crowd, I was given to understand, had been briefed in advance to shoot back at anyone who fired at us.

Clear of this area our guide who, in fact, was a distant relative of Khairo's, lead us safely through to the last of the mountain ranges from where he pointed out a few stone huts situated admist undulating terrain which, I was told, would be our resting place for the night. Before descending on this apology for a village, we had a well earned rest.

One of the more energetic men got up and started to roll large boulders down the valley. In the act of displacing one such he suddenly jumped aside, muttering something. Straightaway the others got up to join him. Naturally, I also joined the circle to be shown a most unusual snake measuring about 9 inches long, remarkably thick for its size with a blunt tail and blending superbly with its immediate surroundings. I had never seen a snake of this species before and presumed it was a deformity, but this was not the case. I was told it was a rather rare snake inhabiting only parts of the Suleiman Range. We stood well back while one of the men worried it with the muzzle of his rifle. At first it was reluctant to do anything about being tantalised, then, to my amazement, I saw it spring vertically into the air to a height of some four feet. Facinated by the novelty, I personally took over the task of ring master in order to observe the take off action more closely. As far as I could see the power came from the blunt tail after a quick contorted movement by which it flicked itself into the air, similar to a spring being held down by both ends to form a loop and then being released.

I was warned not to worry the snake any longer as it was becoming more active and the frequent leaps into the air were its mode of attack and a bite could prove fatal. During the summer this species of snake is supposed to be very active, and can easily flick itself up to heights exceeding six feet, to bite an intruder on the head, face, neck or anywhere on the trunk.

When about half a mile away from the so-called village we were ambushed by a huge vicious dog which had clipped ears and resembled a black bear. Trained to attack strangers it lay in wait for us until we were taken by complete surprise, barking only as it shot out from behind some large boulders to spring at the person leading the column who was knocked down and mauled. Rifle butts were put to use on the dog to repulse the savage attack, despite which it pranced about making desperate efforts to hold back our advance towards the dwelling houses. The barking must have alerted the inmates who had taken up positions to defend themselves against possible hostility.

A loud voice came across a dry river-bed which instantly brought our party to a standstill, followed by a warning from Khairo to me to remain motionless. Words were exchanged between someone in hiding and Khairo's relation, after which he moved forward by himself leaving his rifle resting against a rock. Shortly the two met and I could see them embrace each other. All was well, we relaxed and crossed over to be given a very warm welcome by four tribesmen who earlier must have had their rifle sights on us, itching to squeeze the triggers had we run to take cover.

No sooner had we sat down tea was served, but the first sip I took put me off. I didn't like it and my facial expression must have been observed by the host who said something to Khairo, who in turn told me not to drink it and instead I would be given a "sharbat" (fruit juice). Since no one else appeared to find fault with the tea, I didn't wish to be awkward and forced it down, remembering promptly to place the cup up-side-down on the saucer! There was really nothing wrong with the tea except that a mixture of camel's and donkey's milk had been added to it, producing a rather repulsive odour, not to mention taste!

From a conversation which followed it was evident that something of grave concern was being discussed, but as I was the odd man out I had to wait on Khairo to be told about the matter. The topic was, a feudal tragedy which had occurred some days ago. These stone huts were built on a strategic position, making it well nigh impossible to approach without being seen from afar as we ourselves had experienced only a short time ago. I was told that hostility existed between the host and members of another tribe.

The first attempt made to gain access to the settlement was foiled by the dogs, but while retreating the intruder shot dead two of the three dogs. Taking advantage of the one dog remaining to guard the village, the protagonist acted fast; his intelligence must be given credit, but not the act he committed.

Women have very effectively used their charms on men for ulterior motives and nine times out of ten they accomplish the mission due to the weakness most men have for the opposite sex. A dog, not knowing any better, is more susceptible to this weakness when it finds a bitch in season. Keeping this fact in mind the method used to gain entry to the hut was classic. The raider took with him a bitch which was in season, waited until dark, then approached the outskirts of the village where he tied the bitch to a rock and waited for the dog to be lured to the spot by the instinctive mating urge. The plan worked, the dog in its innocence responded to the laws of nature, leaving the village without an early warning system.

The intruder made a mistake by creeping up to the wrong hut, stood at the door and shot dead the host's brother who was not directly involved in the feud. Naturally, the host was bent on revenge, but not immediately in spite of knowing who the assassin was. From what I gathered, the code is to allow an assassin time to meditate and suffer a mental torture before the inevitable sentence is passed, not by judge and jury, but their own law .....

On preparing to depart Khairo asked me whether I'd like a horse or a camel to ride back on, as the host insisted we went in comfort. To tell you the truth I didn't trust these tribesmen's horses, they were too fiery for my liking so I accepted a camel. The troupe moved off with a horseman on either flank. At first the ride was quite a novelty, later it began to get a bit painful and at the end of the journey I had blisters on my bottom and promised never to ride a camel again!

Having seen what was worth seeing in this province I was pleased to pack up and serve in the Punjab Police with a posting to Lahore where there was still chaos as refugees poured in by the thousands from various parts of India to be rehabilitated in West Parkistan. It was a gigantic undertaking to transport, feed and house these discontented people, afflicted by the partitioning of India. However, the job was done, and with British Governors and heads of departments still in command, with an option to serve on, the regime of the new country was quite stable and we enjoyed the freedom promised by the Governor General of Pakistan, Mr M.A. Jinnah.

Unfortunately, the relationship between India and Pakistan remained strained, which from the family point of view was completely crazy and unreal. When the axe fell we were already serving in an area of the country which would become part of West Pakistan, yet though given the option, all six brothers stayed put, despite our parents being on the other side of the fence, namely India. It was everyone's belief that the initial hostilities between the two countries would soon heal, and conditions would return to pre-partition times. Regrettably, they never did. The imaginary demarcation line separating the two countries was often disputed, especially in Kashmir and the Punjab. Both sides fought piched battles, the United Nations came into existance and the borders, especially in the Kashmir sector, came under United Nations Observer Groups.

Chapter Nine

The Punjab consists of five large rivers which have been dammed at various places and from which canals have been dug; from the canals numerous distributaries have carried a wealth of water to irrigate the plains, making the Province of the Punjab the granary of the country.

Naturally, everything thrives where there is water and food. This province catered for humans and wildlife alike. There was plenty for everyone, including birds which took a heavy toll of the crops. The shooting fraternity concentrated on game birds such as grey and black partridges, duck and snipe. The former was a gentlemanly sport, thoroughly enjoyed by the "Barra Sahibs" (Big Guns) because it was a nine to five affair with plenty of pauses if desired over an easy terrain in dry conditions.

Duck shooting, on the other hand, could be split into two categories – the easy and the hard way. The "Chakoo Jheel" which belonged to the Chenab Shooting Club at Lyallpur, belonged to the former. It had all the necessary amenities such as a decent road to the water's edge, a Club House, boats, butts and trained pickers-up. To shoot on this jheel was a pleasure but no challenge. The majority of the wildfowl were deep water feeders such as the red crested pochard, golden and white eyed pochard. There were also pintail, gadwal, teal, wigeon, ruddy, sheldrake, greylag geese and the shoveller which only the novice shot, but rarely was a mallard ever seen in the bag because they inhabited the impregnable jheels over-run by reeds.

This brings me to the second catergory of duck shooting, the hard way which involved penetrating the reeds on foot through deep water. One of many such jheels provided discomfort, but good shooting and plenty of laughter as on one occassion in early February 1949.

This particular jheel was near a village named Bhalwal in the District of Sargodha. The landlord of the area was a fine chap who always insisted we stay as his guest, his house being close to the jheel. Prior arrangements having been made, we arrived a few hours ahead of schedule, the host making us comfortable and assuring us of wildfowl being very plentiful, especially teal which were in thousands. He was aware that we concentrated on mallard but couldn't give an accurate account of their numbers as they remained undisturbed in the reeds.

It was in our interest, considering we had time on hand, to make a recce into the jheel but not to fire too many shots which might ruin our hopes of a full day's shoot. The only stranger to this jheel was a friend, a Major Hardy, whom I took under my wing, explaining to him that he should be

*Before a partridge shoot. Morning flight over paddy fields
at Panjan, near Chillianwalla, Punjab. Left to right:
Billinda, myself, John, Ainsworth and Charles.*

*One of many good bags of mallard, pintail, gadwal, teal and
geese shot at Bhalwal. Left to right: Illum Din (orderly)
Ainsworth, Reg Goody, Colonel, Jim Coulter and Mervyn Wood.*

careful while walking into the marsh as there was a very uneven bottom with pits and ruts and always a chance of being bogged down.

The situation understood, the party spread out to penetrate the bur reeds. The Major followed in my footsteps until I positioned him at a likely spot where he would shoot a few duck. An English-speaking servant was left with him to retrieve any birds he shot, while I penetrated further interior. I hadn't found a spot to my liking when a shot rang out followed by another, and soon the sky was full of wildfowl, but neither the Major nor I were in the line of flight. However, I was content to watch the duck and where the mallard were settling to get amongst them next morning. I was on my way back towards the Major when I stopped to observe a water snake having some difficulty killing and swallowing a frog. During this short pause I heard splashing as the Major and his servant moved out of the rushes; the servant must have been leading the way because I heard him warn the Major not to follow him as he was getting bogged down. The Major apparently changed course and in doing so walked into a herd of wild pig at which he fired a shot, causing them to stampede to his own detriment, for while attempting to dodge he slipped into a submerged ditch. The hot words uttered in an angry tone, and the replies by the servant in his typical English left little to the imagination.

"Snowball, you're fired!"

"No Sir, I no have gun, but pigs running up and down."

"You bloody ass ... I know you haven't got a gun."

"How I fire shot then?"

"I'll tell you later. Damn it all I can't get out from here, Snowball .. come here quick."

I heard the servant dashing through the rushes to obey the command when the Major's raucous voice rang out again. "Don't come any closer, halt I tell you ... halt. That's a good lad, now throw me one end of your turban."

"What is turban Sir?"

"That ruddy bundle of cloth you have on your head."

"Oh ... this not bundle of cloth, this called pugree."

"Looks more like a birds' nest than a piggery! I need it all the same, throw it across to me Snowball."

"O.K. Sir, I throw."

"You bloody idiot ..... I don't want to wear it! Here, catch the other end and pull me out."

"Very clever idea, now easy pull you out."

"Good lad, you've done a fine job."

"Thanks Sir, but your gun and cartridges all wet."

"To hell with the gun and cartridges. Look at me, I'm covered with dung."

"No Sir, this not dung, only dirty mud. Buffaloes no come here."

"Nonsense Snowball! I saw them earlier on, but that makes no difference now. Just get me out of here."

"OK Sir, you walk in front in clean water, I walk in backside in dirty water."

"And see me fall into another load of muck! No thanks Snowball, I'd much rather walk behind you. Come along .... lead the way out."

I caught up with them. The Major was soaked to the skin from waist down and covered with black oil-like slush.

We emerged out of the jheel at sunset. A watercourse flowed alongside into which I stepped to wash off the muck from my slacks and boots.

"Listen Major, why don't you strip off and let the servant rinse out your clothing."

"And walk back through the village stark naked. No thanks Mick, I don't intend to encourage a nudist colony here!"

"We're in no desperate hurry, you can wear my pullover while your shirt and slacks are washed and dried in front of a fire."

I set fire to a bush onto which I threw odd pices of wood and reeds. The Major started to undress, the servant helping to remove his boots and socks when all of a sudden the Major raised his voice.

"Hey Snowball, what the devil is this stuck to my back?"

The servant sprang to his feet, had a look, then smiled and said, "Oh ho, this Sir is joke, but wait I will burn it!"

"You'll do nothing of the sort Snowball, You can laugh a joke off but I've never heard of burning one off!" Then turning to me said, "Don't just stand there laughing. This is serious Mick, come and have a look."

"Nothing to worry about Major. Care for a cigarette?" I lit his, then my own.

"Did you see that string of geese go over?" I enquired.

"I sure did, but that's beside the point. Tell me Mick, what's on your mind ... what's the joke?"

"Right, I'll tell you. Turn around for a second." Using the burning end of my cigarette I removed the leech from the pit of the Major's back.

"Did you feel anything strange happen?"

"Not really. I don't feel anything there now. What was it?"

I bent down and showed it to him. "Good God, what the hell is it?"

"Nothing to be alarmed about. It's only a leech!"

"A l-e-e-c-h-!! Bloodsuckers! I've never seen one before, neither did I imagine them to be so big."

"It's O.K. for you to laugh Mick, but I assure you it's no joke to have a leech stuck to one's body. And to think that Snowball had the audacity to tell me that a flipping leech was only a joke."

"He's right Major,"

"I thought as much, you were in league with him!"

"Just a minute, give us a chance to explain. You see Major, the vernacular name for a leech is a 'joke'!"

"Well I'm damned! Hey Snowball .... get one thing straight. I'm not at all impressed with your language, nor with your dirty jokes!"

By dusk we had all returned to the house, and after a clean up settled down to a few sundowners while we discussed the prospects for the morning shoot. Everyone had noticed that the mallard were sticking to the interior of the jheel where the rushes were really tall and dense whilst the teal, shovelers and pintail sat out on the open stretch of water. A boat was available for anyone wishing to shoot from it, and in fact the Major asked if he could have it, provided the others had no objections. Since the rest of us were eager to penetrate the centre of the jheel, he was most welcome to the boat with a local oarsman at his disposal.

At dawn the party set off, led by a team of men who volunteered to act as pickers. I don't think they had bargained for what they had committted themselves to, because we had hardly penetrated halfway to our intended positions when they tried to talk us out of going any further. It was desperately difficult walking through the decomposed reeds which had formed a carpet over the water, the depth of which was no more than a couple of feet. We sank up to our waists in a thick black boggy substance and to follow the pickers made matters worse, as not only did they churn up the filth, but also made a rut which deepened as more feet plodded through it.

Reg Goody, a tough rugged man who had often shot with us, brought up the rear and had to cope with the worst end of the line. The decomposed vegetation emitted a gas similar to hydrogen sulphide and Reg complained of it giving him a headache. He tolerated this obnoxious smell for a short period then called a halt and had his say. "I've had enough of this smell.I don't know about you lot, but I've had my fill being at the end of the gas line. What say we split up from here and breathe some fresh air?" Agreeing with him, we took two pickers each and separated. By now it was light and mallard could be seen lifting as they were disturbed by the guns finding suitable positions.

A time had been set to give everyone a chance to be in position before the first shot was fired. During the lull before the storm Reg uttered a warning. "Listen you chaps ..... this area is infested with leeches and snakes." There was a sharp response from someone "Then shoot the bloody things!"

The cross talk disturbed numerous mallard which swarmed low over the rushes, and then snakes and leeches were forgotton as we gave the duck our undivided attention. There was steady consistent shooting all morning with a remarkable understanding between guns; no out-of-range shots were taken, so we didn't wound or lose many birds. Having taken less ammunition than the others, I was obliged to stop shooting and lead the way out with the two pickers behind me hauling bundles of floating duck.

Emerging out of the jheel I was surprised to see a member of our party sitting at the edge of a field in the nude and being given a rub down, while he scratched the accessible parts of his body quite frantically in full view of a group of highly amused kids.

"What's going on here?" I asked.

"Exactly what you see, and it's nothing to smile about," replied "Scratcher," scratching all the harder.

"With all the oil being rubbed on your body, my guess is you're about to dive into the jheel to explore what lies below the water."

"Like hell. Never again will I put foot into this stinker of a jheel."

"But why .... the shooting is terrific. Didn't you get anything?"

"Yes, I got everything! You mention it and I've got it! And what's more, I'll be only to pleased to get rid of it to anyone who wants my share."

"I suppose you fell headlong into a ditch."

"Not really, just that I was shooting in deep water and was attacked by masses of red microscopic insects which have caused this terrible skin irritation."

"Why didn't you move away from that spot?"

"I did, but the damage had been done, and furthermore, having lost my puttees the bloody leeches found their way up the inside of my trousers."

"By the way Scratcher, did you shoot many duck?"

"Of course I did. Between scratching and being scratched by one of the pickers I've accounted for some 40 birds which have been taken to the village."

"Here come the rest of the party Scratcher."

"Oh hell .... be a pal Mick, please coax them away to the village, otherwise they will pull my leg to a standstill."

I walked away and told the otheres of the plight that Scratcher was in, and his request to have not to entertain well-wishers.

"Who's Scratcher?" asked Ainsworth.

"Have a look around. Who is missing?"

"You mean to say…"

"That's right."

"But why do you call him Scratcher."

"Well, you'll see for yourself when he returns to the village."

Of course this gave rise to curiosity and there was no stopping them from paying a visit there and then.

"I s-a-y .... what a prize lobster we have here;" said Charles with a wicked smile.

Before anyone else could chip in with additional remarks, Scratcher was on his feet making a feeble attempt to look serious and said, "You rotten lot, I know I can't bank on getting any help from you, so get lost."

"If I only had my camera with me I could have made a fortune out of you. Just have a look at yourself in you birthday suit. Such a shapely pair of legs."

"Enough of all that Charles," said Scratcher. "I'm in no mood to be pulled to pieces by you crazy lot."

"If you don't sit down or cover youself, the kites may take the liberty of swooping down and removing something essential!" said Reg pointing up to some kites circling above us.

"I can protect my possessions as easily as this" said Scratcher, picking up his shot gun and shooting a kite. "Now, if you so and so's don't get moving one of you is going to end up with a sore backside!"

"That was a smashing shot," said Ainsworth, "I hope you will shoot geese like that in an hour's time."

"Not if it means getting into this bloody water again. I've done enough scratching today to last me a lifetime."

"Oh no, this will be a dry shoot. The geese are sitting out on the damp green plain on the other side of the canal."

Scratcher soon had a sheet wrapped round his waist and became quite sociable in spite of being teased all the way back to the house where he changed into a new outfit and made himself more presentable.

Having had an enormous lunch the natural tendency was to relax a while, which delayed our departure for the goose shoot. However, we got going and arrived at the canal from where a vast green plain was visible. The nearest bridge over the distributory canal was a couple of miles away, and since we were already late it was thought best to wade or try jumping across. Considering the width was no more than 14 feet across and the depth about four feet, we decided to do a bit of athletics by jumping the obstacle.

Scratcher objected to jumping and was prepared for a fast walk to the bridge. To be fair to all, we put the matter to a vote. The majority were in favour of a jump, for better or for worse!

"Its's alright for you blokes with long legs and athletic backgrounds, but I tell you I cannot jump that distance to save my life," said Scratcher very positively, still scratching himself at the sight of water.

"Nothing ventured, nothing gained." I said. Then handing over my shotgun to Scratcher, I set the ball rolling by jumping across with comparative ease. "You see that Scratcher, there's nothing to it ... is there? Now unload your shotgun and throw them over to me one at a time."

The field event started with enthusiasm; the run up was paced out and the take off point levelled and hardened. Charles, a champion long jumper caused some pessimism when he just about qualified, but it was obvious from his run up that he never put much effort into the jump. All were over except Scratcher who was left to make the crossing. He had quite a few practise run ups then told us to carry on as he was not going to join us on the goose drive.

To give him some moral support I jumped back to his side of the bank and with much coaxing he built up the required confidence finally to make up his mind and try the crossing.

"I'll give you a tip Scratcher; run as fast as you can and make sure you gain some height immediately after take off."

"You go first Mick."

"I'd rather not. A coach must help his pupil to the very end."

"You know what Mick! Those blighters on the other side are waiting to have a laugh at my expense, but I think they are going to be disappointed!"

"That's the spirit, now come along Scratcher .... on your mark, set .... go."

"Halelujah! Here I come."

Cartridges rattled in his pocket as he gained speed, there was determination in his run, but as he approached the take-off things went wrong. In trying to correct his footing, he faultered, lost speed, hesitated and in spite of it all jumped. Airborne he was, but his style was more like a hurdler than a long jumper. Of couse, he did a spectacular plunge and when he stood up the water was below waist level!

"Laugh you hyenas! I can now see that this entire business had been planned to provide you all with some entertainment. Hang it all, if I had waded across I would have been far better off. To suit your convenience the canal was fathomed as being at least five feet deep. Anyway, now where are those geese?"

"Forget the geese" said Charles. 'You're soaking wet. Better set fire to these bushes and dry yourself."

"While you blokes shoot the geese! Oh no, I'm going to shoot a goose at all costs after what I've been through today."

Enlisting the services of a few onlookers, they were given clear instructions as to what they were required to do to drive the geese towards a specified direction where the guns would be positioned.

There being little or no cover, it was easy to watch each person as he manoeuvred to intercept the geese when they took off. While the pincer movement was taking shape, one of the party stopped, and the next minute he was on the march again, but in the nude! He was too far to be recognised, yet it was obvious who it was. No one else was in the habit of doing a striptease to enterain wildlife other than Scratcher!

Here and there across this wide plain quite a few horses grazed. At the best of times these village horses are shy of strangers. I passed by two of them which trotted off, then stood up on their hind legs, neighing and behaving as though they didn't approve of my intrusion. Another lot of similar horses didn't take too kindly to the sight of a nude approaching them, and they too reared up, did some buckaroo stunts and galloped wildly all over the plain.

The geese came in the path of the stampeding horses and took to the wing. All that came my way were unruly horses galloping ever faster at the sound of shots. I couldn't have cared less about what was happening elsewhere, my immediate problem was to find an escape from these frisky animals. They reared, fought, kicked, bit and neighed, then would charge past me showing their teeth, only to return and do the same act over again.

Had I been near a tree I wouldn't have worried about their antics, but as I was in a soggy plain with no protection whatsoever, I let fly two shots in the air, well above the one that appeared to be the most menacing. To ensure they kept going at full gallop I fired a third shot in the air! Was I pleased to see the last of them!

I waited until the happy-go-lucky gang came close enough before I joined them. Needless to say Scratcher stole the picture, not only because he was still in the nude,but, had in fact, shot two greylag geese.

"Good heavens Scratcher, that's a whopping pair you have dangling there!"

"They're greylags d'you know. Ains and Charles got one each as well!"

Our departure was scheduled for next morning so we paid off the pickers and relaxed around a log fire in the courtyard of our host's house. After a few bottles of whisky had been emptied I was asked whether there was any truth in a rumour that I got engaged without letting any one know. My reply was straightforward – I had got engaged but told no one because no one asked! However, as the subject had cropped up I let it be known that invites would be out for the wedding at the end of the year, the 28th of November 1949 being the likely date. On hearing the news the consensus of opinion was "that will be the end of your shooting". I made it quite clear that no woman would come between me and my outdoor life. I had already made this point clear with Sheila Sargon to whom I was engaged. The subject ended at this point, congratulations being offered for good shooting after the oath had been taken.

The hot summer months passed by and the month of November saw me a married man. It was now to be seen how we would get along when it came to my habit of pushing off for a shoot on my days off. To my surprise Sheila showed a keen interest to accompany me on a partridge shoot. She stood up to this very well indeed since it was over scrubland and fields. Then it came to a duck shoot. She followed close behind me as I walked into a jheel; the water deepened to thigh level in spite of which she continued to stick to me until at last she reminded me that she could not swim! At the first opportunity I positioned her on high ground where she would be able to get off a few shots and perhaps bag a duck or two while I moved on to a place of my choice.

She fired about half-a-dozen shots after which there was complete silence. Naturally I was perturbed, picked up the birds I had shot and returned to her. She was far from happy. Leeches had found a gap between her boots and slacks to settle down to breakfast! This was the last of her acquatic experiences.

To give her a taste of all aspects of shooting I decided to take her wild boar shooting. On this occasion I chose to wait by a game track in the evening before sunset. Rather than leave Sheila at the side of one such track, I helped her climb a tree where she would be safe and hopefully able to shoot a wild boar. I moved on, leaving her safely perched on a branch of a tree.

Hardly 15 minutes later I heard her shouting for help. I couldn't think what the trouble could be, but hurried across to her assistance. Enquiring what had happened she told me that she was being bitten by red ants! Getting her down from the tree, some of the "red devils" leapt on to me and they were certainly on the war path! What Sheila had done to upset them I cannot say but one thing was obvious, they knew exactly where to make their bites felt most!

I thought this experience would put an end to her desire to accompany me considering she "had been bitten" but not by the "shooting bug". To my surprise she came out again on another wild boar shoot, this time to sit up for them by night! Selecting a potato field I could hardly expect her to sit on the ground by herself so we sat together.

At first she felt the cold which in fact it was. My jacket, however, soon solved the problem. Later she asked if I wanted a cigarette which I refused but she lit one up. I promtly told her to extinguish it. She commenced to fidget and complain of being uncomfortable, something I could do nothing about and insisted she did not talk or move other than in slow motion.

I heard a pig grunt at the edge of the field and was about to use the flashlight to get a good view to see the animal. At this critical moment Sheila coughed! Naturally the pig bolted and we lost the chance of shooting at it. I then whispered to her that this was a game of absolute silence, patience and remaining motionless, in response to which she said "I'm sorry Michael. I didn't mean to cough, neither was I aware that pigs were about. To tell you the truth I'm fed up with this game of 'you can't do this and you can't do that'. Please take me home."

I didn't have an argument about such a trifling matter, instead laughed at her sudden outburst. That was the end of her desire to accompany me out shooting, but she kept to her promise never to interfere with my outdoor life; and for my part of the deal I kept my promise to come back in one piece. This I did with the devil looking after me!

Chapter Ten

Sheila was expecting her first baby and though the Wellington hospital was excellent, she was determined to leave Lahore and be with her parents who were at Sialkot, a town about 80 miles away. Taking into consideration my position as a police officer, on call at any moment of the day or night, I acceded to her wish to be where she would be in good hands in an emergency. The exact time and date of child-birth is hardly predictable, and I could not guarantee to be present in her moment of need. In any case she knew I was not the homely type, content to sit by her side indefinitely and would find an excuse to disappear for fresh air. So I took Sheila to Sialkot and left her in the care of her mother with a request that I be informed immediately when she was admitted to the maternity ward.

During the monsoon, heavy rainfall is an annual event but the year 1950 was abnormal; freak weather conditions brought days of continuous torrential rain, causing chaos everywhere. The entire Punjab was in the grip of torrential storms ... and it would happen when Sheila decided to go into hospital.

In view of a flood threat to the city of Lahore, all leave was cancelled, however, on compassionate grounds, I was allowed to proceed to Sialkot, on the understanding that I would be recalled immediately if the need arose.

Setting off on a Norton motor-cycle on the 9th August 1950 I crossed the Ravi Bridge which was already showing signs of flooding, nevertheless, I continued on my way. On both sides of the road, as far as the eyes could see, sheets of rain-water had collected in the fields and paddy birds, egrets and other waders took to the wing in waves, disturbed by the noise of the motor-cycle. Cattle stood montionless under the shelter of trees, and field rats, lizards and snakes found the raised highway a haven, provided they kept away from the macadamized surface where many had been run over by motor vehicular traffic.

Ahead a storm was brewing. The horizon was bleak with low, ominous clouds blotting out daylight; lightning whipped the earth and thunder clashes like bomb blasts seemed to warn me not to proceed further. It was not long before I was right in the heart of the storm, taking an appalling battering. Without exaggeration, the hail-stones were as large as oranges, and I could hardly believe my eyes when these icy missiles severed branches and made small craters in the slush. I was lucky to be riding through an avenue of trees when this storm struck and escaped the hammering, but the poor birds were not as fortunate; doves, parrots and crows lay dead on the ground, and even the tough vultures sat dazed on the road.

The storm past by followed by steady rain in which I continued my journey until I found myself at the tail-end of a traffic jam. Threading my way to the head of the column I found the road closed to traffic, and Mr Moss and Mr Madden, executives of the Road Transport and Railways respectively, involved in a discussion.

"And where the devil do you think you're going?" asked Mr Moss.

"Sialkot." I replied.

"What! ...but damn it all, weren't you told that the Grand Trunk Road is closed. Take a look at this bridge." To my surprise I saw both the road and railway bridges breached by the force of water being discharged by the Deg, an insignificant little river, more commonly called a nullah.

"Well Mick, do you still think you can get to Sialkot?" enquired Mr Moss.

"Why not?" I said, "where there's a will, there's a way!"

"But face reality" said Mr Madden," there is no way. Anyhow, what's the great attraction in Sialkot to make your trip so essential?"

"Maybe I'm a father by now!" I said, and walked away to inspect the breached road bridge. Though it was impossible for a four wheeled vehicle to pass over the bridge, a motor cycle could be ridden along an 18 inch wide iron girder spanning what remained of the structure, provided balance could be maintained.

Starting the motor cycle I said cheerio to my friends and moved off.

"Good luck to you" said Mr. Moss, "but listen Mick .... in case you don't make it what are your favourite flowers?"

"Carnations will do," I said, then started the trick riding across the girder. I made it but not without some very anxious moments. On the other side I was stopped by a truck driver and advised to return to Lahore as it was pointless going any further due to a causeway being overwhelmed near the village of Sukake, but there was now no question of turning back, my objective was Sialkot, and there I intended to go irrespective of what I was told about road conditions, flood warnings or anything else.

After passing the roadside village of Muridke I arrived at the causeway which certainly presented a problem. It was no longer the causeway I knew so well, with just a trickle of water flowing through it, but a vast expanse of murky water. It was indeed a challenge, a challenge I was prepared to take on in my desperate bid to reach my destination. The water level indicators at the start were promising, showing a depth of about nine inches, yet I was aware of worsening conditions in the centre. Nevertheless, I pressed on regardless, hoping for the best.

Everything was going well, when suddenly the water deepened and the current forced the machine off the submerged road. I tried to keep the engine going, giving her full throttle and making every effort to get the wheels back onto a hard surface, but I succeeded in travelling only another few yards when the water level swallowed the cylinder, there was a cloud of steam and an abrupt end to my motor cycling!

I now stood astride a useless "metal horse" surrounded by water. Close by a yellow bungalow, built on the top of a hillock, was conspicuous in the flat countryside. My courage and determination flowed away with the flood water so, turning the motor cycle around, I retraced my course with much difficulty. Pushing a heavy motor cycle is hard enough without having to cope with a strong cross current and my endurance was fully tested before I arrived back on dry land.

I headed for the yellow bungalow which was a short way off the road. A man who stood in the verandah came along to give me a hand with the motor cycle and, after helping me to push it up to a shelter, introduced himself as Mr Shah. He extended the usual warm hospitality, ordering a servant to prepare refreshments and meanwhile insisted I use a set of his dry clothing until mine could be dried. Soaked to the skin, I was pleased to slip into a fresh outfit.

The servant produced a tray of tea, hard boiled eggs and biscuits apologising for the quality of the food as we sat on the verandah chatting. I spoke in Urdu while Mr Shah replied in understandable, if not fluent English.

His conversation was limited to the Services, perhaps deliberately to get my mind off the worsening weather conditions. However, when I saw a peasant wade across the causeway which only a short time ago wrecked my journey, I became keen to question him, as to what the road was like from where he had come. The information he revealed was by no means encouraging; in fact it was most disheartening because he spoke of a breach in a canal, the flood water from which was threatening the town of Gujranwala, and furthermore, the river Chenab had also flooded causing extensive damage to low-lying areas between Wazirabad and Gujranwala. This meant that my journey to Sialkot was now quite out of the question, for the time being at least. I had a choice, get the motor cycle roadworthy and return straightaway to Lahore, or stay-put with Mr Shah and hope for more favourable conditions next day.

Mr Shah insisted that I stay, assuring me that he had adequate food supplies to last the household for months. A very comforting thought indeed, but I had no intention of staying at his bungalow longer than necessary. Floods were not my only worry, and little did Mr Shah know that it wasn't official duty which was troubling my mind, but the duty a man owes to his wife when she is near her time.

It was very fortunate that Mr Shah persuaded me to stay, because by evening Lahore was isolated by the flooding of the river Ravi, and overnight our site became an island. Many of the inhabitants of the neighbouring villages had already evacuated their crumbling mud huts and collected on our island. Some families had erected improvised tents by suspending sheets or blankets on four poles under which they sat with their bare necessities in a pathetic state of despair.

By afternoon the situation had worsened and more people took refuge on the island; the level of the flood had risen, carrying evidence of its depth and destruction. Cattle were swept along helplessly, primitive farm equipment, remains of thatched huts, chatties, baskets, wooden boxes and chapoys had been washed away in a sea of murky water. It was a most frightening sight, and I couldn't avoid the thought that this was the beginning of the end. I'm sure I was not the only despondent one amongst this ever increasing community; others must have felt the same way if not worse, yet Mr Shah remained astonishingly calm, reassuring everyone that there were better times to come, with more alluvial soil on their lands.

The third morning a Wayfarer aircraft belonging to the P.A.F. made a low pass over the island, banked and then returned lower than before and dropped a string of sacks without parachute attachments. The ignorant villagers, not knowing better, tried to catch the sacks in their arms. Of course, these sacks contained cooked meals and the impact was more than they bargained for! The contents were hardly enough to provide everyone a square meal, nevertheless, it was a great boost to the morale of those marooned on the island.

Mr Shah took possession of the newspaper wrappings which he read out to me. The situation throughout the Punjab was desperate, a national disaster had been declared. The northern plains, extending from the river Jhelum to the Indo-Pakistan border, east of Lahore, a distance of some hundred miles, was inundated by flood waters. We had no reason to doubt the Press reports; after all the Punjab means five rivers – the Jhelum, Chenab, Ravi, Sutlej and Bias – and these large rivers having flooded, joined together and were causing as much damage as they do good to this fertile Province.

After digesting these news reports, Mr Shah commenced strict rationing. He became a hard man and his generosity was a thing of the past; above all, he drilled discipline into the refugees, emphasising the importance of hygiene on the island to prevent an outbreak of typhoid or cholera.

Until now we had killed and eaten his poultry, goats and sheep, but this he said must stop. There are stray cattle, he said on the island which must die before his own stock. The island was about twice the size of a cricket ground, so he had visual control over the whole place from his bungalow. From his vantage point he selected a bull and taking me along with him directed the refugees to form up around him. Standing beside the bull he asked whether it belonged to any of them? There was no claimant so the unclaimed bull met its fate.

Drinking water came from a hand-pump situated in front of the bungalow. This, too, became a guarded installation and no one was permitted to draw water from it without his servant being present. This was the most important machinery we had, and one that had to be guarded constantly because of the heavy demand placed on a pump which perhaps had never been serviced since it was installed. Every time it was put to use I thought I was in the neighbourhood of a piggery! Rather than take any chances of a failure for the sake of a drop of oil, I drained some oil from the motor cycle and lubricated our vital water system which squeaked no more.

My friend was inside the bungalow, while I was busy servicing the motor cycle for a quick get away if and when the chance arose. Suddenly I heard high-pitched screams from a child; the child was hysterical, either from a thrashing or the bite of a snake. Whatever the cause, I hurried over to find out. A lad of about ten had been bitten by a snake, the species unknown, but I presumed it to be a Krait as they were the most numerous in this area. Having been bitten by a Krait myself, I knew the excruciating pain he must have been experiencing.

I made him stand up, tied a tourniquet above the bite which was on the instep and tried to keep him conscious. After a couple of hours his condition was grave and I found myself very upset, recalling how in my case immediate medical aid was available, yet for this unfortunate child there was nothing to be done. By evening he was unconscious, and died while the flood raged on.

I walked away in profound grief and stood by the edge of the turbulent water, gazing across what had once been cultivated land. I meditated in my loneliness; a life had just departed and perhaps at that very moment a son or daughter had been delivered to my wife. Or had the flood waters washed away both mother and child? I had only one consolation in which to place my trust. No news, at this stage was good news. With this thought in mind I looked up into the heavens to see a break in the clouds, some of which did have silver linings!

Quite close to where I stood a small rat, more dead than alive, made fervent attempts to sit up and preen itself after being washed ashore. Within a few minutes it was strong enough to hop away towards a bush where it ended up in the mouth of a concealed snake. At that precise moment an eagle swooped down, grabbed snake and rat in its talons and settled on a nearby tree where it was constantly attacked by crows until forced away, dropping the snake. Later I found the remains of the snake which had provided only a snack for the eagle, but a substantial meal to an army of ants which, within 24 hours, had reduced it to a fish-like skeleton.

On the fourth morning of being marooned another animal sought refuge, a medium-size wild boar. The poor thing had to remain on the move having little or no cover, and all the time being harassed by dogs and humans alike. A pig amongst Muslims could not be tolerated, and its life became a hell in spite of putting up a gallant effort to stay on land. He lost the battle and reluctantly swam away down current.

The next day showed a marked drop in the flood level. As rapidly as the floods had inundated the land so it receded, but the aftermath was still to come. Naturally, low-lying areas, streams, canals and rivers continued to hold the tail-end of the flood waters, yet the immediate outlook was cheerful. I couldn't believe my eyes, I thought I had woken up after a dream. There was no island and where had all the refugees gone? Footprints through the deep slush criss-crossed away from the high ground, indicating a mass exodus from an overnight island, a God-send and a haven to all except a small child who died.

Despite authentic reports of vast sections of the road and bridges having been washed away, I was still bent on getting to Sialkot. Ignoring the advice given by pedestrains and Mr Shah, I set off to fulfil a promise, but the same causeway once again submerged the engine of the motor cycle and I returned to the bungalow where I left the motor cycle in the care of Mr Shah, and headed for Lahore on foot.

I had over 20 miles to walk, and estimated on covering the distance in about six hours. I saw what damage the floods had caused. Almost every bridge had been breached or washed away, some sections of the road did not exist, other portions appeared to have been blown up by explosives, dead animals littered the raised embankments and vultures gorged themselves. About seven miles away from Lahore vehicles were overturned, railway tracks dangled in distorted shambles, thatched huts or their remnants were suspended in the branches of trees and oil drums blackened the soil. Peasants searched amongst the ruins of their mud huts, womenfolk, gathered in small groups to pool their resources to scrape up a meal, and little undernourished children covered with flies and filth, pathetically begged for paisa (money) while the aged lay silent, awaiting death.

Arriving at the outskirts of Lahore I was confronted with the final obstacle of the long trek. There was a low-lying belt of land about a furlong in width, swollen by the flood water of the River Ravi. The gates of a railway level-crossing at this spot had either been washed away or submerged and I knew I'd have to swim to cross the main depression. To get so far I had already been forced to swim many times, and this wider stretch was not going to deter me. I took it easy and started to swim; the current wasn't so swift that I was forced to struggle, nevertheless, seeing a wooden box floating down, I took advantage of its buoyancy and held onto it.

The relaxation afforded by this old box almost cost me my life. It was already providing shelter to a cobra which strongly resented sharing it with me! The familiar loud hiss warned me instantly to withdraw my hand from the box, and as I did so I saw it strike, its hammer-like head missing my hand by inches. Terrified of the cobra following up the attack I swam strongly across to the other side completing the distance in record time! Although I was untouched by the cobra, I imagined I had been bitten. And the more I examined my hand the more swollen it apeared compared with the other hand. I commenced to tremble violently, cold shivers ran through my body and I gave myself about half-an-hour at the most to live! I plodded on through the boggy soil in my misery until I crossed the Ravi bridge from where I was picked up by a patrolling police jeep and taken to my residence. Nothing happended to me, of course and no longer did the fear of death torture my worried mind.

Resuming work I found the situation in Lahore pretty chaotic. In addition to the flood water of the River Ravi having swept through the low-lying areas of the city, the heavy rain had wrecked the drainage system so that stagnant pools of water lay in the streets and residential areas of the city, especially along the north and western surburbs. There was an acute food shortage in this densely populated city in the Punjab. The delivery of food supplies was non-existant, food merchants hoarded their stocks and black-marketing of essential items added to the misery of the poorer classes and the refugees who depended on aid which was inadequate even prior to this terrible flood.

The Government stepped up aid to the worst hit areas and slowly the situation improved until the time was ripe for me once more to obtain leave and renew my efforts to get to Sialkot. Two weeks had elapsed without any news of my wife, and my anxiety was bordering on near insanity. Public transport had not been restored between Lahore and Sialkot, but I got a lift by jeep to Mr Shah's bungalow where, after topping up the motor cycle with petrol, set off for Sialkot.

The road links were undergoing temporary repairs by the Public Works Department and the Pakistan Army. Priority had been given to the Grand Trunk Road to restore the vital link between Lahore and Rawalpindi, so I had little difficulty in getting to Gujranwala, but as soon as I got off this road to head for Sialkot, it commenced to bucket down with rain.

Ignoring the rain, the bumpy pit-riddled road, the dogs which chased after the motor cycle and the bullock-carts that forced me off what was left of the road surface into the deep slush, I was at least making progress in the right direction. Stopping for a smoke and a rest on the canal bridge at Sambrial, I was told by a cyclist that many parts of the road ahead were under water and a causeway in the suburbs of Sialkot could not be negotiated on a motor cycle.

I was not going to give in after coming all this distance. Undeterred I rode on, confident of success, even if it meant walking the last few miles into Sialkot. Long stretches of water covered the road, but fortunately they were shallow and presented little or no trouble in low gear, occasionally putting my feet down to hold my balance.

I was soon clear of this flooded section of the road and headed up a slight gradient which was free from flood damage. After some miles the road levelled out and I saw a sign indicating a causeway.

Stopping at the edge of the water which was flowing through at torrential force I put the motor cycle on its stand and studied the situation. I decided to walk across the causeway to discover the depth of the water. It was just below knee-level and flowing swiftly enough to convince me that once again I'd met my Waterloo!

Already soaked to the skin, a further dousing would be a trivial matter, so I decided to take a chance on two wheels. Riding back a short distance, then turning round and accelerating I approached the causeway at about 40mph, hoping to slice through the water at speed so keeping the ignition system dry. The impact was unexpected and I found myself hurled through the air. Hurriedly I got to my feet and salvaged the machine, dried the spark plugs, and points and, to my utter surprise, after some perseverence the motor cycle started. The performance was not exactly perfect but somehow it kept going, the engine spluttering and back-firing helped clear the crowds off the road and marked my entry into Sialkot.

I found the house and, entering it, I was looked upon as though I was an apparition. My wife sat stunned, my in-laws were bewildered and the reception was so dismal that I was lost for words. Then Sheila stood up, walked slowly over to me, burying her face into my chest and gradually tightening her grip aound my waist. I felt the warmth of her body as she lifted her face and looked at me, pale but beautiful, her eyes full of tears. Her lips quivered as if she had lost the power of speech.

Still firmly holding me she burst out crying. I ran my fingers through her hair, lifted her face and said, "Darling, this is no time to cry ... let's rejoice, bring the baby to me then pour out the drinks." She spoke in a whisper which was absorbed in her sobbing. Perhaps she had given birth to a girl which would be a disappointment to me. Taking the initiative I said "Well, where is the beautiful baby girl? It's time we started the celebrations!" She cried bitterly, then composing herself said, "Michael ... I'm sorry ... we lost our daughter at childbirth."

Shocked to hear the bad news I sat down, Sheila continuing to sob her heart out. I was speechless, thinking of all I had gone through and now to be told of our own loss, as if I had not already witnessed or heard of enough heart-breaking incidents. Fresh still in my mind was the vision of the painful death of the child bitten by the poisonous snake, not to mention the thousands of homeless and starving men, women and children without aid or rehabilitation.

Unable to get back to my district, I reported for temporary duty to the chief of police at Sialkot until road or rail communications were restored. While in Sialkot I met another senior officer's wife who had been marooned there and was awaiting conditions to improve to drive back to Lahore where her husband, Brian Allum, was posted as Commandant, Punjab Constabulary. After telling her that I had got through on a motor cycle, and would be returning in a day or two, she offered to give Sheila a lift with myself as an escort to pave the way across the now uncharted causeways.

A large Urial shot by Father near Margalla Pass, West of Pindi.

Time soon restored life to normal, and the recent calamities became a thing of the past with a few exceptions such as food shortage and lines of communication which still had to be vastly improved. It was now the end of September and the duck shooting season had opened; there were plenty of common and Gargany Teal, with the occasional batch of Pintail still in eclipse to be found heading for the paddy fields. By now, my trigger finger was itching, ready to be exercised!

Selecting a spot for my opening shoot I went down the Multan Road some 17 miles to do an evening flight. There were plenty of birds about but I was selecting Pintail, rather than fire into masses of Teal. After a short while I found I had company. A group of three people were in the same line of flight under which I had positioned myself. Of the three, only one person was shooting, quite briskly too. Having taken a belt of 25 cartridges I finished shooting, picked up the dead birds, and on my way out of the jheel thought I'd check the Game Shooting Permit of the person I presumed to be an army officer.

On my way to do the check, I myself was stopped, recognised and requested to report to his boss. It was a surprise to find no other than Mr W.D. Robinson M.C., O.B.E., I.P. Deputy Inspector General of Police, West Punjab. He had, in fact selected me for the Punjab Police when I left Quetta. He was an unforgettable officer, a lamb when off duty, so much so that he was not very popular with the "powers that be". I paid my respects to his wife Phyllis, discussed the shooting and offered him some Pintail duck then started to walk out of the shallow jheel when he stopped me saying, "Why have you finished off shooting so early?" I told him that I'd come out only for a reccy and had finished my cartridges. He insisted that I help myself to cartridges from his bag and continue shooting. I did so some distance away, but firing very conservatively as I was using his cartridges.

I fired a rather high shot with a No 6 Eley $2^1/2$ in cartridge at a solitary Pintail which, though very badly hit, flew on a few hundred yards then suddenly lost height and came down with a splash. I marked the spot and went straightaway to retrieve it. There was more slush than water, with tufts of tall grass laid flat by the recent floods. At the edge of one of these tufts of grass I saw the Pintail. Thinking it might be alive and concealing itself, I made a grab at it to find, to my utter astonishment, that it was anchored to a snake! I immediately dropped the duck with the snake still attached to it and used the barrels of the shotgun to lever the duck out of the shallow murky water. The snake still held firmly on to the base of the duck's beak, but finally it let go and disappeared into the grass.

I was unable to identify the species of snake; it was dark grey, about 30 inches long and perhaps three inches in circumference. I assumed that the Pintail had a lung wound and was discharging blood from its mouth which attracted the snake to try and make a meal of it. Though I had shot over many marshes I'd never before experienced a snake trying to eat a duck!

*A fair bag of Mallard shot by Ainsworth and myself on a Jhee 1
on the east side of the river Jhelum.*

*Shiela (left) with Birdie King and the children at Kalla
Kahar, standing behind a mixed bag of partridge, chickor
and duck.*

Leeches, on the other hand, I'd often found attached to wounds on freshly shot duck.

At dusk I walked out of the jheel and joined the boss and his wife at their car on the roadside for a few whiskeys. The conversation was very informal and he gave me some bad news, namely that he wouldn't be around for much longer. He wasn't renewing his contract to serve on and was shortly to take up his new appointment as Commissioner of Police, Malaya.

"Sorry to lose you, nevertheless, congratulations", I said,"At least you should get plenty of shooting there! Any chance of getting me a posting to serve with you?"

"Are you serious?" He asked.

"Yes, I think so." I replied.

"O.K. Come and see me in my office, but before you do so I think you ought to talk it over with your wife first." He said.

I did as he advised, confirming I'd be pleased to serve under him in Malaya and left the matter in his hands. Soon, both he and his wife left the country, a great loss to the majority of the officers and men of the Punjab Police, West Pakistan.

I got a letter from him after he had taken over as Commissioner of Police, Malaya, but the contents were not all milk and honey. Things had changed for the worse, and he had decided, for my good, that he was not going to influence my coming to Malaya because if I did, quote "You will be coming as gun fodder! Police officers are being shot-up by terrorists faster than they can be replaced. Under the circumstances I'd feel guilty if anything should happen to you."

I was very disappointed, yet appreciated the frankness of the communication. To some extent there was some compensation, I had been transferred to Rawalpindi, commonly called Pindi. It was my birthplace and where Dad had retired to though not without giving me a taste of his outdoor life, which I remembered, especially when he shot a huge Urial near the Margalla Pass. This short narrow pass bears an obelisk to the memory of Brigadier General John Nicholson who was wounded there in September 1848 while trying to storm the forces of Sardar Challar Singh.

During my posting to the Rawalpindi District I shot chickor and Si-Si partridges north and south of the pass; they are quite plentiful throughout the Salt Range and the North West Frontier. My brother Edwyn was posted at Peshawar, approximately 100 miles away, and he took me to some of his favourite spots such as Razmak, Bunnu, Kohat Parachinar and Landi Kotel. Edwyn had been posted in the North West Frontier since 1940, spoke the language quite well and from what I saw he was very popular with the various tribal "Maliks" (chiefs).

Though a general deterioration was visible everywhere, one thing remained essentially unchanged. Hospitality! Make a friend of a Pathan and he's a friend for life, but make an enemy of him, then your days may well be numbered! Sheila and I were given a feast laid on by the Nawab of Hoti Mardan, a very close friend of Edwyn, after which we were taken into the Khyber Pass. It was a spectacle worth seeing, despite the chance of being ambushed by hostile tribesmen.

Pindi was a busy place being G.H.Q. Northern Command, nevertheless as a Police Officer I was able to mix work with pleasure. Remembering places where I had been taken by Father when I was about a six years old I began to explore them some 20 years later. They were areas surrounding Pindi where one could pick up a few duck, snipe, chickor and partridges. I tried the Margalla Range about eight miles north of the Pass in the hope of meeting up with an Urial similar to the one Father had shot! No such luck so I headed downhill to the gentle cultivated slopes near the village of Golra Sharif.

At the base of these hills I saw partridges and chickor feeding together, which is most unusual. Taking a shotgun from a servant I thought I'd pick up a mixed brace. Wishful thinking! These birds sprint into cover at the first opportunity, and refuse to be flushed. I suspected from this behaviour that someone was using a hawk or hawks in this area which was confirmed by the headman of the village. I also enquired whether Urial existed in the hills. He answered in the negative, though confirming that in the past there were plenty. The few which remained had recently been shot by Pathans who came through from the adjoining North West Frontier to link up with fellow tribesmen assembled at Pindi from where they advanced on Kashmir, joined by "Razikars" (specially trained home guards). A good slice of Kashmir was occupied which from then onwards became known as disputed territory – Azad (Free) Kashmir with its capital at Muzaffarabad.

On the east of Pindi lay the Jhelum District with the Salt Range stretched in between. Duck and geese were to be found in large numbers on the marshes on the East side of the river Jhelum. There are four lakes in the Salt Range, all harbouring a variety of wildfowl, three of which were our favourites, namely Nammal for geese, Martin Sar for mallard and Kabbaki which was difficult to shoot on. (Now a wildfowl sanctuary, thanks to Ainsworth and Chris Savage.) Last, but not least was Kalla Kahar, the beauty spot with two Rest Houses overlooking the lake. Peacocks added their glitter to the gardens while below wildfowl and flamingos, the winter visitors, when disturbed circled the lake filling the air with the swish of wings.

The serenity of Kalla Kahar was such that even Sir Malcolm Haley, later to become Governor of Punjab, used a rock overlooking the lake to deal with his administrative work, read or just relax. This rock, now a monument on which every visitor stands to admire the wonderful scenery, is still upkept and known as Haley's Rock. (Yet elsewhere Queen Victoria's statues and various other dignitaries of the British realm have been removed, including General John Nicholson's plaque.)

Ainsworth took a week's leave in early December to join me, Ernie King of Attock Oil Company and Major Bowells on a shoot in Azad Kashmir. We crossed the river Jhelum at a place called Ghurri, picked up our host and a few porters then commenced a stiff climb to an altitude of about 1,100 feet. We occupied a hut used during the summer months by the host's people who took their cows to this area for grazing. Our objective was a Monal pheasant shoot but it turned out to be a disappointment, nothing like the shoot above Baijnath. However, over a period of three days we managed to shoot a dozen Monal and Four Western Horned Tragopan pheasants.

An interesting observation on this trip remains a mystery. Large footprints were seen in the snow in an area at this time of year uninhabited by man or bear. The porters accompanying me showed fright at the sight of these tracks and described them as being those of a huge hairy man known as "Bun Budda." More interested than worried, I was keen to set eyes on this creature and commenced to follow the tracks. The two porters became rebellious, insisting that we leave the neighbourhood, and warning me that this "man" had the reputation of supernatural powers. Legend or fact, this creature, if it exists, is still to be identified. Until then, come what may, the inhabitants of the Himalayas will continue to live in fear of the "Bun Budda" or "Yetti". Of course, in the Western World it's called the "abominable snowman".

After our return from this shoot, life began to change as our hitherto united family started to leave the sub-continent, finding new pastures in England, Australia and Canada. Only Mother, Father, Ainsworth and myself remained and we were now in two separated countries. A sad state of affairs, especially for our parents who were in India.

On the 12th of July 1952 Sheila presented me with a son to look after in my spare time! Thrilled at the exciting thought of being a father, I settled down to a homely life, giving him all the attention possible. The question of suitable names kept cropping up. I was very keen that Michael be his first name, but this was turned down by Sheila on the grounds that it was bad enough trying to cope with one Michael, let alone two! However, by mutual agreement we named him Ian Winslow, the next of kin perhaps to inherit the wild.

En route to the snow line looking for Monal Pheasants.

A day's shoot. Four Western Horned Tragopan pheasants.

Chapter Eleven

Until the late 1940s a rugged, mountainous territory know as the Gilgit Agency was virtually secluded from Western influence, apart from having been visited by mountaineering expeditions to climb Mount Godwin Austin (K2) and by a few administrative officers in the course of duty. The spirit of adventure led a party of us into this area.

The rapidly ascending and tortuous track leading from Balakot to Gilgit was originally used only by the busy feet of animals and humans to traverse this narrow pass for six months of the year, after which it became snowbound. Then, forced by nature, the meagre population had to migrate to the lowlands to get away from the long harsh winter. In recent years, however, this track has been widened to take the versatile jeep for the purpose of defending the remote frontiers against Communist infiltrators. Of course, the inevitable had to happen – the North West Frontier Government explored the possibilities of introducing a scheduled jeep service up and down the valley. The scheme was implemented and soon a daily service linked the Bubussa Pass via Naran to Balakot.

An enterprising local citizen with an eye to business built a hotel at Naran, alongside the P.W.D. Rest House, and by 1955 the trend was to develop this valley as a tourist attraction. No doubt, in the near future this formerly unspoilt mountainous territory will be highly commercialised and no longer a haven for those wishing to get away from it all. No matter what happens, one thing is certain, for at least six months in the year the gate is shut to everyone by heavy snowfalls.

Our trip took place in the first week of October 1951 when the valley was comparatively unknown to the adventurous holidaymaker.

Arriving at Balakot Rest House, the gear was unloaded, the car garaged and a meal ordered while we whetted our appetites on the verandah. An outstanding feature in the compound of this rest home is a round stone placed on a dais with the inscription "Maryan Stone wt. 240 lbs". According to the locals, Maryan was the most elegant and beautiful girl in this valley, coveted by all those who set eyes on her. But that was as far as they got because, in spite of proposals which poured in for marriage from both the rich and the poor, this stone was always the stumbling block. She carried this stone with the greatest of ease and her challenge to suitors was to do the same. The first to lift this stone could be her husband! The challenge remained open. Men came from far and wide to try to win the affecion of Maryan but, as legend had it, she died a spinster! Like everyone else, Ainsworth, Sydney and myself each in turn tried our very best to lift the stone but, other than shake it, our individual attempts were a miserable failure.

After lunch we walked over to the bazaar which consisted of a few shops and then to the North West Frontier Province Transport Office, where we inspected the jeep which was to take us up and beyond. The trailer was attached, our baggage loaded and we were all set for the trip though we were advised that we might have to return ahead of schedule because it was too late in the season to be certain of the weather.

A one-way traffic restriction was strictly enforced so we had to wait until the down traffic had arrived. Standing on the bridge we watched the Kanhar race down the valley, above which, in the distance, a trail of dust marked a homeward-bound jeep, followed by another and yet another until four of them set up a long dust screen along the mountainside. As soon as they got to base it was confirmed that the last of the convoy had arrived.

Our convoy comprised of three jeeps. Heading the convoy our driver stepped on the gas on the narrow gravel surfaced track and, after travelling about a mile, pulled up at a police barrier where his documents were checked and we were given the once-over by the Frontier Constabulary. A butt salute and we were off, starting a steady climb along the narrowing track. The first mile or so we were worried! The driver was aware of it, calling us backseat drivers, but he very consolingly told us to calm down as this was only the start, the worst was yet to come!

The engine whined as it began to climb in first gear, the gradient varying between 1 in 6 and 1 in 10; the river below us looking ever more threadlike and not a rock or tree to stop the vehicle falling into it if the driver misjudged his steering by a few inches.

The jeeps were moaning as they crawled up a gradient of 1 in 4 in four wheel drive. The track had further narrowed to about six feet wide and some of the hairpin bends could only be negotiated by reversing to and fro before taking the bend. At one point I hopped off when I saw the trailer's wheels on the edge of the precipice.

The scenery was superb, but one could hardly appreciate it when most of the time one's eyes were focused on the perilous track. Not prepared to miss anything, I found a solution to the problem by standing on the attachment between the trailer and the jeep and, since our speed was not in excess of 10 miles per hour, it would be easy to jump to safety in an emergency. The driver saw me standing in this dangerous position and told me sit in my seat. He knew I was scared and suggested that someone blindfold me, a common practice on this track if passengers are nervous. Admittedly I was frightened but not to the extent that I would be subjected to blindfolding.

We drove through a rather barren range of mountains, then started to descend towards the river. Rounding the contour of a precipitous ridge, we found ourselves on a most extraordinary portion of the road which was built out on beams cantilevered from the rock face with wooden planks to provide a base on which shingle had been scattered. I shuddered at the thought of travelling along this ledge in the jeep and on this occasion I wasn't alone in my anxiety. All except Robert Shuttleworth braved it in the jeep and he too was having kittens when the construction creaked and shook under the weight of the jeep.

We reached Mahandhni Rest Home which was the halfway mark between Balakot and Naran. Here we had to wait until the scheduled down service had arrived from Naran en route to Balakot. However, this was a beautiful rest house, tucked away in a mammoth gorge, the river roaring past the verandah and the towering mountains presenting a magnificent picture of what lay ahead.

Leaving Mahandhni, we drove alongside the river on a wider track, making it a more comfortable part of the journey. The driver pulled up to show us a trout farm at Shinwari. Modern in concept and well stocked, the keeper told us that otters frequently got in and played havoc with the larger trout. The driver, on the other hand, believed the keeper enjoyed trout himself and blamed the otters for what he consumed or sold on the quiet!

The comfortable journey was shortlived, for the track again narrowed and the jeep was back in four wheel drive, crawling to higher altitudes. Trouble came when we encountered a herd of cattle on their way down, led by a local tribe known as Koishtanis (similar to Pathans). The herdsman vehemently opposed the driver's order to move his cattle to a more suitable place where the passing could be made safely. Our driver, a Pathan, was as obstinate as the other chap and refused point blank to reverse the jeep. Meanwhile the cattle, terrified of the jeep, had already about-turned and done a bunk. Of course those at the rear soon arrived, herding the cattle back towards the jeep and the argument heated up. Words failed to solve the problem, a rifle appeared and was levelled at the driver, but timely intervention from us saved a situation which could quite easily have ended in bloodshed. The rifle was lowered, the driver switched off the engine and the cattle reluctantly passed by one at a time, rocking the jeep as they squeezed through the narrow gap. One false step and they could have gone crashing down thousands of feet into the river.

The last of the cattle and the women and children having passed through, the driver started the engine. Then, as he moved away, he uttered a shower of abuse at the rifleman who, in his anger, retaliated by firing a bullet, which just missed the front tyre and whistled across the valley. The driver immediately pulled up and appealed to us to lend him a rifle to teach the silly fellow a lesson. Naturally, the driver was told to drive on. Fortunately we were in the lead because when the remaining jeeps met up with us at Kaghan we were told that the rifleman already stirred up by our driver, was in no mood to compromise when faced with more jeeps. The outcome was a free-for-all once the rifleman was disarmed!

The legendary Maryan Stone.

Tree stood as sentinels. Nature's warning to climb no further.
Myself and Syd (right) with the last tree in the background.

The village of Kaghan now below us, we were told the worst of the journey was over. The river once more kept us company until we drove into Naran at dusk. Fiftyfour long miles had been travelled in approximately eight hours over one of the most hazardous tracks in the world. It was a consolation to know that within the first few years only two jeeps, along with passengers, had taken the short cut to the river, never to be seen again!

The one and only Rest House was occupied, in addition to ourselves, by two Americans who were enthusiastic anglers, monopolising miles of the Kanhar River in quest of record size trout. According to them three to five pounders had been hooked, but bigger ones had got away! We were not fussy for the under five pounders would do us fine.

In no immediate hurry to catch our trout, we took things easy, staying in bed and drinking coffee laced with rum. However, by eleven o'clock we were out and about looking at our surroundings. The settlement consisted of a Frontier Constabulary Post, a few shops and the Rest House. The entire population could hardly have been more than 20 people. The valley at this spot was reasonably wide; snow-capped mountains, anything up to 15,000 feet above sea-level, surrounded us and giant fir trees stood like sentinels fringing the perennial snow-line, symbolising Nature's warning to go no further.

We got out the fishing gear and strolled off to milestone 55, as recommended by the Americans. After hours of casting my moment of triumph came. I hooked a trout by its tail! This was the one and only trout caught by the party and weighing over 3 lbs it was certainly going into the frying pan. Disappointed by the day's catch, from now on guns were to replace the rods.

To start with we found duck shooting an attraction. Duck were not plentiful, nor established in the area. They were migrating to the lowlands and a few shots and they were gone. However, during the course of the day a dozen or so pintail and mallard were shot. The late afternoon proved much more interesting when we found large coveys of Chickor on which we concentrated and, despite being a hard bird to hit, our pooled bag by evening consisted of over 30 head. Returning to the Rest House we passed our American friends who proudly showed us their catch, one of which was an 8 lb rainbow trout. Before leaving, shooting etiquette demanded that we offer them some of our game. They accepted the offer and helped themselves to a few brace of birds, yet made no offer of trout!

Late evening a courtesy call was paid on us by one Mohammed Aslam, who was the proprietor of the new hotel under contruction. Seeing that we were interested in shooting, he spoke at length on the subject, telling us what fauna was available in the area, emphasising the "Phurrer" which perhaps could be seen, if not shot. Because I was the youngest in the party, he suggested that it would be worth my effort to go after them with a guide provided by him.

Setting off at the crack of dawn, we climbed for hours, searching the likely places below the snow-line for the illusive birds but never seeing one. The guide suggested another area where, in addition to the Phurrer, Ibex could also be found. He talked me into having another try the next morning but suggested we leave by three o'clock so as to be clear of the tree-line by sunrise.

Ainsworth and Sydney intended to leave a bit later to explore the fringes of the tree-line. According to plan, the guide and I left in the darkness, but failed to get clear of the forest by dawn. At least the delay sheltered us from the cold blustering wind which would have been punishment had we been exposed to it in the open. In the dawn we climbed up a steep valley and then along the edge of a glacier until we were above the last of the trees.

At this time of year the bird life is sparse at high altitudes, and a few snow buntings was all I saw while taking a rest in this valley to watch the sun's rays gradually paint the trees with silver. A soft chuckling noise somewhere above us brought the guide's hand on my shoulder, he whispered it was the call of the Phurrer and we should climb to the precipitous spot where the bird was calling.

Crossing over a glacier, I slipped and almost fell. Fortunately a boulder broke the impetus and I managed to recover; thereafter I treated the glacier with more respect. However, when we got there the Phurrer had moved up higher, from where they took flight , diving down a valley then gradually ascending with the momentum they gained to land about a thousand yards away, again in a barren precipitous area. Though pleased to have seen them, I was unable to identify the birds.

Taking the advice of the guide, we walked along just below the snow-line, stopping every now and then to look and listen. Suddenly the guide spotted these gregarious birds feeding on the opposite side of a wide valley. They were about 300 yards away and resembled hares prancing about. The little I'd seen of them left no doubt in my mind that they were extremely cunning and difficult to shoot. I wondered if an easy way to overcome the problem of getting within shotgun range, was to use the rifle and splinter a bullet amongst them. I took the rifle from the guide and waited for them to cluster at a spot where the bullet would prove most effective. I never got the chance to try the experiment because they moved over a ridge into another valley.

As soon as they were out of view I told the guide to appear above them while I took up a position in the valley below hoping they would fly down the mountainside, as they had done before. The plan worked! About 20 Phurrer came hurtling down the valley in a scattered formation. I wasn't in the best of positions, nevertheless I picked the closest ones and fired. The first shot was definitely a miss, the second was doubtful until it started to spin before disappearing over the crest of a ridge. Convinced of success of finding the Phurrer I waited for the guide before descending in search of it. The mountainside was terribly steep and not seeing where the bird had fallen made finding it difficult. Eventually. by sheer luck, a gust of wind blew some feathers into the air, and I found it lying dead amongst the rocks, its plumage blending with the background. I had never seen a bird of this species previously though there was a similarity to a Chickor, but it was huge in comparison. Some time later it was identified as the Himalayan Snow Cock.

Hunting Ibex would mean climbing to heights of up to 14,000 feet. I just didn't have the will-power to climb another 2,000 feet to the jagged face of a white-veined, snow-crested mountain. So, satisfied with what I had shot, I was pleased to make tracks for the Rest House. En route we found a white colt stuck amongst a landslide of boulders and, trying to free it, I was surprised to see small bloodstained pug marks on the boulders. A closer examination of the colt revealed the truth; both rear fetlocks were inflamed and a chunk of fleash eaten from the rump, out of which blood still oozed.

I couldn't bear the thought of leaving the colt in agony and was about to shoot it when the guide stopped me. He agreed it was the best thing to do but it was advisable first to get the owner's approval. This was all very well, provided the owner was on the scene, but he wasn't and neither was I going to roam about looking for him. The guide, however, assured me that the owner was an old man who was never in a hurry to head for the lowlands as the majority of the people did. He asked me to follow him round the corner where the old man resided. I did so and when he was told about the colt his friendly attitude changed to hostility thinking I'd been responsible for causing the injury. However, he apologised for the outburst after the guide convinced him of my innocence.

Accompanying us to the spot where the colt lay trapped, he had a good look at it, then told me to go ahead and shoot it. Handing him the shotgun, I invited him to do the needful, least he connive with the guide and later make an accusation that I had shot the colt and demanded compensation. The colt was put out of its agony; the animal responsible for causing its death remained unknown, although the old man was convinced it was a lynx which he had often seen in the neighbourhood.

On the opposite side of the river there were plenty of Chickor calling and I suggested to the others we shoot there next morning. There was one drawback; no bridge across the river, though a short distance away at a narrow spot two felled fir trees formed an improvised bridge. To cross would be a dicey business, to say the least; the water was freezing cold and flowing so swiftly that one would hardly stand a chance of surviving the battering on the submerged rocks if you fell in.

No decision was reached as to whether we should risk the crossing for

Two felled tree trunks bridge the river Kanhar.

The weight of the jeep and trailer cracks open an air pocket while crossing a glacier.

the sake of Chickor. We slept on the matter and in the morning, I raised the question again. All except Robert agreed to attempt the crossing. Since I was so keen to shoot on the other side of the river, I was made the guinea-pig! Uncertain of success, I left my shotgun on the bank, stood on the timber, concentrated, then carefully took a few steps, felt giddy and sat down! Then on all fours I crept along like a lizard, occasionally sprayed with water until I reached the other bank safely. The roaring torrent drowned the laughter of Ainsworth and Sydney who were in hysterics at my antics, especially when I had to negotiate the point where the two logs overlapped. My return was equally successful and then it was a question of "he who laughs last laughs the loudest". My moment of amusement came when both Ainsworth and Sydney set off together, with their shotguns. They reached the obstacle but then they clambered in slow motion became dizzy and were forced to return on all fours in reverse gear! With a little persuasion they tried again and this time made it. Robert did not consider the crossing a laughing matter and much as I tried to boost his confidence the further away he moved from the scene, finally stating that "even at the point of a gun he would not put foot on that silly so-called bridge!"

The risk we took by crossing to the other side was well worth it. We came across unusally large coveys of Chickor without having to do much foot-slogging and with steady shooting picked up a fair number of birds to supplement the larder.

A jeep carrying supplies for the Frontier Constabulary arrived at Naran that evening and, since it had no advance booking, we hired it for a trip to the Babusar Pass. We hadn't gone far from Naran when we had to cross a glacier. Everything was going well when, suddenly, the jeep's weight cracked open an air pocket into which we dropped some six feet. I've never seen people move so fast, including myself! There was confusion confounded in the mad rush to get out of the cavity beneath which the gurgle of water threatened further disaster. Having abandoned the jeep, our next move was to enlist the services of what men or animals we could find in the area to pull the vehicle clear of the cavity. With the assistance of helpful hands using pick and shovel, the jeep was driven out after a couple of hours of hard work but it was too late to continue on the planned trip.

In this area is a high altitude lake known as Saiful Malik, situated a few miles above Naran. We were told it was a terribly stiff climb all the way up, yet the scenery, once there, was worth the effort. Leaving in the morning, we followed a small stream up a thickly wooded valley where we saw a lady sitting beside a tent. We thought it a bit strange to find a white woman camping out in the wilderness, so dropped by to pay a courtesty visit.

"Come along gentlemen", she said with an American accent, "join us in a cup of coffee". Out of a slit in the tent a grey-haired, distinguished looking man appeared, introducing himself as Enders. We had a long chat during which they very modestly gave us an outline of the stupendous mission they were about to complete. They had walked the entire length of the Himalayas and now only the Karakoram Mountains remained, where we had met them. The object of their trek along these mountains was to carry out research on rats, animals which Enders believed were responsible for many of the diseases, especially tuberculosis, prevalent amongst the inhabitants of these mountains. He surprised us by producing a collection of stuffed rats, some large, some small, others blind or tailess. Each species had a separate history sheet and, what's more, their parasites were given VIP treatment, packed away in sealed containers! After showing us the rats, he then produced a variety of collapsible traps while his wife, on the other hand, showed us her works of art, pencil sketches and paintings of landscapes. There was no doubt about it, she was a professional artist.

When asked what weapons they caried, Enders answered "None whatsoever, though I could do with one at times". He gave his reason for doing without a gun or rifle that firearms and cameras in this part of the world invariably became a headache when crossing borders. How right he was.

Hearing that we were heading for the lake, and seeing I was carrying a rifle, he asked me to do him a special favour, namely to shoot for him a Marmot, a rodent far too large to be caught in his traps yet a very valuable contribution to his research work. I promised to do the needful provided I saw one.

"You'll see them there alright," he said "and don't call me Mr Enders. I'm known as Bitter End! When next we meet I'll expect to be addressed as such!" He gave me a bag and some cotton-wool with instructions that, as soon as I shot one, the blood should be swabbed up and the Marmot placed in the bag and fastened at the top to prevent parasites, if any, from escaping. "Good luck to you, sir" he said when parting, raising his well ventilated solar topi.

The climb to the lake was long and tiresome with little or no change in the scenery until we were clear of the tree-line. The settlement of Naran was still visible, a prominent landmark of civilization in the peaceful, secluded valleys. We admired the beautiful Lake Saiful Malik and became obsessed with a sense of purity, a purity not only of the air but everything surrounding the lake.

We sat down at the edge of the water to have our packed lunch, and I threw a small piece of bread into the lake. It vanished with a splash, so despite the altitude, the lake held fish. The water was crystal clear and it did not take long to spot numerous trout swimming away from the shallows.

We also spotted a raft of Ruddy Shelduck. In all probability they were migratory birds, though they might have bred in the area. But migratory or not, here was proof that birds, especially duck, are capable of flying at heights of 12,000 feet or more.

The profound silence surrounding this lake was suddenly broken by the shrill whistle of a Marmot, which brought to mind the promise I had made. How could I justify slaughter in this exquisite atmosphere? I was overcome by a strange feeling of pity at the sight of the beautiful creatures as they ran past nose to tail, resembling a thick golden rope being pulled across a green velvet carpet. They stopped by a landslide of boulders to form a knot, begged, then vanished into their underground world. My heart melted and I never as much as thought of the rifle.

A little later a solitary Marmot appeared on a rock and uttered its shrill call. Perhaps because it was much further away than the family I'd just seen, and since I'd reflected on the importance of this medical research, I asked the guide to hand me my rifle. I drew the bolt back, fed in a cartridge and lay down to have a shot, whereupon the guide promptly ordered me not to shoot the Marmot as it was not an edible animal and, furthermore, it was sacred to the mountain people.

Whilst agreeing that it was inedible, I briefly explained to him that it was the wish of the American gentleman that I shoot one in connection with his mission. Doubting the American's business, he said that all he would do with a Marmot would be to stuff it as he done with the rats! Ignoring his remark, I set about getting my sights on the Marmot but it suddenly ran down the rock and vanished. The guide giggled and muttered that if I had fired, the bullet would have gone astray, guided by some supernatural power!

The Marmot was soon back on its look-out post. I again took careful aim and squeezed the trigger but the cartridge hung-fire and the bullet was way off target. The Marmot then acted in peculiar fashion by rushing down the rock then suddenly, as though having left something behind, turned about and took up is original position from where it screeched its head off. I fired another shot with an identical result except that this time the Marmot run up the slope to another cluster of rocks. The guide meanwhile was highly tickled, and reiterated that these creatures were indestructible. Naturally, to some extent I was shaken by the affair, but on the other hand I knew the ammunition was old stock which I would never have attempted to use on game.

Determined to prove that the Marmot was not bullet-proof, I loaded the rifle with cartidges out of a new packet. By now I was not only being teased by the guide, but by Ainsworth and Sydney as well. A series of whistles betrayed the position of a Marmot, but whether it was the same one or not it met instant death. There was no thrill attached to my accomplishment, nevertheless I now had to hurry and comply with the instructions given by "Bitter End". Little did I realise that this would lead to a difficult problem between the guide and myself. He refused to carry the Marmot or my rifle! So my willingness to help the cause of medical research turned out to be the unpleasant act of having to shoot, carry and deliver a creature

From right to left: Mr. Enders, his wife, Sydney and Ainsworth stand above a display of stuffed rats.

The beautiful lake Saiful Malik.

which normally I would never have harmed.

"Bitter End" was more than delighted with the Marmot, but little did he realise the trouble to which I had been subjected in order that his research work could be accomplished by the addition of the largest of the rodent family. Some years later I received news from Sydney Keelan, who was by then Director General, Barrages, Irrigation and Water Power Development Authority, West Pakistan, that Mr J. F. Enders had been awarded the Nobel Prize for medicine and physiology in 1954 for his research work in the field of tracing the source of typhus fever. Furthermore, I was to learn that the Marmot's skull found a place in the Natural History Museum in the USA.

One evening back in the village I noticed our American fishing friends hiding their catch of trout. They were unaware of my presence and as they never had the decency ever to offer us a trout, I cooked up a scheme which involved 'acquiring' three of their fish!

Next day I slipped off to do some "easy" fishing and without any trouble at all returned with three fine trout which I handed over to the cook with instructions that there would be six people for dinner, including ourselves. Contacting the Americans, I extended an invitation to join us for dinner in our apartment. They willingly accepted the offer, drank our whisky and ate our trout, commending the cook for the excellent manner in which he prepared it, with the remark that "fish caught by others always tasted better". "Morning or afternoon catch?" enquired one. "Couldn't really say when they were caught, though I acquired them this afternoon", I replied. But surely there's nowhere one can get trout in this neighbourhood?" asked an American. "Not openly, but you'll be surprised what is available if you know where to look", I said, leaving them guessing and wanting to know what else was available on the sideline!

This was our last night at Naran and our party went on until the early hours of the morning. Every bottle had been consumed before we finally flopped into our beds. On previous nights fleas had been quite troublesome, but on this occasion we were too busy drinking and enjoying ouselves to give them a second thought. On the other hand, it was possible that the fleas themselves got so drunk biting us during the first half, that they were incapable of biting during the second half of the night!

The jeep which we had booked for our return journey was expected at Naran by one o'clock in the afternoon. The first thing we did in the morning was to pack and be prepared to leave by two o'clock, the scheduled time of departure for down traffic. With a few hours to spare, we walked over to a spot where walnuts were growing wild. Picking up the windfalls and cracking them open, we found the contents very much to our liking. The problem was that the demand exceeded the windfalls. The lower branches were bare while at the top there were still some to be picked by anyone who cared to climb for them. Needless to say, being the youngest member, all the dirty work fell on me. I was soon up the trees shaking the branches and watching the "nutcrackers" display their catching abilities as walnuts fell amongst them. I climbed tree after tree until I heard a rustling noise in a hole in a trunk. I stood in the fork with my ear against the hole trying to identify the peculiar noise. Determined to discover its orgin I tore my handkerchief in half and, setting light to one portion, I allowed it to smoulder, then dropped it down the hole.

I thought it could be a snake and stood aside ready to wallop it should it be forced out by the smoke. To my surprise, a pair of flying squirrels dashed out and glided down to the base of another tree. The nut-eating spree was over, our attention was turned on these beautiful creatures which had now climbed to the top of a branch. Although we had seen flying squirrels before in the Murree Hills, these were far bigger and had thicker coats of a golden colour, compared with the grey species. These creatures are nocturnal and therefore are hard to detect, which is to their advantage as the pelts are eagerly sought by the local fur traders to convert into gloves and hats.

The jeep arrived and we quickly became even more tense on the downward journey than we had been on our way up. The driver was a young , loquacious man who had a habit of steering with one hand and using the other to describe the subject, or at times using both hands! In addition, he frequently disengaged the gear (a common practice to save petrol), as a result of which the jeep gained momentum along the terrific descents, only the brakes being used to control it. It was an experience of a lifetime, and my most dreadful one on wheels!

Having spent the night at Balakot Rest House, we left next morning for Rawalpindi. En route Sydney stopped the car at a road fork. The main road led on to Abbottabad while the side road went across a wide, dry river-bed to Muzaffarabad. Sydney turned off left to cross the stone littered river-bed to take the mountainous road. We looked back in awe at this wonderful country where the Himalayas and Karakoram Mountains embrace each other, and the Rivers Kanhar and Jhelum unite at Domail near Muzaffarabad.

At the confluence of these two rivers the colour of the water remains distinctive for about 100 yards, the Kanhar being crystal clear until absorbed by the larger, deep blue Jhelum.

Continuing our return journey alongside the river Jhelum we arrived at the Kohalla Bridge which separates Azad Kashmir from West Pakistan. This bridge is tucked away in a narrow gorge surrounded by mountains over 7,000 feet high. During the Kashmir Dispute after Independence, this bridge became a prime target for the Indian Air Force though without success. On one such attack a pilot got through in what was believed to be a Sea Fury, dropped a 250 lb bomb which ricocheted off the road across the bridge without exploding! This bridge, protected by the towering mountains, has a charmed life, because it survived both the 1967 and 1971 wars between the two countries.

Crossing the Kohalla bridge, the steady climb to Murree commenced, then the final descent to our starting point, Rawalpindi.

Chapter Twelve

During my posting to Rawalpindi District routine checks were made at the Police Post controlling the start of the hill road between Rawalpindi and Murree. Here I often met a landowner, Ayub Khan, who told me all the gossip of the surrounding hills, such as a panther killing off livestock or wild pigs ravaging the crops. On one occasion he appealed to me to come up to his village where pigs were playing havoc with the maize crops.

I met him at the Police Post at the 17th mile on the Murree Road from where we climbed up towards his village. He had already mustered a number of villagers to meet us to start beating through the lower jungles on our way up. My reputation as a "burra shikari", meaning a great hunter, had gone ahead of me. Ayub told me this, though he had never seen me shoot. As a child he had seen my Dad shoot in the same area, followed by Ainsworth, both of whom rarely missed a shot, so he drew his own conclusions. I hoped I would not disappoint him!

The beats were well conducted, nevertheless wild pig and muntjac slipped through without giving me a chance of a shot, and the heat and humidity of the afternoon soon forced a rest by the side of a stream until evening when a final beat up the hill would bring us to Ayub's village. Suddenly there was a buzz of excitement with shouts of "guldar" (panther). The animal broke back between the beaters and all I saw was an ash-coloured streak as it bounded across a stream.

At the base of Ayub's village I could see a wealth of tall maize growing on semi-circular terraced fields. These had been plundered by wild pig which had destroyed more than they had eaten. With the steep climb over and evening setting in, it was nice to relax in an easy chair to watch the hills change from green to black silhouettes against a pink horizon, then hear the strange howling of packs of jackals.

While I sat outside Ayub's house, sinking a few "sundowners", complete darkness set in, the sky became studded with stars while here and there a solitary glinting oil lamp marked a peasant's hut. A stream whispered through the valley, while frogs and crickets grunted and chirped ceaselessly. Moths, beatles and insects swarmed around the bright Petromax lamp hanging from an apricot tree a few yards away to provide a feast for bats. By 8pm the moon appeared above the hills, the crescent-shaped maize fields becoming conspicuous, silver tops of the maize resembling a mass of overlapping sequins.

After a splendid meal Ayub suggested I take advantage of the moonlight and sit up for pig for a few hours. I wasn't very enthusiastic considering a busy day lay ahead. He didn't press the matter but assured me that I would be called upon during the night to deal with any pigs if they invaded the maize.

The room allocated to me was very warm, so rather than be uncomfortable I brought my bed outside and lay gazing at the stars until I fell asleep – but not for long! I heard Ayub's name being called by a man who stood at the door of the house. Ayub appeared and a short conversation followed, after which Ayub asked me to get up and take a short walk to a field where a herd of pigs had been seen to enter. The plan was for a midnight beat!

Silently we descended to the maize fields where the wild pig were creating havoc. Ayub formed the beaters up, and led me across the stream to a large rock opposite the terraced fields. As planned a torch was flashed to signal the start of the beat, and as I was safely out of the reach of these unpredictable animals, the beat by night was no more dangerous than by day. As a matter of fact I thoroughly enjoyed the charge past me of angry boars, sows and their families. I got off four shots which added to the bedlam as the pigs frantically stampeded up a hillside of loose rocks, stones and pebbles. The number of bodies that came tumbling down as a result of those rapid 12-bore shots appeared most rewarding, but when it came to the count it was rather disappointing. However, a few pigs killed does help to cut down their ever increasing population in a country where adequate measures are not being taken to control the menace.

At dawn we were out again. The result this time was good. Four large sows and a boar. During a later beat, I had the unusual experience of having to deal with a domestic animal. We had come down to low undulating terrain, well clad with shrubs and uncultivated olive trees. Ayub was very hopeful that this area would harbour a herd of pig and directed me to go to a bottle-neck about half a mile away while he himself would join the beaters.

I got to this spot and awaited the beat. Some distance away I saw a camel walking rather hurriedly in my direction. There was something strange about it, for it lacked the casual rhythmic walk of a normal camel, but I thought that perhaps the sound of tom-toms and the noises made by the beaters had put the wind up the animal. However, I considered it best to vacate my position to allow the camel a free passage. To my surprise I found that it deviated from its course and came straight after me. Still uncertain of what it was up to I repeatedly took evasive action to keep out of its way without being able to shake it off. This game of hide-and-seek with a camel was no fun; it did not look friendly! I remembered on occasion when a camel got out of hand and almost severed a forearm from the person trying control it. To make sure I didn't lose a limb I fired a warning shot past its head, hoping it would run like hell. Contrary to expectations the camel never flinched and instead became all the more aggressive and

Four large sows...

...and a boar.

frisky. I bolted towards a layer of flat rocks which jutted out just above the mass of stunted trees. Scrambling up I concealed myself amongst these rocks, but my effort proved futile. There was no escaping the camel's long reach. It now had me really cornered; all it had to do was step forward, thrust its long neck out and bite. Camels at the best of times are ugly creatures, but when I saw this one at close quarters it looked like the devil on four legs. A frothy saliva hung out of its mouth like icicles, its skin was mangy and it was terribly emaciated. I had done my utmost to avoid the animal but it was now a question of self defence and I took the easy way out of the predicament by shooting the wretched thing!

The first question asked at the end of the beat was what had I shot. I led them to the spot where the dead camel lay and, with much embarrassment showed them the result of the two shots I had fired. Ayub immediately mentioned that a camel had been abandoned by the owner as he suspected it of having gone mad. In this part of the world one often meets up with mad dogs or humans who have "gone round the bend", but mad camels .... well, there's always an exception to the rule!

Leaving the camel for the hungry vultures to dispose of, we crossed over a series of low hills to a spot where Ayub assured me I would get a few shots at pig. Walking beside him, he abruptly stopped to have a look at a cow then, turning to me, said that the cow had been hypnotised. I found nothing wrong with the cow except that it was rather docile in the presence of the dogs. He told the beaters to sit still while he took me to within a few yards of the beast and pointed out a reptile attached to its rear leg with its mouth to the udder. As far as I could see it was having a darn good drink of cow's milk.

One of the dogs ran towards the cow and the reptile made a dash for the nearest tree. I identified it as an iguana, a large species of lizard which I had thought to be a harmless, ponderous creature. I had certainly underestimated its performance when chased by a dog. The iguana may not be capable of running long distances or putting up a straightforward fight, but keep well clear of that tail which it uses as a whip. The dog reached it before it managed to ascend the tree and the iguana was forced to defend itself. The tail went into action and the dog was lashed across the head several times. There was skin and hair flying and the dog pulled out of the affray, allowing the iguana unimpeded access to the tree.

I couldn't understand why the cow tolerated the iguana's trespass amongst its udder. One would think she would let fly a few kicks to get rid of a creature taking such liberties. Ayub however, suggested that the iguana has some supernatural power by which it casts a spell on the cow before it crawls up the leg for a drink of milk. The after-effects on the cow are such that she will never again milk as well as she did before being suckled by an iguana, so he claimed.

The grand finale to the day's sport came to a painful end. For onlookers the scene must have been highly amusing but I can assure you it was an ordeal not to be forgotten. It occurred by mere accident when I fired a shot at a bird flying through a grove of tall trees. The charge of pellets hit a hornets' nest the size of a football, built of a cork-like substance in which a species of large yellow and brown hornet lives. These hornets are ready to attack intruders for the least provocation, and after having their fortress riddled with lead shot came out at full strength in search of the enemy. Caught on the hop we were unable to take cover or remain motionless, which is the best thing to do under such circumstances. There was no escape and the vicious attack forced a disorganised retreat.

A gun in competent hands is usually invaluable for offensive or defensive measures, but I now found the weapon utterly useless against the onslaught of hornets. The straffing was prolonged, accurate and unmerciful and no one got away without being stung, not even the poor dogs. It was an unforgetable race; we all started off sprinting in the same direction, then the hornets set to work, splitting us up.

There was a wide range of reaction by which each individual expressed the agony of a sting! The general tendency was to yell, some doing so in short bursts, others with long drawn-out horrifying screams, while in addition there was a great deal of rubbing, jumping, flinging about of hands and acts which resembled epileptic fits with remarkably quick recoveries!

Reassembling, we all had one thing in common .... hornet stings! Some had more than others; I for one was lucky to be wearing a pith hat which protected the neck and head, a part of the body the hornet usually attacks.

An antidote for hornet or wasp stings was produced from the lunch basket, plain powdered rock salt. This was diluted with water to make a saturated solution and gently rubbed into the skin at short intervals, wherever the hornets had stung. I was surprised to find how effective this remedy was in reducing pain and inflamation, and afterward made it a practice always to carry a small bottle of salt in my shooting outfit for immediate application if stung; in addition it was handy to get rid of leeches.

This wasn't exactly what I'd call a very successful trip and before anything more serious befell us on this rather ill-fated day, I thought it best to tell Ayub I'd had enough sport and was keen to return to Rawalpindi. There was no point in going all the way back to the village when the motor road was closer, so taking leave and expressing my regret at being the cause of their immense discomfort I walked away, pleased with their strong sense of humour.

In response to a request from Mother and Father to spend our next holiday with them, I applied for a visa to visit India. The visa was granted after some difficulty, and we departed for Roorkee, stopping over at Lahore to spend a day with Ainsworth and Evelyn who drove us to the Indo-Pakistan border. There had been some noticeable changes since I last crossed this border, annoying ones at that; the police and customs posts on either side had been separated by a furlong of "no man's land" over which one had to walk because public transport across this strip was forbidden. However, after much trouble and inconvenience we got a taxi to Amritsar station where I was recognised by a Sikh gentleman who told me I had saved his life during the riots in Quetta. Well, most Sikhs look alike and I couldn't recollect having done him a good deed until he showed me the scars of old stab wounds to refresh my memory, and I recalled how I was instrumental in getting him safely to hospital. In gratitude for what I had done he offered me his car for the duration of my stay in the country. While appreciating the gesture, I politely refused the offer at which he rushed off and made a reservation of a coupe for our travel with all expenses paid. I had no choice other than to accept his hospitality and our journey to Roorkee was very comfortable indeed.

Unfortunately my movements had been restricted, so I couldn't really get around to places I had in mind. Furthermore, Father had aged very much with worry and sadness caused by his children having gone abroad for good, and the pressure being put on him by the Government in an attempt to requisition his property. In view of all this I spent most of the time at home though Dad had obtained a permit to shoot in our favourite forest block. While himself admitting he was too weak to face the strain of venturing into the wilds, he insisted that I went for a day or two.

I know I was under discreet police surveillance, and approached the officer in charge of the district to let him know I was intending to go on a shooting trip. He gave me the all-clear after asking me when and where I was going. Of course, on arrival at Asifnagar I soon spotted the C.I.D. man appointed to keep an eye on my activities. In all fairness I couldn't discredit his work under normal cirumstances, but he was certainly the odd man out in a jungle assignment! For a start he stuck to me for protection, becoming a nuisance until I had to request him to join the few beaters who were not prepared to believe he was a new forest guard, owing to his complete ignorance of wildlife. Finally he got the wind-up on seeing a python I'd shot, which incidentally had swallowed a small sow. On being told to be careful lest he find himself in the stomach of a python, he unobtrusively disappeared from our company and returned to the village. His worst ordeal was hearing I didn't intend sleeping in the village and instead would spend the night in the jungle!

I admired his devotion to duty, and had a quiet word with him, telling him that I was aware of his identity, and he shouldn't make a fool of himself any longer, pointing out that by now he ought to know that I was not on an espionage trip. The game up, he saluted and asked me a favour: "Just let me know the name of any village you may visit so that I can complete my diary!"

I returned to Roorkee after doing the usual honours by providing the village with a change of menu and bringing back a leg of venison for our personal consumption, but failed to fulfil a promise to Sheila that I would get her a tiger or panther skin as a present. If I had shot either of these animals, one thing was certain, it would not have taken the shape of a coat!

Climatically, the latter half of October is a very pleasant month with rather cold mornings and evenings, but warm afternoons. Ian, my son, had found his feet and had become my Father's shadow. Naturally, his tendency was to treat the child in the same manner as he had treated me when I was the same age by introducing him to whatever bird or insect life that existed on the estate at this time of the year. In addition, he had bought Ian numerous presents, one of which was a rubber snake.

One afternoon we found Ian missing from his room. It wasn't a question of rushing to panic stations, but servants arrived at the sound of a bell and were told to search for the child. He wasn't found outside so we checked all the rooms and eventually saw him playing with the rubber snake in one of the bathrooms. Since he could do nothing to injure or drown himself in a basin of water, we let him play on.

After a while he came into the room we were all seated and started nattering to his grandfather. He said something to the effect that he had found another snake which could make a noise, and was also able to "run" when touched! For a moment we took it that he was referring to the rubber snake, but suddenly the reality registered when he said it had hidden itself in a hole. Father asked him if it was a big snake. He said yes and gave an illustration by extending both arms to full length. He had never seen a real snake so we couldn't draw any conclusions as to the species. Taking a shotgun and a stick we went into the bathroom to investigate. The hole he referred to was a water escape leading outside to the main drainage system. Probing the cavity with a stick, a snake uttered a hiss and not being able to find a quick exit through a barrier of wire meshing zizzagged back towards me. With a few strokes of the stick I put an end to the Kariat, a small but venomous snake similar to the one which bit me in my childhood days. If what Ian had told me was true, and I had no reason to disbelieve the story that he had actually touched and attempted to catch it before it vanished, then he had a miraculous escape. Normally, at this time of year snakes should have gone into hibernation, and rather subdued and not too keen to bite at the slightest provocation.

The holiday was soon over and our parting was by no means a cheerful one, nevertheless, Mother and Father promised to pay us a visit provided they found someone responsible to take charge of the livestock and property.

On returning to work I found I had been chosen to coach the police athletic team in preparation for the Inter Police Forces Championships. This assignment was in addition to my normal work, so cutting out or

150

restricting my commitments to shooting partners. The job was done successfully.

By mid October 1954, I was transferred to Multan District. It was a very dull place compared with Rawalpindi or Lahore, with no social life or entertainment. Strictly speaking, this was up my street. I was now in a position to discover new horizons which, on the other hand, became very boring for Sheila. The occasional visit by Ainsworth, Evelyn, Sydney and Joan Keelan was always a welcome excuse to create a party spirit. In addition Sydney, holding the top position in the Punjab as Chief Engineer, Irrigation, took us to the beautiful Canal and Barrage Rest Houses at Punjnad, the Emmerson Barrage at Trimmu and many other water development schemes which made life a little more pleasant for Sheila and Ian.

Rivers had always fascinated me, and with two of the largest flowing through my jurisdiction I was determined to have a holiday on water, with or without the family. Sheila flatly refused to accompany me when she heard of my intention to spend a week with a nomadic tribe on the River Indus.

Chapter Thirteen

The Indus, turbulent in the mountainous regions, enters the lowlands near Attock, and then widens to meander peacefully through the plains of the Punjab and Sind to provide essential irrigation to the otherwise arid countryside along its entire course. During the summer monsoon, however, the river frequently floods, causing widespread damage to crops, livestock and property, yet for the remainder of the year it is calm and clear, breaking up into a network of deep channels across a very wide river-bed, at places extending as far as 10 miles across.

This river has only a few large towns along its course and fewer bridges to span it, and these two factors alone account for this great river being little known, other than to those who inhabit its banks. As a child I used to become fascinated with stories Dad narrated about his episodes along this river when his work involved travel between Fort Munro and Dehra Ghazi Khan during the early 1890's. In those days it was a God-forsaken area and for that matter it still is, yet he took advantage of the opportunities he got to shoot along selected spots on both sides of the river which, according to him had provided the finest sport of all time. Now, the very same area had come within my striking distance and, who knows, I may very well tread Dad's footsteps in my enthusiasm to explore this river, both up and downstream from the settlement of Ghazi Ghat.

On the river is found the Khaal tribe who live on rather large boats which are their permanent floating homes. Of nomadic habits, they spend their lives travelling up and down the Indus River. I often came across a family of them while shooting in the vicinty of Ghazi Ghat from where a series of pontoon bridges span the river to link up with the road connecting the North West Frontier Province to the Punjab. This being an easily accessible place, sportsmen had heavily shot the area, and though black partridge were still plentiful, crocodile had decreased to a great extent. However, my informants led me to understand that there was no shortage of crocodile, or for that matter any other game, north of Ghazi Ghat, namely upstream. The difficulty was to get to these places as there were no mechanical means of transport by which to reach them.

I was bent on a specific journey, one which would take me through the more remote parts of the river. To make this trip possible, the answer was to join up with a family of Khaal's, but the problem was how to set about being invited to live with these people for a week or so. It was obvious that they would object to anyone encroaching upon their privacy on the restricted space of a barge-like craft, yet it was worth a try. I got in touch with a police officer Mohammed Niazi who was very well known to me and posted at Dehra Ismail Khan from where it would be convenient to float down the river to Ghazi Ghat.

Through his influence arrangements were made for me to undertake such a trip and, at the latter end of January 1955, accompanied by our scout Billinda, I boarded the boat to become part of a family of Khaals. The accommodation on the boat was by no means luxurious, and I became pretty dubious about the long journey ahead. My bed was an old charpoy, precariously balanced on a frame of timber under which about four inches of water stagnated. A thatched canopy provided the necessary shade at the stern which had been allocated to me. A pet pelican found the newly constructed canopy very agreeable and I had no objection to it remaining above me as long as it didn't sit on the edge to bombard me or my belongings! There were no toilet facilities while travelling, but I was told if I wished to answer the call of nature the boat would be moored at any stage of the journey. As for a wash and brush up, hot water would be provided as and when required, but a hot bath was out of the question. I'd have to do what others did, bathe in the river.

The boat was stable, had a complement of three sails, and measured some 50 feet in length with a 15 foot beam. All aboard we drifted down the river leisurely. To the Khaal family this trip was just another of their normal passages along this mighty river, but to me it was the start of a great adventure.

I noticed a small boat being towed along which I thought was a lifeboat for me, but I made it quite clear to the head of the Khaal family that there was no need for it, as I was capable of swimming the river in the event of an emergency. He explained to me that this small boat was to serve a very different purpose. I was to be rowed in it from channel to channel in pursuit of crocodile or wild fowl.

At first I eagerly scanned the little sandy islands and banks of the channel we were drifting down in search of crocodile. Turtles, ducks and sandpipers were very plentiful, yet crocodile, my main interest were absent. The glare was terrible across the flat sun-backed countryside, so as advised I left the spotting of crocs to the experienced eyes of the Khaals' while I rested, watching the children run about the boat without their parents showing the slightest signs of anxiety about their safety.

At the outset the Khaals were suspicious of me, knowing I was a police officer they assumed my presence on board for the ostensible purpose of a shooting trip was only a cover. Naturally, people who engage in lawless activities as they did, prefer to keep aloof from the law and as such the atmosphere was not too cordial. They were very careful not to divulge anything which would incriminate them, especially in matters relating to monetary income. On the other hand, enquiries regarding wildlife inhabiting this river were enthusiastically and intelligently answered with convincing authority. To put them at ease I stopped trying to dabble in their private affairs and soon found I was beginning to bridge the gap between suspicion and friendship, and to convince them my motive for living amongst them was to explore the river with shooting as the main object.

A number of "Koonj" (a large species of crane) were spotted on a sandy stretch of the river bed which aroused much interest from the edible point of view and I was asked to shoot a few. Knowing how cunning they were I considered it a waste of time to go after them although the boat had been moored for me to disembark. The tame pelican, however, took advantage of the stop and began to whet its appetite in a shallow tributary where no doubt it had run into a shoal of fish. The boat moved on, leaving the pelican dashing about and I told the Khaals that they had left the pelican behind. I was assured that it would return as soon as it finished feeding. So it did, landing on deck and pompously strutting around before flying onto the canopy to preen itself. The Khaal family had had this bird for a number of years, having originally found it sick and unable to fly. I was aware that the pelican was a winter visitor to the country and was curious to know how they prevented it from joining up with others during the spring migration. They told me that they knew exactly when these birds migrate, so in order to ensure that they did not lose it, its wing feathers were then pinioned.

Excitement came suddenly when, for the first time, the sentence "sahib, sansar daikoo" was uttered, (look ...... crocodile). I glanced across the water in the direction a Khaal pointed to see umpteen turtles and duck yet no croc. However, with the aid of binoculars I saw three crocodiles a considerable distance away, basking on a small island.

Transferring to the small boat I was rowed silently to within 200 yards of the crocs, then leaving the boat I crawled another 50 yards or so to a position from where I was able to select one offering the best shot. This as far as I'm concerned, is the neck in preference to any other part of the body. The 9.3mm bullet found its mark; the croc remained pinned to the sand while the remaining two instantly splashed into the river. The croc was retrieved and taken back to the parent boat where it was skinned after which the carcase was dissected with the skill of a surgeon to remove an organ they called the "tillhi". This gland, I was given to believe, is a very valuable item, used for medicinal purposes and therefore much sought after and extremely lucrative when sold. After the fat was removed and stored away in canisters, the flesh was spread out and slated. Puzzled to know what they intended doing with the fat and flesh I was told the latter was to be eaten by the Khaals while the fat was to be used for cooking; in addition the fat was highly recommended as a remedy for the prevention of rheumatism.

At sunset the boat was moored for the night. The adults wandered off to gather fire-wood, the women made preparations to cook the evening meal while the children dispersed their stored energy by dashing about the unspoilt sands.

I couldn't wait to stretch my own legs so leaving Billinda behind to get cracking with our dinner, I walked across to the main channel to await the evening flight. Just before dark the wildfowl commenced to move off to their respective feeding grounds. They were the usual winter visitors to this part of the country – mallard, pintail, gadwall, teal, shoveller, shellduck, pochard and wigeon. Later, a few flocks of bar-head geese offered a reasonable shot by flying over within range and I shot three which was fair contribution to our personal larder.

Back on the boat the Khaal family had started to cook the croc's flesh. The smell was obnoxious! For a moment I thought I had entered a fishmonger's shop! This crocodile is known as the Gharial or Gavialidae, a very selective feeder living entirely on fish, so the Khaals make no bones about eating it, and consider it better than fish except that it is harder to come by.

I once saw for myself about five or six of these Gharial feeding below the rapids at Punjab Weir. Systematically they swam up the rapids in formation until they could go no further but it was here they found the fishing good in spite of having to fight the tremendous force of the current.

That night, having struggled through a ghastly dinner cooked by Billinda (not that he ever excelled himself in the art of domestic science) I had an attack of indigestion followed by biliousness. I tossed and turned but failed to get any relief. The answer was to leave the boat and go for a walk. It was about midnight when I finally made up my mind to get rid of the discomfort. I failed to notice that the boat had slightly drifted away from its original position slap against the river bank. In the deceptive light I looked down from the side of the boat and could see the bank within easy jumping distance just below me. In a very casual manner I struck my left leg out and lunged forward, hoping to land softly on the sand, but instead I got the shock of my life when I found I had stepped into thin air to land flat on my face in the river! I realised my folly too late. What I thought was the river bank was, in fact, the shadow of the bank cast on the water! To make matters worse, Billinda and a few others awoke with a start and immediately came to the conclusion that I was a burglar, and threatened to batter me with poles unless I stood still. Knowing Billinda as I did, he would have carried out his threat, so I took no chances and identified myself by asking him how he expected me to stand still in deep flowing water.

Ever since my childhood days he had kept a watchful eye on me and in doing so had taken a lot of liberties knowing I would not take offence. Astonished to hear my voice he sardonically asked me (speaking in Urdu) whether I had gone mad to have dived into the river at the dead of night. I didn't take kindly to these words in the presence of the Khaals and told him to watch out for the consequences, meantime to hand me a rope and haul me up. He did as ordered and, getting a good grip on the rope I jerked back, pulling hard at the same time to make sure he hit the water harder than I did. Of course, not knowing my intention he was unprepared for the force I used and came down like a bomb! Being a good sport, he was more tickled than I, admitting that he should have known me better!

I was left to sleep on while the boat was unfastened from its moorings during the early hours of the morning and allowed to drift along. This move had been instigated by Billinda after he had discussed the possibilities of reaching a spot where black partridges were known to be plentiful. When I awoke I was surprised to find we were in a different environment, and Billinda informed me we were heading for a partridge shoot. The spot selected was a "bailla" (large island clad with rushes) through which Billinda organised a beat, flushing more black partridges than a single gun could possibly cope with. In addition he also disturbed a brute of a wild-boar which charged at sight, catching me with an unloaded shotgun. More petrified than brave, I hesitated during those vital seconds it takes a boar to toss you in the air if you can't jump aside. I was very lucky on this occasion because I mistimed my jump and narrowly escaped being disembowelled.

In our absence another Khaal family had moored alongside our boat. There was a lively conversation between the two families, then I saw croc flesh being presented to the others, very generously too, and I said to myself "thank God for that!" After the two familes parted I was told that there was some good news for me. They had obtained information of the whereabouts of an enormous croc which had been seen very recently. I asked them what guarantee there was that this croc would still be there when we arrived. The head of the family put the answer in a nutshell; "A croc will return to its basking place."

On a long narrow island no less than a dozen crocs lay packed together, a rather unusual gathering as far as I was concerned, but the Khaals didn't think so. They told me it was the mating season and all the males in the vicinity collect around a female on heat. To approach within a reasonable distance of these crocs was almost impossible without disturbing them, so I had no choice but to give them a miss. A suggestion was put forward that I fire at them from the boat while drifting past, but I wouldn't hear of such a thing, knowing full well that I would probably wound one. The crocodiles decided the issue for themselves by suddenly making a dash for the water and disappearing. I was puzzled why they had taken fright when we were about 500 yards away. The Khaals knew the answer to that too. Firstly, the wind was blowing towards the croc, and secondly they made a frank admission that they emit a body odour which crocs can smell from vast distances.

A skein of greylag geese, flying as though on a set course across the river, suddenly put on the "falling leaf" stunt and settled on a wide open area between two channels of the river. I agreed to Billinda's suggestion of having them driven to me. But in spite of my best effort to intercept them at a likely flight line they were not to be fooled on a riverbed as wide and bare as this.

Rather than get back on board I felt like lazing it out on the river bank until Billinda produced lunch. I opened a bottle of beer and after emptying the contents threw the bottle into the river. The children who had been watching me immediately dived in for the bottle and after it had been recovered there was a scuffle for its possession. I intervened to quell the trouble and gave my verdict on who was the first to handle the bottle. To keep the peace I promised to give each of them an empty bottle before the journey ended.

This was not a very consoling solution to the immediate problem. The bottle still remained the envy of every child. To take their minds off the subject I coaxed them to a backwash of the river where, after showing them a Rupee coin, tossed it into the water. They swam and dived admirably, on each occasion recovering the coins I threw in until each had a coin of some denomination. I later regretted having introduced this acquatic sport because everytime the boat moored for a break, they clamoured around requesting me to throw coins into the river. I didn't grudge providing the children some fun, but my problem was that I had run out of coins.

Proceeding further, a flock of many hundreds of geese were seen resting on a small island. Again, there was the old problem of no cover. In this instance, however, the Khaals were confident that I could get in two easy shots at them provided I was agreeable to the method they suggested. This was an innovation which I was at first reluctant to try out. It was a cured buffalo skin which they soon inflated, then gave a demonstration of its versatility. Having tested it out I agreed to their wishes and told them to camouflage it with grass while I changed into swimming trunks.

The boat was moored, I loaded my shotgun, then with much difficulty managed to lie flat on the oval contraption, holding on as best I could with hands and feet. As I floated downstream, the buffalo began to get frisky when it met the swifter current, so maintaining balance was a major problem while to manoeuvre was hopeless. However, using one hand as a paddle and my feet as stabilisers I managed to ride the small waves quite well until I was drawn into an undercurrent where the buffalo tried to shake me off by going into a gradual spin together with a bobbing motion. This was not a satisfactory situation as I was nearing the geese.

Try as hard as I did to control the frisky buffalo, it wouldn't settle down to a smooth float-past. Still in the same predicament and a bit off course I approached the apex of the island, and if all went well, I should be able to fire the two shots from about 40 yards. The geese meanwhile began to get suspicious, some honked, others flapped their wings and the majority had their necks stretched up high, a sure indication they were about to fly. By now I was broadside to them and awaiting my chance for the buffalo to place me at the correct angle to let fly. But the geese lifted in a mass while I had my back to them! In making a frantic effort to swing around, I lost my balance but in the act of falling off I succeeded in firing both barrels. The upthrust of the inflated skin when I fell off caused it to bounce out of the water and meet the blast of the second shot to be instantly killed and sunk!

Having accidently shot my buffalo the joy-ride ended abruptly, though it had served its purpose. I swam across to the island to collect my well-earned reward .... three bar-headed geese.

Later steering through a sharp bend, we approached what I presumed was the confluence with the main river. I took a fancy to this place for the evening flight. The boat was moored for the night and climbing up the steep sandbank I walked over to a large tree-trunk with bone-dry roots, resembling an octopus. It had undoubtedly been washed down during the monsoon and deposited at this spot, making a natural hide.

It was while I roamed about the tree-trunk that an extraordinary thing occurred. A croc came dashing across the sand from the river's edge with its jaws wide open, confronting me with a hideous picture. This was a new experience, and frankly I hadn't a clue what to do other than stand my ground and watch this thing awkwardly run along with its mouth open like a mother pelican. It looked as though it was running out of steam after covering some 30 yards, but suddenly there was a burst of speed, its tail worked like a flail and it snapped its jaws viciously. I was so confused that I missed it with the first barrel and the second was equally ineffective, because the pellets ricocheted off the croc's armour. More frightened than hurt, it turned tail and went hell for leather back into the river.

Billinda soon appeared on the scene accompanied by a few Khaals. I sent him back to bring my rifle in case the croc made another attack. While he was away I told the Khaals about the croc's mad behaviour at which they laughed, then went on to tell me that a croc only adopts this attitude when it has laid eggs in the vicinity. An immediate search commenced and it was not long before a large quantity of croc's eggs were found buried in the sand. These were collected, placed in a sheet and taken back to the boat despite my repeated appeals to leave them in their original place to incubate.

I remained at this spot for the evening flight but was obliged to keep a watchful eye on the river's edge and the horizon at the same time. Birds were on the move alright, but either they came over far too high or followed the course of the various channels. The wary Ruddy shellduck or Brahminy duck as it is more commonly called, came over by the thousands, uttering their multi-toned call which can be heard from miles away. Where duck are plentiful the sportsman normally ignores the Brahminy duck because it is not a choice table bird, though the natives rate it above all other species. I think they make this distinction for three reasons. It's a very colourful duck, quantity comes before quality, and being so cunning, and difficult to stalk and shoot, makes it a much sought after quarry. I knew that Billinda loved them and having his interest in mind, I had a right and left at a string of them from my concealed position. One fell dead, the other came down winged and ran towards the river. I gave chase and could have caught it as it entered the shallow section of the river but refrained from doing so remembering that old "snappy-jaw" could well be waiting to get even with me in home waters!

When I boarded the boat I was surprised to see the children already trying to sell hard-boiled croc eggs. I had a count of what remained. There were 24 eggs, of which I could have as many as I wished, with a recommendation that they were better than chickens' eggs, and contained an elixir of life. I took a dozen and told Billinda, in the presence of the Khaals to serve me with two croc eggs every morning. He looked at me unbelievingly but seeing that I appeared adamant, took the eggs and used his favourite sentence which was "bloody fool". He knew the meaning of it as well, because we always told him he was one!

The oldest member of the family was a grandfather who spent most of his time meditating or smoking a hookah (hubble bubble). Now and then he would come and have a chat with me, telling me about the good old days when he used to visit a British officer at the Attock Fort and take him fishing up the Kabul River and on the Indus itself. He told me some typical fisherman's tales with emphasis on how often the famous Mahseer fish had broken a rod and line, and how on one occasion he swam after the rod with a Mahseer attached to the line, retrieved the rod and handed it to the officer who then successfully landed the fish after battling with it for a few hours. He said it weighed one "maund" (just over 80 lbs) and when lifted up was nearly as tall as he was! I didn't believe the story so I just smiled. He read my thoughts and walked away telling me he would find the picture to prove it.

After being called a bloody fool by Billinda, I told him to bring out a bottle and sat down for a "sundowner". When Billinda produced the bottle I whispered to him secretly to take away the croc eggs and bury them in their original place. No sooner had he gone than "grandad" joined me to show evidence of the Mahseer story I disbelieved. By candlelight he carefully unfolded a cloth purse-like arrangement from which he produced two photographs. They were very old and indistinct, nevertheless one picture showed a huge fish with a native standing beside it, the other was of the officer and the monument of the .303 cartridge, a War Memorial to the 40th Pathans, situated on the west bank of the Indus at Attock forming the background of the picture. Just for a bit of fun, I asked him who was the person standing beside the fish. "That's me of course!" he said very proudly. "Can't you recognise me?" I looked at the picture again and then at him, shook my head and then said "no resemblance whatsoever .... you are an old man, the chap in the picture is young!" Under his breath he must have called me more than a bloody fool! However, to boost his morale I gave him credit for his activities, poured him a drink and wished him God's blessings.

Proud of having had a drink with me, he divulged a trade secret by producing a reel of thin wire to which was attached fish hooks of all sizes. Unravelling the wire, he baited the hooks with croc flesh, worms and wholemeal dough, then tied one end of the wire to a hasp, casting the rest into the river so that it would drift away with the current.

At dawn I was woken up by the old man and informed that the dead line was about to be checked and if I was interested to come along with him to collect the catch, if any. I wasn't too happy about being disturbed so early for the sake of seeing fish being removed from a hook, and told him to wait until after sunrise. He insisted that this business had to be done before daylight otherwise some of the fish manage to unhook themselves on being attacked by fish-hawks and eagles.

I arose assuming the dead line was to be hauled up on board. No such luck, I had to entrust myself to his ancient frame to control the small boat in which both of us drifted along examining the dead line. He was delighted when he felt the first tug on the line.

"There's a big fish at the end of that," he said. "Perhaps it's a Mahseer," I said. "Oh no. the Mahseer is only to be found in the higher sources of this river where the water is cold and the current swift."

While he was speaking he pulled the fish in and stuck his thumb into the gills, removed the hook and flung the large fish into the boat. He called this fish a "Mulli" and went on to predict that most of the fish on the line would be the same species because they were easily hooked. He was quite right and the entire catch consisted of fish weighing between four to twelve pounds. I wasn't interested in fish from an anglers point of view, but I did enjoy fried fish that morning!

Approximately 15 fish had been removed from the dead line, of which a few had been consumed and the rest kept alive to be bartered or sold to prospective village businessmen, who preferred dealing with the Khaals and so getting the fish on the cheap rather than from the licensed fishermen.

We moved down the main channel of the river which was the better part of a mile in width. Other than shooting a teal, I found this channel very disappointing and boring, a fact noticed no doubt by the Khaals who, after some time, suggested we select a subsidiary channel which perhaps would provide more sport for me. I agreed, making it clear that they controlled the boat and were at liberty to take whatever course they wished. I was only interested in seeing as much of this river as possible in their capable hands.

While navigating through a network of waterways one of the Khaal's reckoned he could see a crocodile a vast distance away. To make sure I checked the object with binoculars and confirmed that it was indeed a croc, and a big one at that.

Approaching this croc was going to be a difficult task, as a very flat surface and two rather narrow channels stood between me and the croc. The use of the small boat was out of the question which meant that in order to get within range, there was no alternative but to crawl and swim. I couldn't make up my mind whether a croc was worth all that trouble. I had another look at it through the binoculars and on second glance found the temptation irresistible.

Putting on my swimming trunks and loading five rounds into the rifle I set off, walking at first, then crawling over the uncomfortably hot sand. Arriving at the edge of the first channel, I slung the rifle across my shoulder and waded in until forced to swim.

So far so good! I crossed over with no trouble at all, rested a while and made sure the croc was still there, then again repeated the crawling act until I reached the second and last channel which was the wider of the two. From here it was necessary to take things very carefully as I was much closer to the croc and to plan the next move so that, on emerging on the other side of the channel, I would not have to start looking for a suitable place from which to fire a shot. Allowing for a certain degree of drift to bring me out at a selected spot, I swam down silently.

Something struck my feet ... a croc, a fish, a turtle or a submerged tree-trunk. God only knows what it was, but I wasn't keen to find out. I got the wind-up and all that I could think of at the precise moment was self-preservation. Instead of swimming down current, I made a frantic effort to cut the distance short by trying to swim straight across to the other bank. With my feet back on land I had a wonderful sense of reassurance. I lay flat on my back feeling faint, nausea followed and then a growing thirst made me forget all about the croc for the time being.

Having composed myself I drank a few mouthfuls of water, then went about the business of looking for the crocodile. It was still there, although it had changed its position and was now facing me. Satisfying myself that there was no obstruction in the rifle muzzle, I waded along the edge of the river in a crouched position until I got to within 200 yards or so of the croc. Resting the rifle on a heap of wet sand I took aim at its left shoulder, trusting the bullet would penetrate all the way down the length of the body perhaps to paralyse the spine. I fired and the bullet struck the croc with a terrific impact. It struggled a bit then remained pinned to the ground. But before I had time to give it another shot to make certain it remained there, the tail swung into action and zig-zagged the body into the water. I cannot express my disappointment when I saw this enormous croc disappear, but then in a matter of seconds my hopes rose again when the creature reappeared, cork-screwing out of the water at exactly the same place where it entered the river after being wounded. I had the rifle levelled on the spot and took a snap shot which, more by fluke than by judgement hit the croc after ricocheting off the water. Although it did not surface again, ripples continued to form indicating the croc was active underwater and I remained keyed up, ready to pull off another shot. Nothing stirred, time stood still and it seemed as if the river ceased to flow.

I looked across the wide open space over which I had taken so much trouble to crawl and swim to see Billinda and some Khaals amble along using the small boat to cross in comfort. On reaching me the Khaals invited me to hop into the boat and show the exact spot where I had seen it last. Half-heartedly I got in with a Khaal and Billinda to guide them to the scene where the croc had been splashing about. The boat was not big enough to accommodate five of us, so the remaining two held on to the sides to conserve their energy.

The river was quite calm at this spot, which consisted of a number of sandbanks between which the deep water gave the effect of swimming pools of all shapes and sizes. Hitherto, the Khaals had not taken an active part in proving their acquatic abilities, though judging from their offspring I had every reason to believe they would be as much at home in the water as they were on land.

Giving me instructions to shoot from the boat if the croc should surface the Khaals commenced a methodical search by diving to the bottom of the river-bed, at times remaining underwater for an extraordinary length of time. Whilst they revelled in their diving stunts, the chap in the boat used a pole with which he probed other deep spots in he river. Nothing came of the search in the area where I had last seen the croc. The two Khaals stood in shallow water studying the flow of the current, then suggested we move down as turtles and fish could have forced the croc to leave its resting place to escape them nibbling at its wounds. In doing so it could quite easily have been shifted further away by the deceptive currents which passed through this wide expanse of water.

Standing up in the boat we could point out to the Khaals who were wading about in thigh-deep water where the river appeared deepest and they dived to the bottom in their optimistic search for the croc. The boat-man was equally active, probing the deep opaque pockets out of which, every now and then, large fish shot like torpedoes.

While probing one of these deep pockets an alarm was raised, bringing the other two Khaals hurriedly towards the boat immediately to dive beneath us and some seconds later force a huge turtle to the surface. There was some laughter and abuse as well to which the fellow raising the alarm took exception, assuring the others that what he felt at the end of the pole was undoubtedly a croc. The search was resumed with greater enthusiasm, at the same time I was told to be prepared to shoot at sight if the croc should be made to surface. This was all very well, but these people did not understand the power behind a high velocity rifle bullet, and neither was I prepared to place the importance of the croc above the safety of human beings.

Unexpectedly an acquatic battle commenced between the Khaals and a croc, presumably the same one I had wounded. Soon a Khaal attached himself to the croc forcing it to the surface, but it corkscrewed and submerged with a splash taking the Khaal down with it. The Khaal who was with me in the boat handed over to Billinda and joined the others. They stuck to the croc like leeches, making a great effort to guide it towards the boat. Of course, the croc, already in a stupor, had lost its sting and was no match for the energetic Khaals who brought it to within 20 yards of the boat to receive the final treatment. This was when things went wrong!

Just as a fish occasionally revives when about to be landed, so the croc took the Khaals by surprise and shook them off with the greatest of ease with a powerful slash of the tail. The struggle started afresh, the croc heaving itself about and making it difficult for the Khaals to come to grips with it. My grandstand view of events nearly came to an abrupt end when the croc hoisted itself half way out of the water and collided with the boat. As I happened to be in a standing position I fell back, but managed to manoeuvre around to land on Billinda, who, I'm, sure, ,thought I was a part of the croc and tried to shoulder me out of the boat!

The Khaals were in control of the situation again, keeping their distance from the croc's tail which remained the potential danger. Billinda was asked to remove the tow-rope from the boat and bring it to them. He did so leaving me to drift away while he gave a hand to try and subdue the croc. Being inexperienced in handling a boat with the aid of a pole, I made little headway although I did manage to remain where I was by doing a "merry-go-round" manoeuvre. This was an unsatisfactory state of affairs; I was missing the excitement of seeing the croc being tackled and gave Billinda a yell to come and rescue me.

The croc was still quite frisky in spite of a rope being looped around its diaphragm and held at either end by two Khaals. The other Khaal tried to get his hands round the long sword-fish type jaws to which the croc took retaliatory action by snapping furiously every time his hands came close enough. At intervals I directed operations so as to be in a position to terminate this unpleasant scene. Streaks of turbid water flowed away from the disturbed area resembling a wide smoke screen across a blue sky. Exhausted after a relentless struggle, the croc was at last held firmly enough for me to fire a shot at the base of its tail. Telling the Khaals to move back, I put another shot into its neck to end the drama.

To get the croc and the small boat back to the parent boat presented a bit of a problem. Rather than drag the two across considerable distances the

Khaals suggested I accompanied one of them in the small boat while the others returned to the parent boat meeting us further downstream. This was the most practical solution to the problem; the croc was attached to the boat and we towed it along with the greatest of ease. About an hour later the two boats met at the confluence of the channels on the east bank of the river near a village.

I measured the croc and found it to be just over 23 feet in length. Before it was subjected to the knife and chopper, it remained on view to the many villagers who made private deals with the Khaals for its fat, which was in demand for medicinal purposes. Until this episode the Khaal's reputation of being capable of catching crocodiles was hearsay gossip of which I was sceptical but now, as far as I was concerned, there was no room for argument.

At night my sleep was periodically disturbed by jackals howling and dogs barking. This nuisance was at its worst just before dawn when the retiring jackals create a hell of a noise in response to which the village dogs add their say. Some time later while I lay awake watching the vast "Milky Way" I heard a peculiar "whoosh" sound every now and then. I sat up and listened to detect the location of this noise. It came from the water quite near to the boat, but despite having a good look around there was nothing visible on the water-line. Another "whoosh" and I saw a splash; now I knew what part of the river to keep my eyes on. I hadn't long to wait; a creature surfaced, "whooshed" and immediately dived, exposing only a portion of its unidentifiable anatomy. Intrigued with whatever this thing was, I spent much time waiting to see little or nothing of it.

Anxious to satisfy my curiosity I called upon the "wise old man" to voice his opinion. He stood alongside me while we waited until the creatures "whooshed" and disappeared. The old man smiled, then said "woh boolan thar" meaning that was a "boolan". This meant nothing to me, not having heard the word before. He then went on to give me a vivid description, of the legendary mermaid! I thought he was having me on, but, in fact, he was serious and went on to tell me about having seen one netted by a fisherman by sheer luck. He described them as being the size of a human, some pink, others a pinkish grey. They swim extremely fast when they want to, live entirely on fish and are very timid creatures. He went a step further and told me that fishermen had been known to have intercourse with those netted, therefore they are unfit for human consumption.

I came across another of these "boolans" during the day and in spite of the Khaals doing everything they could to help me get a better view of it, I'm afraid I failed to see the evasive creature to identify her, him or it! Personally I think what I heard and got glimpes of was a species of porpoise.

Billinda had taken a trip to the village to contact the right people and obtain information about the shooting potential in the area. They recommended the opposite bank of the river. We spent the better part of the morning negotiating the complex waterways in an attempt to get the large boat as close to the other side as possible, but this turned out to be a waste of time. To cut the distance short there was no alternative other than to moor the large boat and manhandle the small boat over the sand, using it to save swimming across the remaining channels. I appreciated the change to trudge over rough ground in pursuit of bustard and sand grouse, and in addition this afforded me the opportunity of seeing what is now almost an extinct bird, the Giant Bustard.

In my absence another Khaal family had moored alongside our boat and confirmed that they had seen a huge croc at midday at roughly the same spot where others had seen it. This was good news and gave me something to look forward to as it was only hours' sailing time from us. I was advised not to make an attempt to shoot the croc in the evening as it was the wrong time of day to catch them napping, and if I did get a shot and wounded it, they would not be able to recover it once darkness set in

Taking their advice we left next morning to arrive in the locality the croc inhabited by about 11 o'clock. The river narrowed to a bottle-neck and the water was deep and treacherous. The high sandbanks on either side frequently avalanched into the river with loud splashing thuds. However, we soon drifted through the area to enter more likely crocodile basking areas. The boat was moored and we set off on foot in search of the alleged large croc. One of the Khaals reported having seen a croc slip into the river, but could not say for certain whether it was a very large one. Leaving them to return to the boat I went forward to select a nice spot where I dug in and made myself comfortable, prepared if necessary to spend the day in anticipation of getting a shot at the croc if it should come out to bask.

From my hide the opposite bank of the river was about 150 yards and the near side not more than 15 yards. Immediately in front of me was a vortex which sucked in all floating objects which passed within its orbit, spun them around and then drew them underwater.

Watching these little floating objects I became puzzled to know why one of them had escaped being spun, and, whats more, remained static while others whirled around until drawn to the centre and sucked down.

I gave this static object my undivided attention when suddenly another similar object appeared alongside it to be followed by yet another slightly larger one. Together they formed a triangle. The penny dropped ... two marble-size objects side-by-side were the eyes, and the third and larger one forming the apex was the snout of a croc. No doubt it was taking the necessary precautions to have a good look and smell before crawling onto land.

The direction of the wind, if any at all, was in my favour, and other than perhaps a bit of my hair being visible, I was so well concealed that I fully expected to have the croc lying beside me if it decided to come out! For quite some time these objects moved across, down or against the current until the snout and eyes disappeared one at a time. Five, 10, 15 minutes had elapsed and still there were no sign of the croc. I kept my eyes glued to the surface of the water when I noticed something on the opposite bank which at first looked like a turtle at the edge of the water. Keeping an eye on it I could see a gradual increase in length; it was the croc very cautiously crawling out foot by foot and looking as black as charcoal.

Trembling with excitement I watched this croc take to land in slow motion. Fully exposed, it turned broadside as if to oblige me with my favourite kind of shot. I took things easy with the object of converting this wonderful opportunity into a record trophy. There was no danger, no discomfort, no distractions and no exertion – in other words the conditions for rifle shooting couldn't be better.

Placing a Y-shaped piece of wood into the sand and resting the rifle muzzle on it, I took aim. The croc's neck seen through the leaf sight was not clear due to the heat radiating off the sand, furthermore, the sun's reflection off the water was also troublesome. I was trying to be extra careful to ensure that the bullet hit with deadly accuracy. On two occasions I hesitated to squeeze the trigger because of taking too long an aim resulting in the target becoming blurred. I closed my eyes for a few minutes, wiped my eyelids and started afresh. The croc meanwhile was dry and had changed colour to a silver grey resembling a felled date-palm trunk.

I took aim and fired. The blast raised a cloud of sand in front of the muzzle and to my immense disgust I watched the enormous croc instantly splash into the river causing a small tidal wave. Undoubtedly I had missed it and my feeling need not be expressed.

I had not long to wait before the enthusiastic Khaals and Billinda arrived on the scene to ask the usual questions and to get an unusual answer. Billinda was not prepared to believe that I had missed and insisted we cross over to where the croc had lain to make sure it had not been wounded. The small boat took more people than it could hold, but we recklessly crossed over, almost capsizing en route. Examining the spot I saw where the bullet had struck, cutting a miniature trench through the wet sand about six inches above the croc's neck. This prompted me to check the rifle sight, which in fact had inadvertently been rasied by 200 yards by Billinda when he recently cleaned the rifle.

The question now was whether this croc would risk coming out again to bask in the sun after experiencing a bullet whistle past his neck. I was optimistic, spending the rest of the day, and the following day in a fruitless wait for it to give me another chance. There was one compensation, it was unhurt and maybe I'd get an opportunity in the not too distant future to shoot this abnormally sized croc. The contemplated trip never did materialise, and if no other sportsman has had better luck than I, this croc measuring approximately 30 feet must have added to his length by now.

The Gharial measured just over twenty three feet.

The Khaals firmly believed that this croc must have a charmed life to have attained such length and was protected by the God of the River as one of the chosen few, destined to find its way to a selected place somewhere along this mighty river, where, when called upon it would bury itself in eternal rest.

The last leg of this journey became rather monotonous as we were nearing more readily accessible parts of the river. Soon the sound of motor vehicle horns and the whine of their engines as they strained through the sand indicated that I had returned to some form of civilization. It was journey's end for Billinda and myself. The familiar view of boat bridges, the Octroi post and the ancient paddle steamer the "Indus Queen" was a winter landmark of Ghazi Ghat. I refer to it as a winter landmark because it remains moored at this spot for about eight months in the year, and only during the summer monsoon, when the Indus is in spate, does it prove its value by being the one and only means of public transport capable of conveying humans, livestock and machinery across 10 miles or so of turbulent river.

After packing our gear I bade farewell to each and every member of the Khaal family, slipped the old man a bottle of rum and gave the rest of them a handsome monetary reward, the children getting that little bit extra on popular demand ... a handful of coins tossed into the river!

After seeing them all safely on land Billinda and I disembarked, having travelled well over a 100 miles down this wonderful river, free from industrial contamination or filth in its upper regions. The journey was a most enjoyable one, eventful, safe and a trip one looks back on in the hope of doing it again, especially when old age or the heart can no longer stand the pace of a strenuous outdoor life. Looking back as age creeps along, I now visualise the river in three stages to compare it with human life. Firstly, the monsoon season when it flows fast and furious .... our youth. Secondly, the gradual decrease of rainfall when the river flows steadily for quite some time .... our middle age. And thirdly, the long winter at high altitudes when only the fringes of the perennial snow melts, thereby the river being at its lowest ebb for the longest period .... our old age. Unlike the river which flows on indefinitely with the change of seasons, humans unfortunately must fade away irrespective of seasons.

Reminiscing, I can still see the old man as a part of this great river, a man who knew he had past his time and was now a burden on the younger generation, teased, ridiculed and humiliated by all other than the women. Yet I admired him for what he stood for – tolerance and wisdom. By now he must be in his happy "fishing grounds" where hopefully he has a school of disciplined pupils, teaching them, in addition to other things, the subject of ethnology in which I personally had an interest, adding the sagacious Khaals to my unprejudicial interest in God's people.

A few weeks after my trip along the Indus, I was invited to a village near Fort Munro from where I was to be taken for a Markhaur shoot. My host, a member of the elite Legari family, namely Usman Khan, a Pathan-like tribe inhabiting the Dehra Ghazi and Fort Munro area of the North West Frontier. The mountains where I was taken were about 8,000 feet above sea level but barren and very, very precipitous. I encountered the first Spiral Horned Markhaur resting below a protruding rock. It wasn't a big head so rather than disturb the area I moved on with Usman climbing all the time through this wilderness of mountains.

In a narrow gorge we disturbed a herd of these large goats, amongst them a few young males, once again carrying small horns. They disappeared out of sight while we rested when to my delight Usman handed me the binoculars pointing to a spot where a Markhaur sat, its neck and horns only visible. It was the best head we had seen so far and worth bagging. Of course, to get a reasonable shot we had to get closer and above it hoping that it would not be disturbed. All went according to plan, Usman circumvented the mountainside to bring me within about 200 yards of the Markaur.

By now he had seen us, standing motionless he was quite a good size, offering a fair target Removing my pith helmet I placed it on a rock surface, rested my hand and rifle on it, took steady aim and fired. I was pleased to see the animal collapse on the spot because a wounded Markhaur would be one hell of an aimal to track down amongst cliffs suitable only for lizards and the goat family.

Usman, sure footed as the Markhaur himself went hurriedly to carry out the religious obligation of 'hilalling' (cutting the throat of the Markhaur). Leaving me at the spot, Usman told me he would be back within the hour with a few of his men who had been instructed to await him at a prearranged spot.

He returned with his men sooner than expected, presumably they had heard the shot reverberate through the mountains and come to meet him on route. The Markhaur was skinned, gutted and carved, the choice portions wrapped in the skin, the head being taken care of separately. When back in the village I was asked if I wanted the skin, I declined the offer but said I'd have the head to keep as a trophy.

I knew that the word Markhaur originated from the Persian language meaning "snake eater". There are four species of Markhaur, all inhabiting the same type of terrain, though they differ in size, the Pir Pinjar species being the largest. I have travelled through from the Hindu Kush to Baluchistan without finding evidence that the Markhaur in fact is a snake eater. However, there is a strong belief, especially amongst the Punjabis who inhabit the outskirts of the North West Frontier, that if they kept a piece of Markhaur skin in their homes, a snake would never enter therein because it would get the scent of the Markhaur, the snake eater! A similar kind of superstition is attached to a piece of snake's skin if kept in a wallet or hand bag. In this case such wallets or hand bags should always be well loaded! I've kept a piece of Cobra skin in my wallet but I can't honestly say that since then my wallet has been bursting at the seams! Far from it, yet I've never been short of a penny or two to keep the wolf from the door.

Chapter Fourteen

My posting to Multan District had been in Autumn 1954 so I had yet to have a taste of what it was like in summer. It was heat, more heat, extreme heat, dust and sand storms, camels, donkeys and graveyards! A British Garrison had always been posted there. A look at the tombstones in the cemetery was proof of the number of military personnel who failed to make it to other more choice stations. Mind you, Multan did have a reputation of being a punishment posting in the old days but since various irrigation schemes had been introduced, the district has been converted from a bleak countryside to a fair amount of greenery.

By the end of March 1955 we got a taste of the hot wind known as the "loo". This heralded the dust and sand storms which made spring cleaning almost a permanent feature! What with these storms, the sand flies and the heat life became very uncomfortable. The day temperatures averaged 120 degrees Fahrenheit, though by night it became quite cool.

Elsewhere the monsoon had broken at the usual time about the end of June but here we were in the middle of August with no signs of rain to bring any relief. Since Sheila was expecting another baby I took the remainder of my annual leave which we spent at Murree, our favourite hill station nearly 7,000 feet above sea level. It was certainly a cool retreat from the hot sultry plains, but with very inclement weather we could not get out and about in comfort.

The holiday over, we returned to Multan, the rain being incessant almost all the way. Our bungalow was surrounded by water, fortunately not entering the house itself though the servants quarters had been flooded. Generally speaking the whole district was somewhat waterlogged, ideal conditions to attract the migratory wildfowl to these areas earlier than usual. There was one drawback, to get to the good jheels was almost impossible because of the road conditions. However, I found some spots where I was able to pick up some good bags and provide the lower subordinates mess with a change in menu. Sheila, on the other hand, wasn't very happy about these trips as she was nearly due to go into the maternity ward; but I had already made arrangements for Police Transport to run her to hospital in an emergency.

Exceptionally heavy rain in the catchment areas of the River Ravi and Chenab brought flood warnings. Emergency measures were put into action immediately to avert the catastrophe of the 1950 floods. The most vulnerable barrage in the district to face the impact of flood water was the Sidhnai Barrage. The canal had already absorbed more water than it could take, resulting in the breaching of its banks. The discharge from the barrage itself was at its maximum and there was more and more flood water racing down into the barrage. Reinforcing the embankments and the discharge gates with ballast and sand bags didn't seem to make much difference at the time.

I can recollect standing on the barrage at night; the vibration was frightening as the flood water thrashed the weir and the foam spurred over in huge gusts. It was cetainly not a safe place to be if the barrage should collapse. At this moment my mind went back to Sheila and all the rest of the people in Multan which lay in the path of the flood water if the barrage should burst.

The barrage stood the onslaught but all the time I had the flood of 1950 in mind, wondering whether Sheila and I were going to be separated again. Fortunately all went well and she produced another boy whom we named Michael Clive. He came into this world after four false alarms and thereafter was troublesome and restless, in spite of being adorable with plenty of life in him. A "typical Harrison" as Sheila would call him whenever she had had enough of his nonsense.

Ainsworth and I were invited to visit a friend who was commanding a section of the Desert Rangers on a sector of the Indo-Pakistan border along the Thar Desert. On the way to his Head Quarters we were very impressed with the efficiency and mobility of a fully equipped Camel Squad which moved faster than our jeep across the sand dunes with incredible silence. Nearing the border we were puzzled by the absence of any landmarks to indicate the exact location of the border between the two countries.

We were told they were few and far between, but sufficient for the inhabitants of the desert to make the distinction. The black buck, once plentiful, but now a rarity on the Pakistan side of the border is occasionally seen if it should stray across. We witnessed a buck, "on the wrong side of the fence", make a dash for survival at the sight of our jeep. It ran flat out with our jeep in hot pursuit until it suddenly stopped about a couple of furlongs ahead of the jeep which was also brought to a stop. The reason, believe it or not, was that the buck had crossed back into Indian territory, and knew from past experience that the Pakistan jeep would give up the chase! Sadly, the unsporting practice of shooting such animals from jeeps has reduced their numbers drastically, almost to the point of extinction. Hopefully, the black buck and the Chinkara (gazelle) will take advantage of the political situation between Pakistan and India to make the border their refuge, thus to some extent avoiding vehicles and the camels or other animals on which the unscrupulous hunter rides to make an easy kill.

Our host had laid on a good shoot east of Fort Abbas. With little or no cover, the Imperial Sand Grouse still flew past in all directions providing us with some fine sport. Bustards, however, were more wary, much fewer in number, but nevertheless, gave us a few shots at this big deceptive flyer, even though we had to do quite a bit of sprinting to get within shooting range. Needless to say, we rarely did!

I had spent over a year in Multan when I received promotion in March 1956 and transferred to Head Quarters Lahore. Despite the unfavourable things said of Multan it had, nevertheless, been a restful posting to which we had adjusted. A move to Lahore was not something to look forward to, especially as far as I was concerned, because Lahore was always a headache for police officers. If it wasn't political demonstrations, it would be State Visits by Kings, Queens, Presidents, Prime Ministers and various other V.I.P.'s from abroad and within the country. To cope with the ordinary course of events was bad enough without the extra responsibilites, half of which were absurdly unnecessary. Naturally, all this activity would leave little time for shooting.

On taking up my new appointment, amomg various other matters, I perused a file relating to an Indo-Pakistan agreement on a reciprocal basis whereby refugees going back to the time of independence and the partitioning of India, were able to return under escort to recover valuables buried or hidden, in or nearby, their evacuated homes.

I was told by subordinate officers who had been on such escort duties that quite a few valuables such as jewellery had ben dug up from beneath floors and trees, and in one case from a well. Though it was not expected of me to go on such escorts, I did so on one occasion, more for a break from the office than a joy ride. The village visited was about 15 miles north-east of Lahore.

Nine years had elapsed since the country had been partitioned; since then Sikhs had not been seen in the Punjab and the one escorted to this village became the centre of attraction, especially by the children, the majority of whom had never seen a member of the Sikh community before! This Sikh gentleman took us directly to a large house with an enclosed courtyard which he claimed, belonged to him before India was partitioned.

The inmates of this house, now the lawful owners of the property, were told of the reason for the visit by this Sikh gentleman, and asked to allow him to enter the premises. Permission was granted without Police interference. The Sikh's declaration of valuables to be recovered from the house was described as gold.

Without any hesitation whatsoever, he went straight to a wall and removed items of cloth from three pegs which protruded about nine inches out of the wall. They were black, nothing out of the ordinary and as a matter of fact, very crudely finished, yet typical of village house fittings. He asked for them to be removed which caused some concern because they did not conform to the description of solid gold!

"They're gold alright", he said after scraping a thick black layer of paint off a peg to reveal the hidden truth, a glitter of gold! He did the same with the two remaining pegs to claim his valuables. His mission was completed successfully to the amazement of the inmates who had been dwelling in a gold mine!

Over the years I'd observed a gradual change taking shape in the machinery of the Government and it was becoming obvious that British Officers were becoming conspicuous by their absence. This was most noticeable at places such as the Lahore Cathedral, gymkhana and golf clubs. However, British and American Diplomats and visiting businessmen did make social life bearable, but were certainly no incentive to forget the past or hope for better things to come. Sadly, the days of the Raj were over, discipline was on its way out and nepotism on its way in, filth spread faster than rumour and there was a general deterioration which even Martial Law failed to eradicate, though in the initial stages Field Martial Ayub Khan almost restored the polished image of the good old days.

Try as I might to maintain a high sense of discipline, the subordinate staff, in complying with my orders, often got themselves into trouble, not to mention putting me into embarrassing situations. Eventually I found I was on the wrong side of the fence. Losing interest in doing my usual conscientious job over and above working hours without overtime, I began to take more time off to go shooting when the opportunities arose. In doing so I spent hardly any time with the family which naturally caused friction. Well, friction at home, friction at work didn't help make life pleasant.

I put up with all the elements, ignoring the worst and enjoying the best until one day Sheila made me realize that I had a wife and children to think of. She asked whether it had ever occurred to me to do what the majority of my colleagues had done by resigning and quitting the country.

Sheila was undoubtedly concerned about my shooting interest being given preference over everything else. She wasn't far wrong; I spent most of my leisure hours shooting, yet it was at times like this that I gave serious thought to the future of the children, but in view of their tender age there was no real cause for immediate worry. I kept in mind the saying "don't trouble trouble, until troubles trouble you." At the same time something else was playing on my mind, "if you can't beat them, join them!" I was reluctant to do that but meanwhile Sheila increased the pressure to do something positive, and soon, before it was too late to create a new life in the U.K. In spite of the pressure from the home front, I still didn't think the time was ripe for making a snap decision.

I was directed to attend a high level Police meeting specially convened to discuss the security aspect of the State Visit to West Pakistan by HRH Prince Philip, Duke of Edinburgh in the very near future. It was anticipated that as soon as the country came to know of his visit, the old politicians would renew their campaign on the Kashmir issue which was, and still is, a sore point. The majority of the inhabitants were Muslim, therefore as India was partitioned on the grounds of religion, Kashmir should have formed part of West Pakistan, just as East Bengal which was predominantly Muslim became East Pakistan. The people of Pakistan still believe that the partitioning of India was unfair to them, and the person responsible was Lord Mountbatten, the Viceroy of India. It was known that Prince Philip was a close relative and like Lord Mountbatten, should not be made welcome. His visit would have to be considered a security risk, and that was to be avoided at all costs.

However, as expected the arrangements went ahead to welcome him. Early in February 1959, Prince Philip arrived at Lahore Airport in a Comet Jet passenger aircraft along with his entourage. It was an occasion for two "Firsts". The first visit by British Royalty to West Pakistan and the first commercial jet aircraft to be seen in the country. Both hit the limelight.

The main attraction of the visit was for Prince Philip to witness the National Horse and Cattle Show, a headache for the Police yet an annual event much looked forward to by the nation as a whole. Highlights of the week to mention but a few were tent pegging, dancing horses, camel fights and races, a charge-past by the Desert Rangers on their fully battle-equipped camels, Khatak dancing (Pathan tribal folk dancing), a Police Tattoo and a mass band display by the Pakistan Armed Forces. The show lasted a week, commencing each night at 9pm and continuing until about 11.30 pm. One night I remember seeing a camel fight, which involves the skill and technique, similar to wrestlers. Naturally there is some biting as well! On this occasion the camel which lost the fight ran out of control, chased by the winner. Both camels headed across the vast "Maidan" (field) enclosed by spectators, finding an exit through the standing enclosures. Needless to say, there was chaos amongst the crowd as the camels ploughed through knocking people over left, right and centre. There were some casualties, but in this part of the world injuries mean nothing if caused in good faith!

Prince Philip was a guest of honour at the Punjab University. When he walked out of the building a young girl holding a pen and notebook bowed then asked him for his autograph. He smiled then said "I'm sorry, I never learnt to write!" The girl was led away and told by a university official that Royalty do not sign autographs.

Sightseeing occupied a few days of Prince Philip's busy schedule. He visited the famous places built during the time of the Mogal Empire such as the Shalimar Gardens, Noor Jehan's Tomb, Lahore Fort and Hiran Minar which means antelope turret. Near the turret was a waterhole where black buck came to drink and were shot at by Mogal Kings or guests with bow and arrow. Alongside the turret a deep pool has been closed in with steps leading to the water with sitting space and apartments surrounding it. These days the pool provides anglers with sport at the reasonable cost. Being some 20 miles east of Lahore, the black buck disappered by 1939, exterminated by modern weapons.

Foot note. During the India Pakistan war, East Pakistan was over-run by Indian forces in 1971 to be now known as Bangladesh, an independent country. West Pakistan then became Pakistan.

In addition to a polo match, Prince Philip was taken out to do some partridge shooting to break the monotony of the usual receptions etc. The place was Balloki about 25 miles south off the Lahore Multan road. The shooting trip had been put on at the last moment and the area cordoned off overnight. Selected beaters were screened first thing in the morning and taken to the spot where they were each told to get themselves a thin stick to rattle the bushes when the beats commenced. The normal thick "lathis" (staves) were not permitted for security reasons. Mingling amongst the beaters were a fair number of plain clothes Police together with uniformed officers to maintain discipline in the beat formations.

I was well acquainted with this area on the east bank of the River Ravi. The partridges have excellent cover, breeding well with a good survival rate in spite of vermin being very much in evidence. With plenty of water, sarpat, wheat, mustard and sugar-cane crops, the V.I.P. shoot was set to prove very successful.

The President of Pakistan, Field Marshall Ayub Khan, Prince Philip, the Inspector General of Police Mr Anwar Ali and General Mohammad Azam Khan took to the field. The beat started very quietly compared with a big game shoot; there were no tom-toms, rattles or shouting. Black partridges rocketed in front of the beaters, then levelled out to fly over or across the line of guns. The shooting was good, but at the end of each beat the grey partridges, which prefer to run ahead until the very end, suddenly burst out of cover to fly low and fast, taking the shooters by surprise. After several beats the shooting ended with a very good bag and lunch was taken at Balloki Weir under brilliant open air conditions. The late afternoon shoot was available but very wisely Prince Philip declined the offer, he had enjoyed the shoot, and, as the saying goes ... enough is as good as a feast!

Escorting the entourage back to Government House, I walked around the picturesque grounds, the miniature flower-clad hillock and the lake, bringing back memories of 1950 when attached to Government House I had witnessed the departure of Sir Francis Moody, the last British Governor of the Punjab, and saw in the first Pakistani Governor of the Punjab, namely Abdul Rab Nistar, surprisingly a Pathan, yet popular and welcomed by the Punjabis.

That evening Prince Philip was to attend his last function at a reception given by the Deputy High Commissioner (UK). It was at this reception, after having shaken hands with Prince Philip, that I realised now was the time to quit this land which had meant so much to us in the good old days. "What good old days?" I've been asked recently by young Indians and Pakistanis. I've had to tell the truth, hurtful as it may have been. "You were not around to make a comparison between then and now!"

Decisions must be made in everyone's lifetime, some small, some big, some pleasant, some unpleasant. The one I was obliged to make was big and

176

most unpleasant. I had to resign my job and forfeit 14 year's service.

Before tendering my resignation I was very keen to have my parents spend a holiday with us yet at the same time give them no indication whatsoever of our plans to quit the country for good. They agreed to do so. We met them at Wagah, helped their entry into West Pakistan and drove them to our house at Lahore. They brought along a real treat for us, something ordinary, yet unavailable in the country ..... a leg of ham! Though I shot numerous wild pig, roast pork was about the only meal we managed on the quiet in a Muslim country.

As usual Father declined going to cinemas and clubs. On the other hand he needed no encouragement to join me on shooting trips, especially for partridges. I was delighted by the manner in which he still handled a shotgun, taking some remarkable shots. In fact, it gave me immense pleasure to observe the pleasures rather than the pains of old age which Father was displaying.

Their visit was a pleasure, and try as we did to prolong their stay Father was determined to get back because of his pets which had a high priority on a list of worries when away from home. On parting I was naturally very upset, and try as I did, I could not say a word of farewell, because I was guilty of hiding the truth that this would, in all probability be the last time we would ever see each other. I watched Mother sobbing, then she gave Father a supporting arm and walked away. At this point my vision became blurred and that was the last I saw of my dear Father, the immortal sportsman who just faded away. Not the greatest, not even great, but above all a man of honour, respected by the poor and gentry alike.

I deleted the date fixed for our departure on the calendar, a date I was not too keen to see because it indicated the end of an era which began with my grandfather's posting to the North West Frontier in the 81st Foot Regiment. Only colonials know the heartache of selling up property to return to their land of origin.

As the time drew nearer farewell parties commenced; the sale of my weapons was negotiated, homes were found for the dogs, budgies and chickor, jobs found for the servants, not to mention inumerable other issues which kept cropping up. However, with all these matters settled I decided to have, so to say my last fling. I went for my last wild boar shoot to a favourite spot. Here a wild boar appeared at a most unexpected place as though "planted" as a parting present. The loaded rifle with its safety catch positioned on Safety was being carried by a trusted army NCO who, excitedly rushed forward, undoubtedly switching the safety catch to the firing position and passed the rifle negligently to me muzzle first, and in doing so accidently pulled the trigger. The blast at point-blank range vibrated through my chest almost knocking me over backwards more by fright than by force. The experience was dreadful for I fully believed the bullet had passed through my chest, so much so that I felt afraid to look for blood or feel for the bullet hole! Fortunately it missed by a hair's breadth, but I was too shaken to feel confident enough to face an unpredictable wild boar. In the past I had had experiences of near mishaps, but this was undoubtedly the closest I'd ever been to a fired bullet. I took this incident as a warning that I might be running out of luck, so handed my firearms over to the people who had put down deposits on them.

With my firearms gone and the pets and poultry missing from the compound, the bungalow looked dismal. The dogs followed us from room to room, watching our every move as though sensing this was not just another transfer but a parting forever. How true, how sad, yet it was some consolation to know that their new homes would not be too stange to them as their masters were keen sportmen who would not deprive them of the sport they enjoyed so much.

The day of depature soon showed up on the calendar. There were still those last minute matters to attend to before setting off for the railway station to board the train to Karachi. I expected friends to give us a send off, but I was very moved to see the platform near my carriage so thronged with fellow officers, subordinate staff and our loyal scout Billinda who had come from his village near Sargodha to bid us farewell.

The traditional custom of garlanding commenced with the children and Sheila then it was my turn to get the more elaborate garlands enriched with gold and silver tinsels and sequins. I could hardly see through this curtain of flowers which steadily increased until I was covered from head to waist. It served a very useful purpose because behind those garlands I was able to hide my emotions.

The train pulled out and Billinda ran alongside our carriage, waving his hands, then finally came to attention and saluted. That was the last sight I had of him. I heard later from Ainsworth who was posted at Tehran at the time, that Billinda wounded a boar and was following it up when it charged and gored him very seriously. He remained ill for a long while. On his death bed his last wish was to request Ainsworth to come out and see him. Ainsworth obliged, but he was a day too late. Thus the sad end to a brave man and an unforgettable character.

The long journey down the hinterland was a melancholy one, each mile travelled was a mile nearer a resolution I had made that when I got to the UK I would give up game shooting and turn to the conservation of wildlife instead to try and give back, even if it be a mere fraction of what I had destroyed, during the time of my love for the sport.

I stood at the door of the carriage, absorbing the last view of the countryside which by evening had changed from lush green vegetation to scrubland and desert. But here, too, I knew that somewhere in the tranquility of the interior roamed herds of gazelle, antelope, foxes and the marauding wolves. With the approach of winter would come the migratory bustards followed by swarms of sand grouse to cheer the hearts of the desert

The monument of the .303 Mk VII cartridge, a War Memorial to the 40th Pathans (height: 25ft). The inscription on the plaque reads:

"To the memory of all ranks, British and Indian, of the 40th Pathans fallen in action, particularly in honour of those who gave their lives in the Great War.
This monument was raised by the comrades on the 4th anniversary of Ypres Day 26th April 1919."

Sheila (left) and Evelyn (right) standing at the base.

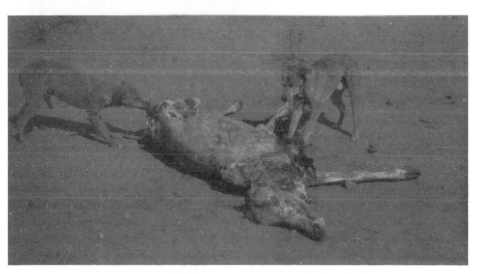

Where animals have no graves: pariah dogs help reduce a carcase to a skeleton.

inhabitants by filling the sky with the sound of their music.

Rising early next morning, I opened the shutters to see the usual blue sky. Roller birds flew off the telegraph wires displaying their rich blue plumage, cows and buffalos lazily roamed amongst groves of date palms feeding on the tender shoot while the frisky goats bolted across the sun-baked plain to keep a safe distance from the speeding train. To end the overland journey I saw a familiar sight, an old acquaintance, something I'd learnt to live with and undoubtedly the most irreplaceable gift to this land. A whirling mass of vultures, nature's unfastidious undertakers, disposing of a carcase.

We spent the day shopping in the hustle-bustle of Karachi, a city of contrast where the ancient utility of the donkey and camel continue to dominate the traffic in spite of being overwhelmingly outnumbered by he latest automobiles. The shopping spree over, we were entertained by friends until it was time to board R.M.S. Celicia on the 3rd of June 1960. Soon after sunset the ship pulled out of harbour; the decks were packed with passengers amongst whom my wife, children and I stood watching the lights of this mystic land disappear to an orange glow on the horizon.